D1615922

RADICALDECENCY

A Values-Based Approach to
a Better Life and World

Jeff Garson

Radical Decency

©2020 Jeff Garson

Print ISBN: 978-1-09837-133-3

eBook ISBN: 978-1-09832-100-0

DEDICATION

To my Beloved Wife Dale

We learn and grow through our experiences in life. Dale, my partner of 38 years, is a person of compassion, guts – and deep integrity. She always expects the best from me and never settles for anything less. Whatever wisdom I have been able to grow into over the years has everything to do with the inspiration she offers as I strive to be the partner she expects and deserves.

FOREWORD

I met Jeff Garson on a trip to Egypt about 9 years ago. He was, I learned, a person who had practiced law for many years and, then, switched to psychotherapy. Also a blogger, his weekly "Reflections" offered social commentary, oriented around Radical Decency, his values-based approach to living. He also quickly became "camp counselor" for my boys, 8 and 11, entertaining them in the back of the bus as we toured Egypt. Interesting background! Good guy! Returning home, we stayed in touch, occasionally getting together for drinks and dinner.

Few years ago, however, my understanding of Jeff changed dramatically and, with it, our relationship. Only then, after years of more casual friendship, did I realize that while Jeff is, indeed, a writer – hence this book – he is first and foremost an activist thoroughly invested in finding ways to implement his ideas in the world.

●●●●●

According to Jeff, we need to practice Radical Decency in every area of life – with friends and family, at work, in politics, and in how we treat our self. Otherwise, the culture's predominant compete-to-win values will, with time, overwhelm the smaller islands of decency we seek to create. But putting his activist hat on, he adds another key point: We need to find a key leverage point in the culture where a decisive shift toward decency might actually bleed into every other area of living, building serious momentum toward the world to which we aspire.

On this crucial point, Jeff's "go to" place is not, as you might expect, politics. As important as it is, these efforts are (in his phrase) mostly "puffs of smoke." Yes, things are accomplished. And yet, with depressing regularity, reform energy recedes, moving on to the next issue or electoral fight. Then, the culture's me-first, self-aggrandizing ways quietly reassert themselves, reversing previous reforms or finding creative, new work arounds.

Jeff – the activist – instead focuses on business. The reason? Most every institution of any size and enduring presence depends on money provided by business or the people it has made rich – from our political parties, to our higher education and religious institutions, to the media and entertainment industry. If we can change the way business operates, everyone else – intent on maintaining their flow of funds – will change with it.

•••••

In 2011, after 20 years on Wall Street, I shifted gears. Choosing to pursue my life's passion, I became a farmer in Central New Jersey. And seeking to farm in an economically and socially enlightened way, in the years that have followed, has been quite a challenge.

Fortunately, the money I made on Wall Street allowed me to confront these issues. Unlike almost every other farmer in the US – aside from a tiny handful of mega-farms – I haven't been consumed by a grim, relentless effort simply to survive. And so, over the last few years, through trial and (a lot of) error, I've come to understand that a technologically driven shift to centralized processing, over the last 50 years, underlies so many of the problems we face; not just farming's unsustainable economics but also its enormous environmental impacts, unstable distribution system, and highly processed, increasingly unhealthy food. Thus, a return to "on the farm" processing is key to reversing agriculture's dismal condition.

Recent technological developments now make this shift possible. The needed equipment – once costing millions – can now be purchased for a few hundred thousand dollars and can be operated, onsite, by local farmers. The key impediment to making this happen is that small farmers, already struggling with onerous operating loans, can't access the funds needed to finance this shift. Offering the money and know-how to make this possible – and, with it, a transformation in farming – has become my consuming mission in life.

•••••

About 3 years ago, Jeff and I realized how congruent our ambitions are.

• If bringing Radical Decency's values-based approach to business is key, what better place to start than agriculture; an absolutely essential, trillion-dollar sector of economy.

And, equally,

• If we hope to transform agriculture, more dollars in farmers' pockets isn't enough. We also need to offer leadership in using those funds to tend to the environment, produce healthy food, reverse our stunning cruelty to animals, and help to revitalize our local communities. The work needs to be thoroughly grounded in Radical Decency.

Understanding this, Jeff and I have joined forces. We have created the Decency Foundation whose mission is to operationalize Radical Decency in the world, with a focus on business. Toward that goal, we have created a metric – Nu – that allows our business partners in the initiative to measure their social return on investment with the same precision with which they now routinely measure their financial return. And, of course, our inaugural project – Nu.Ag – focuses on farming.

•••••

Because Jeff is, first and foremost, an activist, you won't be surprised to know that all proceeds from *Radical Decency* are going to the Decency Foundation. I know you'll enjoy the book. Jeff's ideas are smart, provocative and wise. But know as well that you are also helping us in our efforts to contribute to a better, more decent world.

Jon McConaughy
Double Brook Farm
Hopewell, New Jersey

CONTENTS

MY STORY

We live in a world that values getting ahead and being a success above all else. Into my early forties, I was riding that wave. A partner at a prestigious law firm, I had a wife I dearly loved, a beautiful suburban home, three bright, energetic kids, and a steadily growing income. The story the world told me – and I told myself as well – was "you have it all."

But then I pushed too hard in the preparation for a key hearing, which led to complaints about me from one of our client's key executives, followed by my removal from all the cases I was handling for this, my most important client. Just like that, a third of my practice evaporated, an event my law "partners" – all too predictably – used to bolster their practices and undercut my position at the firm.

Suddenly, after almost 20 years, my career trajectory was in doubt. I could no longer tell myself that I was safely on the "winner" side of the ledger.

• • • • •

I am a child of the Civil Rights era. I still recall the thrill of attending a fundraiser at Jackie Robinson's house in Greenwich, Connecticut, as a 13-year-old, listening to dignified and eloquent Civil Rights leaders speak of past injustices and their hopes for the future. Similarly vivid is my memory, 3 years later, of sitting with my feet in the Lincoln Memorial's Reflecting Pool, on a blazingly hot late summer afternoon, as the melodic cadences of Martin Luther King's "I Have a Dream" washed over me.

The successes of the 1960s Civil Rights movement left me with an abiding belief that creating a more just, equitable and decent world was a relatively straight-forward and achievable goal. It just required smarts, guts and hard work on the part of well-intentioned people. Fired by this naïve belief and the inspiring example of the Civil Rights activists of my youth, I considered a career in the public sector.

But a second, equally naïve belief, also taken from my growing up years, was that you can have it all. You can be a fierce competitor in our me-first, dog-eat-dog culture and still be a dedicated social reformer. So I chose, instead, to combine a busy, commercial bankruptcy practice with leadership positions in organizations such as Common Cause/Philadelphia, Philadelphia's Public Interest Law Center, Habitat for Humanity, and the National Constitution Center.

My belief in the comfortable compatibility of competitive success and a values-based life was smashed by my mid-life career crisis. I realized to my dismay that, like so many others, my bottom line was not decency. It was instead a success story thoroughly dependent on the accumulation of status and money.

Precariously balanced on this one-legged stool, I toppled over – falling into a major depression, triggered by this reversal in my upward career trajectory. At the time, it felt like the end of my life. It was, however, the thing that saved me.

●●●●●

Insight into who I was, and an understanding of the person I aspired to be, came hard. Most painful was the realization that, for all those years, far too many of my day-by-day choices put career and ambition ahead of the people I most cared about – my wife and children.

I tried to be a loving and attentive person, sort of. But far too often I would express my earnest desire to be at the teacher's conference, or a full partner in the baby's late-night feeding and then reluctantly say "sorry, I just can't" – because of work commitments. Even worse, I'd beg my wife to "understand."

The truth, of course, is that I could have taken on those tasks, and many others. But I didn't. The reason: The compulsion to compete and win – to get more clients, produce more revenue for the firm, come out on top in every case – was too strong. And the deeper, disquieting truth was that, while I eagerly sought the success-driven highs that this life offered – big new clients, victories in high stakes cases and, of course, more and more money – the real driver in my life was an abiding fear of failure.

Regularly anxious and preoccupied, I felt powerless to let up more than just a little bit. And if I did, it was only for short, carefully controlled spurts of time. If I wasn't ever vigilant, who knew who or what might trip me up. So I chronically pinched on time, not only from those closest to me (to their detriment and mine), but also from the simple joys of rest, relaxation, my love of reading and music, and so many other of life's possibilities.

As I struggled to climb out of the dark emotional place that my career crisis triggered, a powerful realization also grew, the one that led to the writing of this book: My personal choices reflected a pervasive cultural context that reinforced and rewarded my single-minded focus on success and penalized any meaningful deviation from it. Recognizing that I was not alone in being caught in this trap, it has become my abiding passion to find ways to free myself and others from this spirit-draining trap. Hence the philosophy and practice of "Radical Decency."

●●●●●

Radical Decency's informing perspective is that:

1. The culture's current default setting – a set of values I shorthand as compete and win, dominate and control – is deeply flawed; and

2. If we hope to live differently and better, we need to systematically replace it with a very different approach, practiced in every area of life.

This is what Radical Decency is all about.

Applying this philosophy in my own life has profoundly changed me. I gave up the practice of law and returned to school to train as a psychotherapist. And for the past 18 years, my old legal clients, with their moneymaking pre-occupations, have been replaced with therapy/coaching clients who are earnestly seeking to create more decent and loving lives; a shift in focus that has deeply nourished and enriched me.

I also have a new personal bottom line. Weaning myself from my old, flawed "success" story, I'm focused, instead, on being the best possible spouse, parent, friend, community member, and citizen I can be – and on being kind and loving to myself as well. I continue to deal with many challenges, of course. But I now have a much better sense of the cultural forces that so deeply affect and influence me. And, best of all, I have a way of managing them, day by day, that allows me to live a far more satisfying and generative life.

Sharing my ideas and life experiences in the pages that follow will, I hope, provide you with insight, support, and inspiration. Radical Decency has worked for me and I passionately, unreservedly, commend it to you.

PART 1

RADICAL DECENCY: WHAT IT IS, HOW IT WORKS, WHY IT'S IMPORTANT

Unlike many other programs for living differently and better, Radical Decency fully integrates change in our personal lives with change in the larger culture. Chapter 1 explains the crucial importance – at this particular point in our history – of this approach.

Chapter 2 then describes: (1) What Radical Decency is; (2) how it works; and (3) why it's an effective response to the particular circumstances with which we find ourselves in today's world. Describing the pervasive indecency that our compete-to-win culture has spawned, it makes the case for Radical Decency as:

- A clear, practical, and effective pathway to a more generative and spirit-affirming life: and, at the same time,

- A way of becoming a far more effective force for change in the world.

The Section concludes with a discussion, in Chapter 3, of what it means to be "Radical" and "Decent," providing:

- A working definition for each of Decency's 7 Values – Respect, Understanding, Empathy, Acceptance, Appreciation, Fairness, and Justice;

- Key ways in which these Values interconnect and reinforce one another; and

- A roadmap for their "Radical" application – that is, at all times, in every context, and without exception.

CHAPTER 1

Catching Up with Our History in Perilous Times

This book is about personal healing and growth, offering a detailed roadmap for organizing our lives around Decency's 7 values. But this focus on individual life choices makes it easy to overlook a core belief that is not only central to Radical Decency's approach but is, in fact, the aspect of the philosophy that makes it different and worthy of special consideration: The vital importance of bringing Decency's values to all areas of living, from the most personal and private to the most public and political.

My insistence on this across-the-board approach is based on two key beliefs.

1. Due to recent seismic shifts in the ways in which we humans live, we've reached a point in human history where change strategies that focus on personal choice but fail to deal, in a focused and sustained way, with our choices in the business/public/political sphere, are no longer viable.

2. Given these same historical developments, if we fail to embrace an across-the-board approach to change, such as Radical Decency,

the risk of devolving into a nightmarishly dystopian world, both environmentally and socially, is far too great.

Since these beliefs are so central to the approach to living I describe in the Chapters that follow, I begin with an explanation of each.

PERSONAL GROWTH'S UNIQUE CHALLENGE IN OUR TRANSFORMED WORLD

For virtually all of human history, we lived quiet existences, distant from affairs of the world. And with this as our taken-for-granted-reality, a decision to create a more self-aware, valued and purposeful life was a private matter, largely unaffected by outside pressures imposed by the mainstream culture. But then, just a few short years ago, a seismic and wholly unprecedented shift occurred in the ways in which we live that, like it or not, has thoroughly injected the larger culture into our lives.

If Decency's 7 Values guided most everyone's choices in life – if they were our dominant values – this wouldn't be a problem. The culture would seamlessly support and reinforce our private decency choices. But, unfortunately, that isn't the case. We live in a world in which the prevailing mindset is to get ahead, to compete with others, and to win. And because these values are now – for the first time in our history – a daily, relentless, in-your-face reality, thinking about personal growth separate and apart from change in the larger culture is no longer a viable strategy. If we do, the mainstream culture's corrosive values will, almost inevitably, invade the smaller islands of decency we seek to create in our private lives.

Moreover, because these historical changes have happened so quickly, our thinking about how to go about personal growth hasn't caught up with the realty of this dramatic change in context. We continue to assume that we are independent agents – captains of our ship – who, deciding how we want to live, have the ability to "just do it."

In the first half of this Chapter, I describe the seismic historical changes that have so fundamentally altered the ways in which we live. I then explain how the cultural forces they've unleashed inhibit our ability to create more meaningful lives; a hard reality that makes Radical Decency's comprehensive approach to change so vitally important if we hope to get from "here" (our current self-aggrandizing norms) to "there" (the more nourishing and generative life to which we aspire).

$$\bullet\bullet\bullet\bullet\bullet$$

We Homo sapiens have been around for about 300,000 years and, in the course of our history, there have been many dramatic changes in the ways in which we live. But one seemingly unalterable fact – unalterable, that is, until the last 140 years or so – is that we lived in small tribes or villages and we were in meaningful connection with only a relative handful of people.

In those years, there were of course times when the larger world would tear at the fabric of our existence through, for example, wars or epidemics (such as the Black Plague that killed a third of 14th Century Europe's population). But the larger reality was that these interruptions, however catastrophic, were episodic. When they ended, a predictable, isolated rhythm would return to our lives for decades – if not centuries. In other words, for virtually our entire history as Homo sapiens (99.95% of that time), the larger world only had a minimal impact on how we chose to conduct our lives; that is, on our personal growth choices.

To understand what the world was like, even as recently as the last years of the 19th Century, consider Thomas Hardy's *Far From the Madding Crowd*, a novel published in 1874. In it, the author describes a world in which townsfolks occasionally went to Casterbridge, a fictitious town a day's walk from their village. However, no one ever visited – or even talked about – London, even though it was only 150 miles away!

In *The Rise and Fall of American Growth: The U.S. Standard of Living Since the Civil War*, economic historian Robert J. Gordon exhaustively documents the particulars of this old way of life. In 1870, the starting point for his analysis, 75% of Americans still lived in small (2500 residents or less) farming communities. And just as it had been throughout our history as a species, our isolation from the larger world was quite stunning.

Travel beyond our village was by foot or on horseback over dirt roads (even in 1900, there were less than 250 miles of paved roads outside of our largest cities). We washed and cleaned with water carried from a well; lit our homes with candles or lamps fueled by oil or kerosene (a recent invention, still offering only a tenth of an electric light bulb's wattage); and relied on the kitchen stove for warmth in otherwise unheated homes.

In addition, the Sears mail-order catalogue – the breakthrough innovation that brought national consumer products to rural America – was still 25 years in the future. As a result, virtually all our goods were either homemade (e.g., almost all of our clothing) or bought at a local general store. And, needless to say, there were no cars, phones, TVs, computers, social media networks, or worldwide webs.

For some, 1870 might seem like a long time ago. But, in historical terms, it's just the day before yesterday. For thousands of generations people lived one way. Then, in the generation of my grandparents Eli and Daisy Garson (born in 1870 and 1875 respectively), things began to change. In other words, virtually all of the monumental changes that have transformed our way of life have occurred in just 3 generations.

•••••

When we lived the isolated existence that Hardy and Gordon describe, change strategies that focused on our private lives, but largely ignored our interactions in and with the larger culture, made sense. In that world, adopting a different, non-conforming approach to living might well have run into strong head winds, subjecting a person to harsh judgment and, even, ostracism. But these consequences, however painful, were still local; operating within a known and understood universe – a person's village and a group of people with whom he had and would always live.

But now we're wired into the larger world in ways that were simply unimaginable back then. And, with that, has come a similarly unimaginable increase in our vulnerability to judgment, manipulation, marginalization and control by the larger cultural forces that surround and envelop us.

•••••

Adjusting to these massive changes, already very challenging, is (ironically) made a lot more difficult by our innate nature as highly adaptable beings. A new product appears – televisions, computers, the internet – and, for a brief moment in time, we're amazed. But then, just like that, it becomes so much a part of our taken-for-granted way of living that we seldom reflect on its impact on the tenor and tempo of our existence.

This point was nicely illustrated by the standup comic who told the story of a guy who, settling in for a 5-hour New York to LA flight, started cursing in frustration when his personalized TV screen, an innovation added just months earlier, didn't work. Noting that not so many years ago "the trip would have taken 7 months and he could have died on the way," the comic, while making fun of his fellow passenger's sense of entitlement, also offered an excellent example of how quickly we adapt to and, then, see a new innovation as utterly routine.

Consider, as well, the taken-for granted assumptions of the "futurists" to whom I was exposed as junior high school student, back in the late 1950s. Well-known public thinkers, they would predict, often with remarkable accuracy, the amazing technological innovations that would come online by the dawn of the 21st century. But, then, they would just as confidently forecast the three-day work week to which these innovations would lead.

Because they were speaking from the perspective, not of the 1870s but of the late-1950s, these thought leaders had experienced decades of dramatic change – radio, TV and movies; cars and airplanes; national brands and multi-national corporations. And yet, even at that late date, they still assumed that our ongoing technological revolution would have little effect on the individual autonomy we'd enjoyed throughout our history. Hence, their belief that "of course" these new tools would be used to relieve life's drudgery, freeing us to pursue our private passions.

In retrospect, this prediction seems laughably naïve. And yet, for the reasons described above, it is also entirely understandable.

●●●●●

In the last few decades, new reality-altering technological developments have exploded into our lives at warp speed: Personal computers (in the 1980s), the internet (in the early 2000s), smartphones (in 2007) and, in the last decade or so, the now ubiquitous algorithms that monitor most every aspect of our lives, in real time, and use this data to mold and guide our behaviors.

These developments, eclipsing even the bold predictions of the futurists of my youth, have had a massive, debilitating effect on our personal autonomy. Tethered to our smartphones 24/7, we're now force fed an avalanche of information and commentary and are wired to thousands of "friends" and public figures through Facebook, Instagram, Twitter and whatever incredibly popular phone apps have come out since this book was published. In addition, the internet has become the go to place for more and more of life's activities: Shopping online; entertaining ourselves with video games, podcasts, online books and YouTube; communicating with friends and loved ones via text and email; tele-commuting to work.

When the alarm on our smart phone wakes us up in the morning, we reflexively plug into the world – even before we brush our teeth – checking our emails, or the news, or the latest posts to our favorite Twitter accounts.

And so it goes, throughout the day, with the larger world intruding into our lives as we "relax" on a remote tropical beach, drive to and from work, lie in bed at night – even as we sit on the toilet.

Moreover, the content with which we're bombarded, and the behaviors it evokes, are not benign. Social media is a place where, seeking to maximize our likes, followers and friends, we're conditioned to broadcast our successes and hide any trace of vulnerability – or to use our cloak of anonymity to attack others. In addition, we're deluged with ads filled with images of people who are invariably smart, funny, attractive, and always upbeat and positive; constant reminders of the unrealistic ideal against which our life will be judged.

●●●●●

To understand how profoundly these developments have affected our ability to change the ways in which we live, consider the situation faced by a person, let's call her Fiona, who goes to a weekend retreat where she learns about a new spiritual life path based on empathy and loving acceptance. Fired by this message, her challenge now is to incorporate these values into the life she left behind when she left for the retreat center, on Friday afternoon.

Living in today's world, think about all the pressures she'll face. It begins with her job, a reality with which she'll have to contend first thing Monday morning, when the alarm jars her awake and she hustles out the door for her commute to work.

On the face of it, work would seem like a terrific place to begin making the required changes. After all, it dominates her existence; removing her from her home and loved ones every morning, soaking up the best hours of the great majority of her days. What better place to dial back on her competitive, self-protective instincts and to focus instead on being more compassionate, open and honest?

But you can imagine how hard this would be. First of all, she no longer works at a local business where her boss lives around the corner and joins her at church each Sunday. To the contrary, she's employed by a corporation, located in another town, a 30-minute drive from home. She also works with people who only came into her life when she took the job. And while most of her co-workers are outwardly friendly, they understand that they're competing with one another for recognition, raises and promotions and, thus, keep each other at arms-length.

In this environment, if she gets the job done and doesn't cause trouble, she's probably ok. However, even then, if the company decides to relocate or downsize, or her boss has it in for her (fair or not), or if she just doesn't fit in, she might still get fired – with little advance notice and no ability to protest if the dismissal is unjust. Faced with these realities, Fiona simply can't afford to bring the weekend's spiritual teachings to her workplace in any serious and sustained way.

Moreover, the spillover effect that work has on her "free" time is massive. Getting home at 6 – assuming rush hour traffic cooperates – there's no time for relaxation and reflection. Instead, every minute is devoted to dinner, homework, and the kids' bath and bedtime rituals. And the weekends are more of the same. Between the kids' extra-curricular activities and the seemingly endless chores that accumulate throughout the week, Fiona hardly has time to breathe, let alone make major changes to her life.

Looking at her situation more broadly, things are equally challenging. Like all but the most privileged among us, the money she makes at work is really important. With their combined incomes, she and her husband are getting by month by month. And it helps that they recently moved into a "little too expensive" home in a suburb with good public schools, thus avoiding the crushing expense of private school for their 6-year old daughter.

But they're still paying $10,000 a year for their son's daycare and will be for another 2 years. In addition, the expense of college for her husband's

15-year old son, from his first marriage, is very much on their minds. Back in the "old" days – 1975 – the average yearly cost of tuition, room and board at a 4-year college was $2,275. Today, average tuition is $34,470 and room and board adds another $11,000. And, in a cruel and ironic twist on the financial vise in which most of us now live, Fiona (like so many others her age) is still paying more than $400 a month on her own college loans!

While Fiona and her family are getting by, there's no margin for error.

●●●●●

Suppose, despite all these concerns, Fiona meaningfully alters her priorities and, as a result, winds up making less money or, even, finds herself out of work for a period of time. The effect on her family's finances would be bad, to say the least. And if unemployed, she'd be thrown into the demoralizing world of online job searches. She'd sit at her kitchen table – day by day, week by week – filling out forms and hitting send. And then? Nothing. She'd wait in isolation, with no feedback from anyone unless, that is, she was one of the lucky few called in for an interview with an actual, in-the-flesh person.

Suppose, further, that to keep her family going between jobs, Fiona ran up additional debt, stretched out payment on some of their bills, or took out a home equity loan? If so, she'd then have to deal, as well, with its effect on her FICO credit score.

This number – which didn't even exist prior to 1989 – is now being used, not just by lending institutions to evaluate loans, but also by employers to screen job applicants and landlords to qualify tenants. Needless to say, Fiona could ill afford a major hit to this now pervasive number that, with brutal finality, separates the financially and socially suspect from the "good" people who deserve access to jobs, housing and loans.

Finally, huge psychological factors would inhibit Fiona's desire to create a different life. In a culture that places such a high value on "success," most all of us strive to follow its prescribed path: Go to the best schools and get the best grades, so you can get into the best college, so you can get a good job where, climbing the ladder of success, you can make the most possible money. And, on the flip side, we're equally weighed down by the ever-present fear of being a "loser," marginalized and dismissed in the eyes of the world.

For all of these reasons, getting off the treadmill is just so hard. Far better for Fiona to play it safe, lest the consequences of her choices sabotage the respectable middle-class life upon which her identity and self-worth – and that of her children – so heavily depends. The result: Lacking an effective strategy for dealing with these issues, Fiona will reluctantly put aside the inspiration and hope that the weekend retreat instilled in her and continue to live her compromised, mainstream life:

- Working the extra hours her boss demands;

- Managing the spirit-draining anxiety that is the product of her long and stress-filled hours at work; and

- Squeezing her deeper longings and aspirations, as best she can, into her over busy nights and weekends – and an occasional spiritual retreat.

Sadly, Fiona's situation is utterly typical.

•••••

Given these new realities, the inescapable conclusion is this: If we hope to create more meaningful and nourishing lives, we need detailed change strategies that encompass every aspect of our lives. Absent that, we (like Fiona) are far too likely to wind up leading compromised lives; resigned to the fact that we'll never be able to eliminate or, even, meaningfully ease the many indecencies that litter our world.

A UNIQUE MOMENT IN HISTORY?

As described above, Radical Decency's insistence on a change strategy that encompasses all areas of living is grounded in a belief that, in today's world, it's a practical necessity. However, it's also rooted in a second, equally important belief: Because we're at a pivotal turning point in our history, the very future of life as we know it depends on it.

Needless to say, this is a bold statement. Making it, I'm painfully aware that I am dancing on the knife's edge of a classic "on the one hand, on the other hand" question.

On one side of the equation is the certainty that such a moment will come. After all, we all know about the dinosaurs. They reigned as the earth's dominant species for 200 million years. But then, about 65 million years ago, they disappeared. And as best we can tell, in the 3 billion years or so in which there's been life on Earth, several pre-Dinosaur species also took their turn as the planet's dominant species. In addition, the archeological evidence suggests that there have been 5 additional events that, short of wiping out the dominant species, nonetheless led to cataclysmic mass extinctions, killing anywhere from 75% to 96% of the then existing species, with the earliest happening 450 million years ago and the most recent 70 million years ago.

Given this history, it would be foolish to think that we humans won't, at some point in time, confront our own moment of truth. Really, it's a matter of when – not if.

On the other hand, I recall the joke my father once told me about the bored kid whose teacher said, "in 37 billion years, the earth will turn into a fiery ball and everything will be destroyed." Jerking to attention, he said, "what did you say?!" Then, when the teacher repeated his prediction, he slumped into his chair in relief saying, "phew! I thought you said 37 MILLION years!"

For countless generations, visionaries and alarmists have seen theirs as the pivotal end of time moment in our history: French Bishop, Martin of Tours, in the 5th Century; Pope Innocent III in the 13th Century; the Jewish mystic Sabbatai Zevi, Cotton Mather, and Methodist Church founder John Wesley in the 17th and 18th centuries; and the Jehovah's Witnesses, Sun Myung Moon and Jerry Falwell in our era. For this reason, I'm slow to conclude that we now, in the first half of the 21st Century, may be approaching such a moment – if not next year or the year after then, perhaps, in mere decades.

But let's look at the evidence.

Environmental Storm Clouds

The case for such a moment being upon us begins with the truly alarming situation we face due to climate change and global warming.

The polluting effects of the Industrial Revolution have been apparent since the 19th century. However, in the last few decades there has been a stunning uptick in its consequences; a reality brought home by the environmental writer David Wallace-Wells who reminds us that fully half of the fossil fuel carbon in the atmosphere has been emitted in the last 3 decades.

In his book, *The Uninhabitable Earth: Life After Warming*, Wallace-Wells offers a catalogue of environmental consequences with which we're already living:

- Since 1980, there has been a 50-fold increase in the number of dangerous heat waves;

- Of the 10 years with the most wildfire activity in the U.S., 9 have occurred since 2000;

- Flooding has quadrupled since 1980 and the melt rate of the Antarctic ice sheet has tripled in 10 years;

- The number of disease cases from mosquitos, ticks, and fleas has tripled in the U.S. over the last 13 years;

- Since 1950, the good stuff in the plants we grow – protein, calcium, iron and vitamin C, for example – has declined by as much as a third;

- In the developing world, the air in 98% of the cities is above the threshold of safety established by the World Health Organization.

We're used to hearing reports such as these piece-meal and in dry, data-laden scientific language. So when it's all pulled together in one place, as Wallace-Wells has done, any reasonable person has to conclude that we are now, at the very least, in a dangerous situation.

But Wallace-Wells doesn't stop there. Reviewing the best scientific research, he also pulls together a series of predictions for what might plausibly lie ahead in the coming decades:

By 2050,

- Up to 5 billion people will have poor access to fresh water;

- As many as 150 million people in the developing world will be at risk of protein deficiency as the result of nutrient collapse, and 1.4 billion could face a dramatic decline in dietary iron, pointing to a possible epidemic of anemia;

- As the tropics creep north and mosquitoes migrate with it, plagues such as yellow fever and malaria will be globalized, affecting hundreds of millions in now temperate climes;

- Up to 1 billion politically destabilizing "climate change" migrants will be unleashed on the world.

And by the end of the century:

- Sea water levels will have submerged the Maldives and Marshall Islands, Jakarta, most of Bangladesh, Miami Beach and much of Southern Florida, Santa Monica and Venice Beach, St. Mark's Basilica in Venice, and the White House;

- Whole regions of Africa, Australia and the U.S., parts of South America north of Patagonia and Asia south of Siberia will uninhabitable due to direct heat, desertification, and flooding;

- The world will suffer a projected 23% loss in per capita earnings, with mid-latitude countries such as the U.S. and China losing up to 50% of their potential output, and large parts of countries and regions near the equator –Africa, Southeast Asia, India, Mexico and Brazil, for example – losing up to 100%.

•••••

Understanding and, then, predicting the future of the Earth's entire climactic system is, needless to say, impossibly complicated. So specific predictions, such as these, are probably wrong. They may be unduly pessimistic. Things may not be so bad. Or, perhaps, with our amazing creativity and ingenuity, we'll invent technologies that deal with these threats in new, unanticipated ways. On the hand, maybe this unfolding cascade of interrelated events might occur faster and with even more serious consequences.

In the end, however, these kinds of speculations are beside the point. If you lived on a busy road, and your 5-year-old was a pretty level-headed kid, you wouldn't shrug and say, "sure, go ahead and play ball on the street, you'll probably be ok." But isn't that exactly what we're doing when it comes to climate change?

Indeed, the final draft of this book's manuscript was completed in early February 2020, a long-ago time when the Corona virus pandemic was beyond our imagination. Now, just 3 months later, total cases stand at 3million worldwide (1 million in the US) with total deaths at 250,000 (70,000 in the US) – and counting. And as shocking and unsettling as these realities are, consider this comment from research microbiologist George Alkire:

> The Corona virus is highly contagious but not all that deadly while 2013's Ebola hemorrhagic fever was very deadly but, fortunately, not that contagious. Really, it's really just a matter of time when – in our high speed, interconnected world – we'll be confronted with virus that is both **highly** deadly and **highly** contagious. And that will make the current crisis look like a garden party.

So yes, predicting the future is impossible. But coming to grips with the deadly serious possibility – indeed likelihood – of unanticipated species-threatening consequences, if our stunning indifference to our physical environment continues, is not.

Me and my fellow Baby Boomers will be gone by 2050. But Roman and Claudia, my 2 and 4-year-old grandkids, will be in their early 30s. And what of their kids who will still be in their prime in 2100? Given our behavior to date, the indictment by Sweden's teenage environmental activist, Greta Thunberg, is deserved – and stunningly pertinent:

> You say you hear us and you understand the urgency. But no matter how sad and angry I am, I don't want to believe that. Because if you really understood the situation and still kept on failing to act, then you'd be evil. And that I refuse to believe.

To me the dangers are, self-evidently, too great. We urgently need to re-orient our ways of living so that, through our choices, we become more and more effective advocates for a shift in how our businesses and private and public institutions operate so that, instead of plundering the world, they are conscientiously and consistently decent to it.

Our Perilous Future in an Algorithmic World

In *Homo Deus: A Brief History of Tomorrow*, Yuval Noah Harari makes this provocative comment:

> Until today, only conscious beings – us humans – could perform tasks that required a lot of pattern recognizing intelligence, such as playing chess, driving cars, diagnosing diseases or identifying terrorists. However, we are now developing new types of intelligence that can perform these tasks far better than humans. For all these tasks non-conscious algorithms may soon exceed human capabilities.

The implications of this emerging, new reality are massive. For all of our history, until now, intelligence and humans were a package deal. Pointing this out, Harari asks an obvious question. If you were running a company, which would you prefer: A fallible human who might call out sick, bicker with you and his co-workers, and steal money? Or an algorithm that never sleeps, never complains, and never drops a decimal point?

Really, it's no contest. And the consequences of this no-brainer choice are already deeply affecting our lives – and will continue to do so on an increasingly massive scale.

Robots and similar technologies have already gutted manufacturing jobs. And, according to a 2013 study, computer algorithms are likely, by the mid-2030s, to replace all of the following: Telemarketers, insurance underwriters, paralegals, waiters and bartenders, veterinary assistants, security guards, and archivists. Harari also notes that, with computer algorithms already handling 50 to 60% of all financial trades, a similar fate likely awaits stock brokers. And since self-driving vehicles, linked into a single network, will be far safer than roads loaded with human drivers, he also predicts the disappearance of truck, taxi, and Uber drivers.

Note as well that even high-end, prestigious professions are at risk. Using doctors as an example, Harari offers this dramatic contrast between a human doctor and her algorithmic competitor:

"My physician has only a few minutes to make a correct diagnosis. This allows for no more than a few questions and perhaps a quick medical examination. The doctor then [relying mostly on her flawed memory] cross-references this meagre information with my medical history and the vast world of human maladies."

By contrast, an algorithm using artificial intelligence:

"Will be intimately familiar with my entire genome and medical history, that of my parents, siblings and cousins, whether I recently visited a tropical country, whether there have been cases of intestinal cancer in my family, and whether people all over town are complaining this morning about diarrhea.

●●●●●

In addition, it can hold in its databank information about every known illness and medicine in history, and can update these databanks, not only with the findings of new researches, but also with medical statistics gathered from every linked-in clinic and hospital in the world.

●●●●●

Understanding these trends, the question we need to confront is this: What will all of these dramatic changes do to us humans? And this is where Harari's speculation really gets scary.

As he sees it, there is a pertinent historical precedent. Seventy thousand years ago, we humans did not dominate the world. To the contrary, we were one of a number of species competing on a more or less equal basis for scarce resources in Africa's Serengeti. But, then, everything changed. We populated the world and became its dominant species.

And what have we done with the animals we now so thoroughly control? Indifferent to their fate, many disappeared. But those that remain have been mercilessly harnessed to suit our needs.

To illustrate the point, Harari describes the fate of pigs. Highly intelligent animals, they are able, with training, to learn and play simple computer games. And as curious and social creatures, they use a rich variety of vocal and olfactory signals to communicate, care for, and play with one another. And yet, as their masters, we've been remorseless in our exploitation:

> Pigs are locked in tiny gestation crates, usually measuring six and a half by two feet. The crates have a concrete floor and metal bars and hardly allow pregnant sows even to turn around or sleep on their side, never mind walk. And, whereas piglets would naturally suckle for ten to twenty weeks, in industrial farms they are forcibly weaned within two to four weeks and shipped to be fattened and slaughtered. The mother is then immediately impregnated again, going through five to ten such cycles, before being slaughtered herself.

Like the futurists of my youth, many cling to the belief that our new algorithmic marvels will lead to a world in which our unique value as individuals will be unleased as never before. But Harari offers a starkly different vision. He sees a world in which a small number of uniquely skilled humans continue to be valued and materially rewarded at astonishing levels. But the vast majority of us, having lost our economic value, will wind up being utilitarian cogs in this new, algorithmically driven world; consigned to jobs – and existences – where we're monitored and controlled as never before.

Maybe we won't be consigned to pens and deliberately slaughtered when our economic utility is at an end. But like pigs, the nonhuman decision-makers that rule our world – harnessed to the twin gods of efficiency and profit – will ignore and run roughshod over our needs and desires, creating for an increasing majority of us a dismally dystopian existence.

•••••

When I first read Harari, this prediction struck me as the stuff of science fiction; disturbing but highly speculative. But then I read *On the Clock: What Low-Wage Work Did to Me and How it Drives America Insane.* Reporting on her experience as a worker at Amazon, a call center and McDonald's, the author, Emily Guendelsberger, brings to life a reality that makes Harari vision look a lot more like a real and present danger.

Working at one of Amazon's many "fulfillment" centers, Guendelsberger worked 11½ -hour shifts, 5 days a week. And like every other "picker" – the people who roam the aisles pulling merchandise out of bins for shipment to customers – her every step was dictated and controlled by a scanner hanging from a lanyard, draped around her neck.

Logging in at the start of her shift, the location of an item would pop up on the scanner. Off she'd go, with a relentlessly receding blue line, at the bottom of the scanner, counting down the 2½ minutes she was allotted to retrieve the item. Failing to beat the clock, a de-merit would automatically show up on an efficiency scorecard, constantly updated for review and monitoring by her managers. Completing the task, the scanner would flash an ironic "THANK YOU!" – followed, immediately, by a new item location and countdown clock. And so it went, throughout her day.

Intent on preventing workers from "stealing time" from the company, Guendelsberger limited time off – 30 minutes for lunch, two additional 15-minute breaks – was also carefully timed by her omnipresent scanner. And these time limits were relentlessly enforced. One minute late coming back from lunch or a break? She was charged half a point, under a system in which just 6 points resulted in automatic dismissal (and a single mom is charged 1½ points if, after being all night with her sick child, she calls out from work).

Many other aspects of her workplace also reflect the brutal damage Amazon's efficiency-obsessed algorithms inflict on their employees. Working in a windowless building (designed, no doubt, with input from a cost-conscious algorithm), they are trapped in a sterile, sunless environment. And the widespread pain endured by pickers, like Guendelsberger, who spend the entire day on their feet is handled, not with modified schedules but with Advil dispensing vending machines.

Guided no doubt by detailed empirical evidence of abuse, Amazon also bans cell phones and MP3 players, short-circuiting workers' ability to deal with unexpected emergencies at home or, even, to relieve their monotony with a favorite music soundtrack. Guendelsberger notes, as well, that the algorithmically plotted "pick paths" that dictate workers' every move were "brilliantly" engineered to keep people from getting within speaking distance of one another. And while this helped to avoid logjams in narrow alley ways, she also speculates, very plausibly, that it was designed to maximize efficiency by making worker interactions impossible; nevermind the psychological damage that enforced isolation has – not just on crate-confined pigs – but on humans as well.

•••••

This emerging algorithmically driven world is also inflicting serious damage on peoples' lives away from work. Using sophisticated metrics, companies now calculate the minimum number of workers required to deal with anticipated traffic on any given shift. This, in turn, has led to shift assignments that, changing from week to week, make it almost impossible to schedule a doctor's appointment or daycare coverage for the kids. It has also led to "clopening," a nightmarish new phenomenon where the scheduling algorithm – unanswerable to any human – assigns a worker to the last shift in the evening and the first shift the following morning.

More subtly, with staffing stripped to an absolute minimum, these scheduling systems assume something that is almost never true: That all workers will show up on time and everything will go right. As a result, with understaffing being the rule and not the exception, employees are chronically overworked; an outcome that's been embraced by companies like Walmart and McDonalds because (no surprise here) it improves the bottom line – worker well-being be damned.

•••••

While artificial intelligence has only been around for a few short years, it is already deeply affecting our lives. And while these new algorithmic tools could just as easily be used to improve people's lives, the cold truth is this: So long as our culture is dominated by competitive, profit-driven mindsets, the great likelihood is that applications indifferent to our well-being will be far more prevalent than uses that honor and support it. Thus, we need to seriously consider Harari's comparison of pigs' fate, in a human dominated world, with our potential fate in an algorithmically dominated world. To do otherwise would be as foolhardy as shrugging off all the environmental risks we'll be facing in the decades ahead.

WE'RE ALL IN THIS TOGETHER

One danger we face as we contemplate the twin threats of an environmental cataclysm and out of control algorithms is a silent, often unaware assumption that, while bad, they won't REALLY affect people like me. On the environmental side, the implicit operative assumption is that the really bad stuff will happen, not in Philadelphia, but in Bangladesh or a remote Pacific Island – or to some future generation long after I'm dead.

Moreover, while we feel bad about the life Amazon workers have to endure, we assume it won't happen to us. To the contrary, as smart and determined people, we will find jobs or career paths where, because our contribution is so valuable, we'll be treated – not like pigs in a crate – but with a reasonable modicum of respect and consideration.

But here's the thing. If companies are so determined to extract every last once of efficiency out of $15-an-hour warehouse workers, why in the world wouldn't this mindset increasingly bleed into their treatment of their high-priced executives – and lawyers, accountants, and consultants? Why wouldn't they just as meticulously surveil and monitor their computers, phones and offices to prevent these individuals from "stealing" their – exponentially more valuable – time from the company.

Given the unique challenges we face, an "I am exempt from the forces of history" mindset is no longer viable. Instead of sitting on the sidelines, we urgently need to re-think our ways of living "from the ground up" – not just in our private lives but also at work, in our communities of choice, and in the ways in which we deal with one another in the political sphere. In the memorable words of Brian Clancy, long-time leader in the micro-lending movement, we need to re-align our choices in life with a (hopefully) growing movement to "reboot the culture's operating system" so that, going forward, it more and more fully reflects the humane and decent values that represent the best within us. And that is what Radical Decency seeks to do.

A JOURNEY OF POSSIBILITY AND HOPE

If you share my concerns about the future and decide to seriously consider the ideas described in the pages that follow, please also consider this final, crucial point: We can't embrace Radical Decency out of fear. Why?

First of all, it won't work. Being decent to self, others and the world, at all times and in every context, is a hard and demanding discipline. If you embrace it because you feel you have no other choice, you'll be forever looking over your shoulder, worrying that others are doing less and, thus, getting an edge over you in the relentless competition for money, status and success. Unable to let go of this mindset, a slide-back to the culture's compete-to-win norms will be almost inevitable.

More fundamentally, embracing Radical Decency because "we have to" would drain the philosophy of its power to inspire and sustain us. As explained in the next Chapter, central to its approach is the belief that living according to Decency's values, in addition to being the right and prudent thing to do, is also the surest path to a more nourishing and meaningful life. It's impossible to overstate the importance of this perspective as we seek to stay motivated and focused as we implement Radical Decency's ambitious and, so often, perplexing and uncomfortable goals.

So let the urgency of this moment in our history fill you with a sense of urgency and purpose. However, if you're drawn to Radical Decency, I urge you to incorporate it into your life – not out of fear – but with a vibrant sense of possibility and hope.

CHAPTER 2
The Case for Radical Decency

At the very core of our culture is a very specific set of values – compete and win, dominate and control. While not inherently bad, these values are wildly over-emphasized, infecting virtually every area of living, creating in their wake a world in which:

- 44% of teenagers feel "a lot" or "overwhelming" pressure to succeed in school, no matter the cost;

- Close to 9 out of 10 college students report mental distress exceeding that experienced by their average 1930's counterpart, with research pointing to an obsession with material gain and success as the likely culprits;

- Personal debt, fueled by our addiction to status-defining consumerism, has exploded from 90% of GDP in 1981 to 190% in 2015;

- A recent study finds premature white-blood cell aging, "ominous" cardiovascular and metabolic health numbers, and an elevated risk of diabetes among young African Americans rated as highly diligent and success-driven; and

- 72% of adults report stress about money, with 25% rating it as "extreme."

Reflecting on the stark evidence that these bullet points exemplify, I have come to a bold, unequivocal conclusion: We live in a failed culture.

Why do I say this with such certainty? Because, if we were to create a culture from scratch, virtually all of us would want it to support us in pursuing at least one of these goals:

- Being decent to ourselves,

- Being decent to others, or

- Being decent to the world.

Sadly and remarkably, our current culture fails to support us in any of these purposes!

If you're unsure about this, take a moment to ask yourself these questions.

With regard to how we treat ourselves: Does the culture support us in doing the things that truly nourish us? Or do we feel compelled to devote the most productive hours of most of our days to making money? Does our work and the hours and energy it consumes nourish us or does it more typically deplete us and distract us from our deepest aspirations and longings?

With regard to how we treat others: Does the culture make concern for other people a priority? Or is its focus, instead, on how other people's actions affect us or, even more narrowly, what they can do for us?

With regard to how we treat the world: Does the culture encourage us to marshal the environment's resources with care, and to actively consider the fate of the planet and other living things? Or does it place primary emphasis on how these "resources" can be exploited for profit and short-term convenience?

A VALUES-BASED RESPONSE TO A VALUES-BASED PROBLEM

If you agree that our culture perversely pushes us in the indecent direction these questions imply, the compelling question is this: How can we wean ourselves from these ingrained habits of living, freeing ourselves to craft ways of being that truly nourish and sustain us and, at the same time, treats others and the world more humanely? The answer, as I see it, is the values-based approach at the heart of Radical Decency.

Here's why.

In our effort to live differently and better, the first order of business is to fully embrace the reality of the situation in which we find ourselves. Electing the right leader, changing "this" or "that" public policy, or finding a better job, relationship or therapy to quiet our fears and anxieties – all of these things are important.

But if we hope to change things in an enduring way, we need to confront the fact that, living in a compete-to-win world, a fundamental, values-based disease fuels and magnifies all of the seemingly endless indecencies that litter our world. Given this stark, inescapable reality, what is called for is a values-based response with the power: (1) to wean us from our current habitual ways, and (2) to simultaneously support us in crafting a different, more nourishing and spirit-affirming way of living.

Radical Decency is designed to meet this challenge. It is the strong values-based medicine we need in order to deal with the virulent, values-based disease that plagues us.

ACCOUNTING FOR WHAT AND WHO WE ARE

One virtue of Radical Decency's approach is that it accounts for, and offers strategies for overcoming, two of our culture's most ingrained change inhibiting realities: (1) our virulently partisan, me-first mindsets,

The Case for Radical Decency

and (2) the inconvenient fact that nature has wired us to be creatures of habit, doing in the future what we've done in the past.

Moving Beyond Partisanship and Individualism

There is nothing unique in Radical Decency's values-based approach to living. To the contrary, it's an idea that has been eloquently expressed by many others, including some of history's most inspiring leaders and visionaries from the Buddha and Jesus to Martin Luther King, Jr. and Nelson Mandela.

Radical Decency embraces this wisdom tradition and seeks to be a part of it. But it also seeks to adapt it to the special circumstances in which we find ourselves today.

We are immersed, as never before, in a world that is both deeply partisan and tribal and, at the same time, heavily invested in an individualistic, "do your own thing" mindset. As a result, the wisdom of our forebears is, to an alarming degree, summarily dismissed when it isn't expressed through our chosen religious or political tradition or, even more narrowly, when it doesn't come out of our own brain.

Because Radical Decency isn't a part of any established religion or political ideology, it is able to restate these enduring values in a way that is unencumbered by our tribal roots, thus making them unusually accessible to a diverse audience. In this way, it allows well-intentioned people from different traditions – with their ideological and sectarian blinders loosened – to more easily explore their shared, values-based concerns. Then, hopefully, they'll be able find more cooperative and collaborative ways to work together in service of creating better lives and a better world.

Overcoming Our Habitual Brain

Radical Decency also fully accounts for the fact that nature has wired us to be profoundly creatures of habit; subject, in all that we do, to Hebb's Theorem which eloquently and succinctly states that: "If it fires together, it wires together."

To illustrate what this means, consider the example of a barking dog that startles a baby, triggering a chain of neurons in her brain to fire in a particular sequence. Because this chain of neurons has fired once, when the baby is confronted with a similar stimulus in the future – perhaps the unexpected crash of a dinner plate on the kitchen floor – this same chain of neurons is more likely to fire once again. Confronted with that stimulus a third time, the likelihood that it will fire still another time is even greater, and so on.

In other words, absent conscious intervention, our brain will do in the future what it did in the past; a behavioral pattern that governs everything from the characteristic way in which we wrinkle our nose, to our frequent use of certain phrases, to the expectations we bring to our most intimate relationships.

For our purposes, the pivotal reality that flows from Hebb's Theorem is this: Far more than we care to acknowledge, the me-first values that so thoroughly permeate our culture are deeply baked into our habitual behaviors. In large ways and small – through a myriad of cues, incentive and sanctions – they are woven into the very fabric of our lives, pulling us toward the "safe," "smart," and "obvious" choices that, in the end, reinforce the self-aggrandizing ways that are our unfortunate birthright.

For this reason, our journey toward a different and better life and world cannot operate solely at a cognitive level: Identify the problem, craft a solution, implement. What is called for, instead, is a massive and sustained war of attrition in which we systematically cultivate new habits of living that can, with practice and persistence, replace our status quo ways of operating.

This process of replacing old habits of living with new ones, in turn, sets up the following "good news/bad news" dichotomy, inherent in the Radical Decency's approach and key to its potential as a life-changing force:

- If we commit to being decent "radically" on an across-the-board basis, we have a puncher's chance of weaning ourselves from our mainstream habits of living.

On the other hand,

- If we adopt a pick-and-choose approach – being decent with family and friends but not at work, in our self-care but only half-heartedly in our communal involvements – we will fail. Given our habitual brain and the pervasiveness of the culture's mainstream values, its compete-and-win mindsets will inevitably invade and compromise the small, private islands of decency we seek to create.

A PURPOSEFUL, NEVER ENDING JOURNEY

Presented with this enormous challenge, the initial reaction of many is to see Radical Decency as an impossibly daunting task for us mere mortals. If "picking and choosing" where to practice decency is doomed to failure, does that mean that only saints can succeed? If Radical Decency is doomed to failure unless it's applied at all times to everything, must I be the equivalent of a Buddhist monk?

This reaction is, I have come to realize, an unwitting and wholly unnecessary re-creation of the very mindset we're trying to get away from. In asking "am I radically decent," we are, like the perfection-seeking competitors we've been groomed to be, tallying up the evidence and making a judgment: Have I succeeded in being radically decent? Or am I a self-absorbed shlub? Am I a saint or a failure? Am I a winner or a loser?

Seeing this instinctive reaction for what it is, the far better approach – the one that truly reflects Radical Decency's 7 Values – is to view the philosophy as an aspirational ideal. With this mindset in place, "being" radically decent is no longer the Holy Grail. Instead, the measure of success is our willingness to make decency our highest priority along with the focus, persistence, and sheer guts with which we pursue it.

Think, in this regard, about the Buddhist approach to meditation. While you are taught to focus on your breathing, you're also told that, inevitably and repeatedly, your thoughts will drift to memories from the past and thoughts about the future. When this occurs, you're instructed to simply notice what has happened and, without judgment, refocus on your breath.

Similarly, with Radical Decency, we focus on each moment's endless possibilities for being decent. But then, inevitably and repeatedly, our attention falters, distracted by old, mainstream habits that cause us to:

- Limit our time with loved ones as we strive for "success;"

- Dial back on our social/political involvements – or on the support we offer to a troubled friend;

- Manipulate and control "this" conversation or "that" business transaction, with too little regard for overall fairness and the needs of others.

When these things happen, we need to notice our faltering attention and, then – without judgment – return to our Radical Decency practice: Learning from our lapses; doing the necessary repair work; stretching toward new choices that more effectively balance and harmonize decency to self, others, and the world.

Committed, long-term meditators never succeed in eliminating their brain's distractibility. But this does not mean that they've failed. To the contrary, persisting in their practice over the years – trying and falling short, trying again and "failing" again – they fundamentally shift their outlook and way of living.

A similar process is at work with Radical Decency. A dedicated decency practice slowly chips away at entrenched, socially determined ways of being, deeply changing us in the process.

RADICAL DECENCY ON THE GROUND

Ann is a woman who, when you meet her, exudes a piercing intelligence, and genuine warmth and curiosity about who you are. Comfortably commanding confidence in others, she has an innate ability to compete and win.

Choosing a career in law enforcement, Ann became, at 24, the youngest Senior United States Probation Officer in the country. From there, she moved to the private sector. Beginning as a trainer at a company offering re-entry services to former inmates, she quickly moved up the ranks, eventually becoming the company's COO, managing a $30 million budget, 150 employees, and seven service centers.

But Ann could see that her life and values were incongruent. A big part of her job was managing the mercurial moods of the company's brilliant but erratic CEO in ways that buffered the rest of her staff from the effects of his behavior. Fighting every day to preserve oases of decency within this fundamentally indecent environment, she could see that she was paying a heavy price. Did her work really need to be an unfortunate exception to her most deeply held values – at the very center of her life?

But change was difficult. When you've done everything "right" and been richly rewarded, how do you cut the cord? For Ann, the turning point came when a co-worker, poor and pregnant with her fifth child, approached her about adopting her new baby. Now in her late 30s and still single, Ann realized this was something she had to do.

Saying yes to her co-worker, everything changed. Within a year, she'd left her job, re-locating to Albuquerque – a city she fell in love with in her 20s – for a lesser position with a more community-oriented company.

This too, was a learning experience. Her new life reminded Ann of the importance of the supportive community she'd left behind in Philadelphia. It also helped her to more deeply understand the difficulty that even well intentioned businesses have in translating positive motivations into more decent ways of operating.

Recently, she returned to Philadelphia, buying a house in her old neighborhood and becoming the CEO of a smaller nonprofit whose mission – to provide services to the City's most vulnerable citizens – is more fully congruent with her values. And, very importantly, her new leadership position gives her the ability to create a work environment in which she and her co-workers can thrive, both professionally and personally.

Ann's new life is, without question, more complicated. The money, security, and professional prestige are far less certain. But as she is quick to note, adopting her daughter and, then, re-orienting her life in ways that more and more fully reflect her values are among the best decisions she's ever made. Clear about her priorities, Ann's life is now sustained by a rich sense of appreciation, possibility and hope.

•••••

Now, let's turn to the look and feel of Radical Decency in the public/political sphere (an area we'll return to in greater detail in Chapter 10). Steeped in our compete/win mentality, most of us are fixated on the next election or current high-visibility partisan fight. If we can only elect "this" person or pass "that" law – we tell ourselves – things will be better.

But the show-stopping reality of our politics is this: The driving motivation of mainstream politicians is to win, and to maintain and increase their power. As a result, the substantive programs they propose are, mostly, a meaningless shell game that whips up the partisan fervor of their supporters but, unfortunately, distracts us from the profound and far more important policy failures that so deeply infect the quality of our lives.

On this point, the record couldn't be clearer. For 40 years we have been electing:

- Republicans who promise to free up the wealth-creating potential of private markets by reducing government – but who allowed the Federal budget to double under Ronald Reagan, to expand it by 53% under George W. Bush, and to grow it by another 16% in the first few Trump years; and

- Democrats who promise change through governmental initiatives – but who dismantled the welfare and bank regulatory systems (under Bill Clinton) and poured $1.59 trillion in bailout funds into the financial system without seeking any meaningful re-regulation or accountability in return (under Barack Obama).

Saddled with a political system that perfectly reflects the mainstream culture's compete-to-win values – and makes wining far more important than good public policy – a meaningful shift toward policies that reflect Decency's 7 Values is highly unlikely.

Even in this dismal environment, we should of course continue to push for better laws and public policies. But the vital contribution that Radical Decency makes in the political sphere is that it focuses us on a second – daunting but crucially important – goal: Creating a political conversation that decisively diverges from our current adversarial, right/ wrong, attack mode of public discourse, progressively replacing it with one marked by respect, understanding and reasoned compromise.

How would this look in practice? Imagine – if you can – a Sunday morning talk show in which the "liberal" spokesperson's remarks on abortion, without any hint of cynicism or manipulation, includes the following: "Your reverence for the process by which life is created is inspiring, and deserves our deepest respect and consideration." And a response from the "conservative" that includes this: "Of course the many painful dilemmas that confront women with unwanted pregnancies need to be fully understood and factored into the choices we make."

Bringing Radical Decency into the political sphere would also encourage a dramatic change in the scope of our collaborative initiatives. No longer constrained by the mindsets of their liberal/conservative, Republican/Democratic political tribe, the many people who share Decency's 7 Values would increasingly come together, fueled by their shared desire to understand one another and to craft policy initiatives that balance and harmonize their varied outlooks and concerns.

●●●●●

Finally, consider our dealings with the many people in what philosopher Martha Nussbaum calls life's "Middle Realm." This area of living includes strangers as well as casual acquaintances, store clerks, your landlord, and the person at the other end of the help line. Our Middle Realm relationships are the background music that infuses every other area of living. As a result, how we act in these relationships is a vitally important since it will, inevitably, deeply influence our ways of being in every other area of living as well.

Recently, I had to deal with a hitherto casual acquaintance who was pushing for a relationship more intimate than any I was interested in. In my old, pre-Radical Decency days, I would have avoided her, making excuses until she "got the hint." But mindful of my decency practice, I instead told her over lunch that, while I liked spending time with her, my busy schedule meant that I'd likely disappoint if she expected more regular contact.

Her response was surprisingly positive. After a moment of stunned silence she said, with perceptible relief: "You know, I have a busy life too. Spending more time together probably wouldn't work for me either." But it didn't have to go that way. In that situation, another reaction – probably the more likely one – would have been hurt and blame: "Fine, if that's the way you feel, I'll stop calling. I never should have expected more from someone as busy and pre-occupied as you."

Notice, however, that my choice in that moment was not dictated by a desire to avoid an awkward or unpleasant outcome. Instead, my mindset going into the conversation was that if I focused on being decent, then, whatever the outcome I'd be able to manage it. In that moment – and, increasingly, in others like it – my clarity of purpose sustains me.

Another Middle Realm example involved a recent shopping trip to Target. Unable to find the environmentally correct baby wipes my daughter needed for her newborn, I reached out to a sales person who not only scoured the shelves for this elusive product but also called the store's supplier to see if it could be express shipped. Before leaving the store, I paused to call Target's hotline to report, in detail, my interactions with this unusually helpful salesperson.

In the Middle Realm, especially, we are challenged to be more decent in the innumerable smaller moments that so regularly come up in our lives:

- Acknowledging a waiter's efforts, even when he's distracted and not fully attentive;

- Quieting the anger that flares when the guy in the next car over cuts in front of us;

- Showing up on time for all of our engagements, including the church fundraiser and our aunt's dreary holiday party.

We are also challenged to live up to our decency vocation in far more consequential Middle Realm moments as well:

- Responding with acknowledgment and support, rather than self-serving silence, when someone else's mistake gives us an edge in a financial transaction.

- Using our money, as investors and consumers, to support businesses that share our decency commitment, even when the "experts" – focusing on price, convenience, and profitability – insist that the "smart" move is to go with companies with long and shameful histories of environmental and social indifference.

•••••

As you can see, there is nothing Pollyanna-ish about a committed Radical Decency practice. It is demanding, unrelenting and, often, confusing and uncomfortable. But, happily, the philosophy does not force us to choose between a nourishing and fulfilling life and stoic self-sacrifice. To the contrary, as I explain in the sections that follow, a radically decent life is a richly rewarding one, without regard to its financial or other "real world" outcomes.

DECENCY'S SPIRIT-AFFIRMING DANCE

My friend Alan was a remarkable person, devoted to family and friends, and active throughout his legal career in efforts to improve the lives of disenfranchised people. A few years ago, he died of a fast-moving cancer.

Those of us who knew and loved Alan mourned his loss. At his funeral, his brother remembered his trip to Mississippi in the 1960s, to work as a Freedom Rider in the civil rights struggle, as well as his standard response when asked why he joined this risky mission: "Because it was the right thing to do."

This answer is a fine one – as far as it goes. But leaving it at that obscures, I think, another vitally important point. A lifelong fighter for fairness and justice, Alan was also a joyful man who:

- Regularly grabbed his wife, Adelaide, as the pasta boiled, twirling her around the kitchen to old Motown songs;

- Inspired co-workers at the stodgy, self-important law firm (where we both worked) by posting an ever-changing collection of cartoons, quips and jokes on his office door, a shrine to his infectious spirit; and

- Joined the kids at most any party, leaving them (literally, at times) collapsed with laughter at his fish face and other antics.

Life – as we know, but seldom acknowledge – is capricious. The only certainty is the inevitability of pain and loss including our own decline and death. But within the confines of this unforgiving reality, how we choose to live makes an enormous difference. The coming together of a dedication to decency with a vibrant, nourishing existence, so beautifully exemplified by Alan's life, is no lucky accident. To the contrary, as explained below, while life offers no guarantee, the ways in which we're neurologically wired make it the expectable outcome of a radically decent life.

DECENCY'S DEEP BIOLOGICAL ROOTS

As an ever-growing body of scientific research confirms, we humans are, quite literally, programmed by nature to be in intimate connection with one another. As Louis Cozolino, one of our leading neuroscientists, states flatly in his 2014 book, *The Neuroscience of Human Relationships*, "a brain without connection to other brains will shrink and eventually die;" a conclusion backed up by this powerfully revealing description of how our brain and body work:

Gaze, pupil dilation, facial expressions, posture, proximity, touch, and mirror systems are all reflexive and obligatory systems that working with other systems, yet to be discovered, create a high-speed information linkup between us [humans], establishing ongoing physiological and emotional synchrony.

The internationally recognized psychiatrist and author Daniel Siegel makes the same point when he describes the brain as a complex nonlinear system that exists within a larger complex nonlinear system consisting of it and other brains. In other words, it makes no sense to think about a brain in isolation. We are, quite literally, wired to be in relationship with one another.

The implications of this reality are profound. A baby's brain is molded, not in isolation, but through his ongoing interactions with his primary caregivers. So mom and baby share a small happy moment, one of many. What is happening? In developmental terms, she is modeling for her child the look and feel of a mature brain's expression of joy. Then, as the baby moves into sadness or frustration, mom moves with him, modeling a more mature brain's expression of these emotions as well.

In addition, there are those innumerable shifts in mood; when, for example, a dark cloud and cry envelops a baby who, just a moment before, was all happy and giggly. These moments of transition – from happy to sad, distracted to engaged, calm and relaxed to irritated, and so on – are crucial. They are the moments that, again through interactions with mom (and others), shape the baby's brain in ways that will allow him to handle the often sudden and unexpected emotional shifts he'll inevitably confront in life.

Note, importantly, that this process does not end in childhood. Throughout our lives, our growth and evolution are deeply and fundamentally influenced by our interactions with others. And when it comes to the ways in which we choose to live, the implications of this insight are pivotal – indeed life changing.

DECENCY IS ITS OWN REWARD!

Understanding these neurobiological realities, Radical Decency's promise as an alternative to our current problematic ways couldn't be clearer. Our me-first, self-aggrandizing habits of living are thoroughly anti-relational. They encourage and reward dominating and manipulative behaviors – as well as envy, greed, score keeping, and judgment. And, equally, they minimize and suppress more vulnerable emotions that, while more connecting, might be perceived as weak: Uncertainty, vulnerability, confusion, and so on.

Pre-occupied with dominating others and hiding large chunks of our humanity, our ability to create and sustain the essential nourishment that intimate contact provides is sharply diminished. Small wonder, then, that we suffer from an epidemic of emotional disorders: Depression, anxiety, and the many addictive behaviors – drugs and alcohol, sex, workaholism, and so on – that we use to anesthetize our isolation and pain.

Radical Decency reverses this dismal equation. When "decency" is "radically" embraced, our debilitating pattern of emotional isolation is replaced with new, habitual ways of living that allow intimate contact to flower and grow.

Here's how the process works.

When we make across-the-board decency our priority, our goal in life shifts from some ill-defined, future goal – how to be successful and rich, or happy and fulfilled – to the intensely practical day-by-day, moment-by-moment task of being decent in every area of our lives. And, with this shift in focus, good things start to happen.

It begins with a seamless shift toward curiosity, and away from a utilitarian "what can you do for me" mindset in our dealings with others. Why? Because we quickly learn that, in order to make more decent, here-and-now choices, we need to deeply understand other people's motives (and ours as well). Striving to do so, we actively cultivate curiosity as well as emotional openness and receptivity; hallmarks of a more emotionally connected and, thus, more nourishing existence.

Radical Decency also requires unwavering, day-by-day attention to the many small moments that challenge us to balance decency to our self, others and the world. Consider, for example, these dilemmas:

- Should I spend Tuesday morning at mom's nursing home despite the relentless demands of my work? How about next Tuesday morning? And the next?

- When a quarrelsome and unpleasant co-worker makes a mistake, do I say something or remain silent and uninvolved?

- Is an appropriate amount of my resources being invested in the communities of which I am a part – my church, synagogue or mosque, the city or town that has been my home for all these years, the organizations that promote and maintain my profession's best practices?

- Am I taking enough time for the things that really nourish me – time with loved ones, pursuit of my private passions, rest and relaxation?

In the mainstream culture, the standard way of dealing with these sorts of issues is to either: (1) ignore them; (2) "solve" them by going to one extreme or the other (self-absorbed obliviousness or self-abnegating sacrifice); or (3) latch onto some convenient excuse to explain them away ("quality time makes up for more regular attention to my kids;" or "taxes take care of my contribution to society").

Radical Decency, by contrast, challenges us to notice and fully address these sorts of issues. Doing so, we grow important, life-nourishing relational skills:

- Our emotional awareness and analytic capabilities;

- The courage to act in uncomfortable situations and the patience and self-control to forbear when that's the better choice; and

- Our ability to more capably love others and ourselves.

And where does this lead? What happens when all that we do is approached in this radically decent way?

Living in the present, which leads to less shame, guilt, and remorse about the past and less fear and anxiety about the future, replacing them with the far less complicated and cluttered emotional landscape that is the natural extension of our here and now focus;

Appreciation, empathy, and acceptance for our self and others, which leads to less judgment, jealousy, greed, and need to control, experiencing instead more warmth and joy within our self and in the company of others;

Clarity and coherence about our priorities and choices, which leads to less confusion and anxiety, and an increased sense of ease and well-being; and

A spirit-affirming sense of purpose, which leads to less, "is that all there is" hopelessness and, instead, a growing sense of vibrancy, aliveness, and pleasure in living.

To me, these are the elements of a good and satisfying life. Thus, while Radical Decency is the right thing to do – as my friend Alan might have said – the really exciting news is that it's also its own reward.

CHAPTER 3

Being Decent, Being Radical: A Primer

Seeking to describe Radical Decency's underlying values, "Decency" is a good start, suggesting that some behaviors are better than others. But a far fuller description is needed. Toward that end, I have evolved the following working definition of Decency: (1) Respect; (2) Understanding; (3) Empathy; (4) Acceptance; (5) Appreciation; (6) Fairness; and (7) Justice.

Testing this definition's utility, over time, I always refer back to these intensely practical questions at the heart of Radical Decency. Committed to its values-based, across-the-board approach to living:

- Are my day-by-day choices becoming more purposeful and generative; and

- Are my relationships becoming more nourishing, productive and mutually supportive?

I invite you to do the same.

●●●●●

Each of Decency's 7 Values is commonly viewed as a stand-alone value, at best only loosely related to the others. But in fact, they are deeply intertwined. As we operationalize Radical Decency, we need to understand not only what each of these terms means but, also, how they interconnect and reinforce one another, magnifying the impact of each.

RESPECT

Respect is Radical Decency's entryway value, providing the orienting context in which the other 6 values can be most productively cultivated. As I use the term, Respect encompasses politeness and civil expression, behaviors typically associated with the term. Built into it as well, however, is a presumption of good will in both thought and action.

Given the mainstream culture's judgmental habits of mind, it's particularly tough to consistently honor this presumption. Our instinct when someone criticizes us is to return the fire, responding with counter criticism. We also habitually dismiss a political partisan on the "other side" as a heartless conservative or knee-jerk liberal. In these kinds of situations, we need to lean hard against these dismissive and judgmental tendencies. At the same time, however, we need to remember that the presumption of good will *is* a presumption only. Sometimes, as we learn more about a particular person, it needs to be abandoned.

To illustrate both sides of this balancing act, consider President Trump and his supporters. What separates me from Trump is not the kind of principled disagreement that separates people of good will, operating out of different worldviews. So with him, I strive to retain a mindset that is polite, civil, thoughtful, balanced in its judgments – and, even, empathic and understanding with regard to the struggles of this obviously troubled human being. But I don't offer him the benefit of doubt; that is, a presumption of good will. In fact, I do the opposite. My default position is NOT to trust.

At the same time, I work hard to distinguish Trump from his supporters. As I interact with them, I assume going in that they're good people, with very real economic and social grievances, doing their best to get by in an unforgiving and perplexing world. Doing so can result in unexpectedly meaningful interactions, ones that bring out the best in me and encourage movement toward Decency's 7 Values on their part as well.

An example of this process at work occurred the day after Trump was elected President. Walking into my waiting room, a new client smiled at me and said: "Well, we don't have to deal with that lying woman anymore." A Hillary voter, my immediate instinct was to deliver an impatient rebuttal. But I stifled it and said instead: "I think I know what you're getting at. She seems to carefully calculate everything she says. While I wouldn't call it lying, it does feel manipulative. And I don't like it either."

My comment brought him up short. Unexpectedly finding common ground across our assumed partisan divide, we went on the discuss our shared belief that many, perhaps most other politicians are big-time manipulators as well, including many people on "his side." His final comment, delivered just before he disappeared into my co-worker's office: "I wish we had time to talk about abortion. I'll bet we could do a lot better than the guys we've put in office."

Wow!

To think the two of us could have hammered out a wiser public policy on an incredibly partisan issue like abortion is, of course, naïve. But there is nothing at all naïve in believing that, when a presumption of good will guides our interactions with others, we enhance the possibility for discussions that are more open, honest and nuanced, even on the thorniest of issues.

UNDERSTANDING AND EMPATHY

Primed by our habit of Respect to be curious, rather than judgmental and dismissive, there is a natural flowering of our ability to be aware of and emotionally receptive to differing beliefs, behaviors and communication styles: To see the world as others see it (Understanding), and to experience in our bones what it feels like to be them (Empathy).

One of the great gifts of being a psychotherapist is the daily challenge of living up to these values. Karen is a woman in late 40s, sharp-tongued and funny, deeply honest and inspiring in her loyalty to those she loves. She was born with a chronic immune disorder that has triggered an endless series of additional injuries and diseases. As a result, she lives with chronic, unrelenting pain and the disappointment of a life that can't include children or the nursing career she loved but had to abandon in her 20s.

Just a few months into our work together, I pretty much understood the facts of her life. But witnessing her week by week in the years that have followed – seeking to inhabit at least the foothills of her daily psychic reality – has been a life-changing lesson in the challenges and rich rewards that come with a sustained commitment to Understanding and Empathy.

I'll never forget the day, several years into our relationship, when I harshly criticized her long-time husband Joe who, weighed down by the years of struggle, suddenly turned sullen and withdrawn. Her fierce and passionate response was a dramatic reminder of who Karen – a person I thought I knew so well – really was: "Stop it! You're wrong about Joe. He's going through a difficult time but he's still the same loving partner who has stuck by me, time and time again, when I've been at my worst. He deserves no less from me."

The poet Naomi Shihab Nye beautifully described Karen when she wrote:

> Before you know kindness as the deepest thing inside,
> you must know sorrow as the other deepest thing. . . . Then it
> is only kindness that makes sense anymore . . . only kindness
> that raises its head from the crowd of the world to say, it is I
> you have been looking for and then goes with you everywhere
> like a shadow or a friend.

The harsh hand Karen has been dealt in life taught her this lesson and, in our interaction that day, she helped me to better understand and empathize with it as well.

While Karen's story illustrates the redeeming promise of Understanding and Empathy in an intimate relationship, these values richly reward us even when intimacy isn't our goal. Whether it's a co-worker, the receptionist at the doctor's office, or the person at the other end of the help-line, these values lead to choices that are wiser and more satisfying, not just for the person we are interacting with but for us as well.

Sadly, many people instinctively resist these values in life's competitive, "real world" environments. Seeing them as soft and fuzzy, they believe they only invite victimization. Consider, in this regard, the many attorneys who feel compelled to take on a tough, never back down persona in order to attract clients and be taken seriously by their peers. Consider, as well, the reforming politician who is passionately committed to those who are marginalized and neglected, but who nevertheless feels compelled to belittle her opponent and run demeaning attack ads.

If our goal is decency, this "fight fire with fire" approach will never succeed. When we adopt it, even a "win" becomes a loss since it perpetuates the very compete-and-win, dominate-and-control value system we're trying to overcome. We will never be able to bully or manipulate a co-worker – or the world – into being more relational and decent.

The good news is that we don't have to choose between Understanding and Empathy and thriving in the real world. In Chapters 9 and 10, I describe how doubling down on Radical Decency, at work and in politics, actually enhances our effectiveness in these realms. In other words – done right – Understanding and Empathy (as well as Decency's other values) are personally satisfying and rewarding and, at the same time, make us more capable and effective in the rough-and-tumble world in which we live.

ACCEPTANCE AND APPRECIATION

The norm in our culture is to see our side as "good" and the other side as "bad" or "less than;" a mindset exemplified by the shock we inexplicably continue to feel when still another of our public heroes proves to be a drunk, philanderer, or crook. What this good guy/bad guy mindset obscures is the simple reality that we all – all of us – have within us the full range of human thoughts and emotions, from the most loving and generative to the most hateful and destructive.

How, then, can we best account for our inevitable human complexity in a more decent way? By understanding and acting on its hopeful possibilities. Yes, hateful feelings lurk within us. But, on the flip side, in each of us – even those who seem permanently stuck in ways of living that inflict pain on others – is the ability to nurture our better instincts and to lead a more decent life.

When we fully embrace the upside of this equation, Decency's 4th and 5th values, Acceptance and Appreciation, take center stage. Embracing these values, we create an emotional context in which, seeing the best in others, we encourage them to respond in kind. And since the way we treat others and the way we treat our self will inevitably converge, treating others with Acceptance and Appreciation cultivates a similar generosity of spirit when we deal with that person we see in the mirror each morning.

"Acceptance" is grounded in the Buddhist belief that, because the full range of human emotions is within all of us, it makes no sense to react to another person's "bad" behaviors as though they are aberrational or an affront. Better to view them as inevitable parts of his humanness and, thus, with a sense of acceptance and equanimity. And, so too, with our problematic behaviors as well.

"Appreciation" grows out of an insight succinctly expressed by relationship expert Harville Hendrix in *Getting the Love You Want: A Guide for Couples* (1988): "Everyone makes complete sense" – if, that is, we know enough about a person's innate disposition, personal history, ways of adapting to that history, and hopes and dreams for the future. Given this reality, Appreciation for the pain, confusion, and struggle that others experience as they seek to get by in life – no matter who they are – is a realistic and worthy goal.

In this regard, I think of my father. A privileged but neglected child, he became a warm, fun-loving but self-indulgent adult who, tragically, deeply hurt both my mother and beloved stepmom with his faithlessness. Through the years, however, I came to understand how alone and unappreciated he felt, and how his compulsion to find other women anesthetized that pain. While never forgiving his choices, I was able, by the end of our journey together, to Accept, Appreciate – and love him.

Another vital aspect of Appreciation lies in the fact that meaningful healing and growth occur, not in a vacuum, but instead when we face and overcome adversity. Thus, instead of feeling aggrieved and angry, far better to embrace – Appreciate – an adversary as a part of living that is not just inevitable but, also, essential to our growth.

●●●●●

Decency's second and third values, Understanding and Empathy, are essential building blocks as we seek to cultivate a mindset that is habitually Accepting and Appreciative. In order to Appreciate another person, we need to Understand her on her terms, recognizing that her worldview has an internal logic that makes sense to her. Then, building on these insights, we need to cultivate Empathy for the fears and vulnerabilities that drive her. Only then will we be able to realistically Accept and Appreciate her as just another person who, like us, shares in our flawed, struggling reality as a human.

This can be a difficult journey even when we know someone as well as I knew my Dad. But the challenge is far greater when we're dealing with a public figure or more casual acquaintance. In these relationships, the presumption of good will, discussed earlier, is also an indispensable ally.

Slowing down our instinct to dismiss this person gives us the emotional space to imagine, and to test out, ways of seeing him that are more nuanced and, thus, more Accepting and Appreciative.

●●●●●

Note, crucially, that we are talking about Acceptance and Appreciation of a person and not of his beliefs and actions. When someone takes a position or engages in behaviors with which we fundamentally disagree, we can and should be forceful and determined in our opposition. But the hallmark of our approach should be to vigorously resist and neutralize his behaviors – not his personhood.

FAIRNESS AND JUSTICE

Being Fair, we fully consider the impact of our actions for our self, others, and the world. When we decide how and where to allocate our time and money, we consider not simply our own needs, but the needs of others as well. And, we expect other people to do the same.

Being Just, we seek to understand the many cruelties that our current ways of operating inflict on others – and our self as well – and actively look for ways to lessen them. And here too, we seek productive ways to hold others, especially those with power and privilege, to this same standard.

In the complex and flawed world in which we live, Fairness and Justice are aspirational ideals that can never be fully realized. Thus, the goal is not to judge our self and others as fair or unfair, just or unjust. Instead we need to make an ongoing, fearless inventory of our choices, and the choices of others, in every area of life.

- In our political and communal engagements: Are we investing adequate time and resources in activities that promote a fairer and more just world? Are we supporting political candidates and other communal leaders who are invested in these goals?

- In our personal relationships: Recognizing that bullying, manipulation, and indifference to others perpetuate inequity and injustice, are we cultivating more decent ways of interacting, not just with family and friends but with everyone with whom we interact?

- In how we treat ourselves: Are we standing up to unfairness and injustice when it is directed toward us or toward a group of which we're a part?

Then, building on this ongoing, fearless inventory, we need to make forward-looking choices that consistently challenge ourselves and others to more effectively deal with the inequities and injustices that litter our world.

The importance of these values cannot be overstated. A full-throttle commitment to Fairness and Justice is the crucial, rubber-hits-the-road test of our commitment to Radical Decency. It is at this point, and this point only, that we become active agents for the fundamental change we seek.

HOW DECENCY'S 7 VALUES INTERSECT

Earlier, I described how Understanding and Empathy allow us to Accept and Appreciate the humanity of others more fully. In this section I describe other key ways in which Decency's values intertwine and reinforce one another.

Consider, for example, Respect. In the absence of Understanding and Empathy, Respect is likely to be pallid and incomplete, exemplified at its worse by the cold, even cruel person who is unfailingly polite.

On the flip side, the presumption of good will, inherent in Respect, is vitally important to our efforts to live up to Decency's other values. Allowing it to fall out of the equation, we'll be quick to judge others, shrinking our instinct to be Empathic and Fair, especially when it comes to people who are different from us.

In that regard, I always remember the nonprofit executive who bitterly told me that his donors eagerly supported "pretty little white girls in wheelchairs," but felt very differently about "overweight, abrasive African American teenagers." History also offers many examples of groups, outwardly devoted to the soaring principles of their religion or political sect – from the medieval Catholic Church and the French Revolution, to the Russian Revolution and the Taliban – that systematically hunted down and murdered nonbelievers.

Another example of the effect that Decency's values have on one another involves Empathy, on the one hand, and Fairness and Justice, on the other. Suppose, for example, you find out that the object of your initial, Empathic response is acting in duplicitous and manipulative ways. At that point, considerations of Fairness and Justice may lead you to place a higher priority on supporting and protecting the people affected by his behaviors.

One messy, real world example of this process involved an employee – let's call her Tess – at an organization in which I had a leadership role. When she joined us, we knew she was highly emotional. But her enthusiasm was infectious and, at her best, she did good work. The end came when, feeling unappreciated by her co-workers, she resigned.

Shortly after Tess quit, she sought me out, wanting me to validate her hurt feelings. Moved by her pain, I listened to her sense of grievance and outrage over lunch and on several lengthy phone calls. But then things deteriorated. She started bad-mouthing her former co-workers, and then threatened to "expose" our organization to some of our key clients. At that point my Empathy intersected with my sense of Fairness and Justice. After a final attempt to explain our side of the dispute provoked a furious counterattack from Tess, I cut off contact with her, focusing my concern instead on my unsettled co-workers.

A final example of how Decency's principles reinforce one another involves the way in which Acceptance and Appreciation solidify the other 5 values. How – you may ask – can I maintain an attitude of Respect, Understanding, Empathy, Fairness and Justice when "that" idiot shows up on the TV screen? When all I want to do is yell at him or switch the channel? How can I possibly maintain my Decency practice when the entire effort feels like a grim, uncomfortable and, ultimately, untenable exercise in pretending to be someone I'm not?

This is precisely the point at which Acceptance and Appreciation come to the fore. Cultivating these values as our habitual way of being, we are better able to:

1. Vigorously resist the unfair and unjust byproducts of that person's outlook and choices; and, at the same time;

2. Accept the fact that she is just another human being struggling to find her way in the world;

3. Appreciate her essential humanity; a humanity that is, in the end, no different than ours; and, thus,

4. Interrupt and displace our knee-jerk reactivity, allowing us to engage her with Understanding, Empathy, Fairness, and Justice, and (at least) the civility to which our practice of Respect leads us.

BEING RADICAL

Viewed in isolation, Radical Decency's component pieces are unexceptional. Be Respectful? Understanding? Empathic? Appreciative? Accepting? Fair? Just? Ask any person – even someone who is thoroughly invested in the mainstream culture's competitive, win/lose mindset – and he's likely to say, "Sure, no problem, all of these things are good."

However, driven by the need to survive economically or, as we move up the scale of wealth and privilege, by our compulsive need for more status and power, this response is typically code for: "I'll happily be understanding and empathic but only when it doesn't interfere with my headlong pursuit of money and status. I will honor the idea of fairness and justice, but only when it requires no meaningful sacrifice on my part."

With these unspoken caveats, this person is expressing a deeply ingrained, mainstream approach to living that I call "pick-and-choose" decency. Be respectful, fair, just and so on when it doesn't cost you anything. But when it really counts – when you're competing for a promotion, or a significant amount of money is at stake – do what you have to do.

This approach is, of course, not decent at all.

Radical Decency is distinctive, not because it promotes its 7 Values, but because it applies them, not partially and when convenient but at all times, in every situation, and without exception. In other words, the philosophy's transformative potential lies in its radical application.

Let's take a closer look at the concept of "radical application" and how we might manifest it in our lives.

Not Just a Goal, A Way of Life

In the mainstream culture, "radical" or "radicalism" is commonly defined as "going to the source or foundation" or, more specifically, "favoring basic change in social or economic structures." These definitions may seem reasonable. However, they contain a serious flaw in that they focus on the ultimate goal and effectively ignore how we get there.

This disconnection between means and ends can have unfortunate, sometimes disastrous, consequences. At one end of the continuum are the many movements around the world that call themselves "radical" because of their commitment to broad ideals such as freedom or justice, but then use tactics that are thoroughly coercive and even murderous. Needless to say, they don't offer a useful model for creating the more decent life and world that is our philosophy's radical goal.

On the other side of the equation are the many people who focus on "means" but act as though getting to the "end" will just kind of take care of itself. In the words of Howard Lesnick, author of *Listening for God: Religion and Moral Discernment* (1998), these people seem to believe that if enough of us just "do the right thing," we'll magically coalesce into a movement that will positively change the world. Lesnick, with critical and biting accuracy, calls this mindset the "avalanche theory" of change.

To me, neither of these approaches makes sense. The term "radical" needs to be reserved for the relatively rare people and movements that pursue justice in ways that fully integrate means and ends, the most visible examples being Gandhi, Martin Luther King, Jr., Nelson Mandela, and (as nearly as we can tell) the historical Jesus.

This is the model to which Radical Decency aspires. Yes, our "end" is ambitious. We hope to create a world in which Radical Decency is the new norm. But we then add a second, "means" focused prong to our radical vision: An ongoing commitment to making Decency's values a priority in all our choices. The perplexing question we unflinchingly address, with this second prong, is how to craft a change strategy calculated to be both transformative in its ultimate effect and, at the same time, fully decent as we translate it into our here-and-now life choices.

The "As If" Factor

Some might see this discussion of means and ends as overly academic with little connection to how we live, day by day. However, it's anything but. Consider, for example, this intensely practical question: Why should I make choices that contribute to a healthier environment such as purchasing green products, buying locally grown foods, or using public transportation? After all, these choices take time and effort and their impact is cosmically small.

The typical answer is that, even though you're just one person, you need to act "as if" your choices matter. If we all do this, we can change the world.

But here's the problem. This approach doesn't offer any but a purely theoretical reason for actually making these day by day choices. Even worse, because we're prone to feelings of guilt and self-judgment when we fail to do the "right" thing, this mindset can actually discourage the change it seeks. Far easier to put the whole uncomfortable topic aside as we hurry home from a long day at work, picking up a box of frozen hamburger patties at Safeway for dinner.

A second defect with this "as if" approach is that it invites the following, all too human line of thinking, even from the most committed among us:

> I understand the environment is your priority, but mine is education reform (or women's rights or religious freedom). I know I should act "as if" when it comes your priority as well, but I just don't have the energy to do so – to say nothing of the other compelling issues, different from mine, that also require "as if" choices.

Or this additional, even darker thought:

> Why is it that, even as you implicitly judge my lack of initiative on your issue, you fail to make "as if" choices in the areas I'm most passionate about? If you're not with me on my issues, why should I be all in on yours?

In other words, at its most insidious, this "as if" approach, far from facilitating a coming together of committed people, can actually fracture reform efforts and promote competition for scarce resources.

Then – Why Do It?

Radical Decency offers a far more effective answer to the all-important "why do it" question. Here's how it works.

As I describe in Chapter 2, while Radical Decency is the right thing to do, it is also a smart and effective way to create a better life – right now – without regard to ultimate outcomes, creating:

- A more vivid experience of living in the present and, with it, less guilt and remorse about the past, and less fear and anxiety about the future;

- Greater empathy for yourself and others;

- Increased clarity about your priorities; and

- An ennobling sense of purpose.

But here's the thing. Our mainstream ways of operating relentlessly pull us in a very different direction. Thus, we can only make these outlooks habitual if our day-by-day choices cultivate them at all times, in every context, and without exception.

So why should I stretch to buy green products, or to leave my car at home and take public transportation? Because doing so is still another way in which I can deepen and extend my decency practice, trusting that as these choices accumulate I am not just doing the right thing. I am also cultivating the habits of living that are the surest path to a more vibrant and nourishing life.

Being Positive and Forward-Looking

Saul Alinsky, the legendary radical organizer, argues that, to succeed, a radical movement needs a designated enemy around which to coalesce. This model is reflected, for example, in labor's struggles against management; the mid-20th century civil rights movement vs. the Deep South's defiant racism; Reagan and the Tea Partiers vs. the "spend-and-waste" Federal government; and so on.

For me, however, this "us vs. them" approach contains a fatal flaw. It fails to come to grips with the authoritarian, win/lose mindsets that are the root cause of our culture's endemic indecency. Ignoring this reality encourages the belief that, because "we" are good and right and "they" are bad and wrong, the actual process of making change, once we win, will be easy. Our self-evident rightness will point the way.

With this mindset firmly in place, radical movements frequently spend little time on what is, in the end the crucial question: Given the opportunity, how will they deal with the complex and intractable problems they'll face once in power? The result: The leaders of so many successful radical movements – steeped in this self-righteous mindset – lack the more subtle skills needed to actually implement their visionary goals.

To the contrary, after years of struggle, what they know best are the ruthless, win-at-all-costs ways of operating they employed in order to beat the establishment forces at their own game. Thus, it's no surprise that, when they do take control, they so often wind up replicating the indecent ways of the people they supplanted; a lesson graphically illustrated by the fate of so many of history's best known radical movements – the French and Russian Revolutions, Maoism, and so on.

Radical Decency seeks to avoid this trap. It starts, it is true, with an in-depth analysis of the mainstream culture's dysfunctional ways of operating. But the goal is not to demonize and defeat an enemy. Instead, it seeks to understand the ways in which the mainstream culture neutralizes radical reform efforts so that we can avoid these pitfalls.

Then, it focuses on the positive, forward-looking agenda that is the essence of Radical Decency: Understanding what decency looks like and crafting strategies that implement it in all areas of living. Doing so, it avoids the trap of merely ranting against "what is" without offering a detailed, thoughtful plan for living differently.

Being Strategic

We live in a highly individualistic culture. And while taking charge of our own life is a good thing, this self-focused, "do your own thing" mentality has a dark underside. It allows us, too easily, to lose sight of the ways in which we might coordinate and merge our efforts with others, thus creating a more effective change movement. The result? With our change initiatives fractured and uncoordinated, the culture's status quo, compete/win ways continue to operate without serious challenge.

Prevailing attitudes about charitable giving offer a good example of this phenomenon. People are urged to give, it's true. But strikingly absent is any societal pressure to coordinate donations with others so that, overall, they meaningfully address the culture's most serious problems. Instead, a gift to a college with a multi-billion endowment is just as commendable as a gift to an organization that serves the neediest among us. And a contribution of any size is just fine – the recipient of effusive praise – even when it represents an infinitesimal fraction of the donor's net worth and income.

To be truly radical, we need to continually examine and re-examine our priorities. In other words, we need to strive, always, to be more strategic in all of our choices.

This process is complicated and often uncomfortable. How can I best allocate my time, talent, and financial resources – day-by-day – among my family, my immediate communities, the larger world, and my own needs? How do I choose between this change initiative and that one? There are no easy answers. But as we willingly grapple with these wisdom-stretching questions, we more fully make good on the goal of creating a decency practice we can legitimately call strategic and, thus, radical.

Engaging in this process, we need to pay special attention to ways in which we can collaborate and integrate our efforts with those of others. The slope is just too steep to climb solo. We can't take the easy, more comfortable route of pursuing our special passions only, offering little or no support to other important initiatives. This vital, collaborative aspect of "being strategic" is a subject to which I return in the book's final Chapter.

Being All In

Joseph Stalin was a mass murderer, responsible for the death of 60 million people. Jesus has been an inspiration to countless millions for two millennia. But they were both radicals and, in one respect, their message was identical.

When the wealthy man asked Jesus what he needed to do to get eternal life, His response was: "Give your possessions to the poor and follow me." (Matthew 19:16–30; Mark 10:17–31; Luke 18:18–30). Similarly, after the collapse of the 1905 revolution, when so many of his compatriots got married and found jobs, Stalin thundered that you can't be a householder and a revolutionary.

Being "all in" is a tough discipline, a fact the Bible highlights when it reports that the wealthy man, hearing His message, was "saddened." And lest the point be lost, Jesus goes on to say that "it's easier for a camel to go through the eye of a needle than for someone who is rich to enter the kingdom of God." (Matthew, 19:24; Luke 18:23-24).

Jesus and Stalin were right when they said that, when fundamental change is your goal, you can't be committed halfway. To be truly radical, you need to be "all in" – as Jesus was when he risked all, entering Jerusalem with his radical, anti-establishment message and as Nelson Mandela was throughout his decades of unbending resolve as a prisoner on Robben Island.

Being "all in" in the context of Radical Decency presents special challenges. Unlike many other radical approaches to change, it is not exclusive or rejectionist. Instead, it urges us to live joyfully in the world as it is – an essential aspect of decency to self – while, at the same time, actively making choices that foster greater decency in our immediate environments and the world. With these wide-ranging goals in mind, the philosophy typically unfolds quietly, in the privacy of our day-by-day choices.

This means that the great majority of the choices that put us "all in" will be invisible to everyone except us. As a result, it's easy to fake it, making visible but easy contributions while quietly neglecting riskier, more uncomfortable decisions. Needless to say, we need – always – to vigilantly guard against this tendency.

• • • • •

The choices I have made in my life exemplify the trickiness of being "all in." For many years, I was active in the community but, at the same time, devoted the great majority of my time to building a legal practice. And during that period of my life, I regularly congratulated myself on how committed I was.

But was I "all in"? Not by a long shot. The great majority of my time and energy was given over to helping banks and other large investors wring as much money as possible out of companies in bankruptcy – and, of course, to lining my own pockets as well.

Since leaving the practice of law I have, I think, done better. But even in my new career as a psychotherapist, I continue to grapple with difficult and perplexing decency choices. Do I build a private practice that rejects lower-paying, insurance-based clients, thereby earning more money but limiting my practice to privileged, high-income people? When I am sitting with a client, late on a Friday afternoon, who has no money to buy groceries, do I play by the "ethical" rules of my new profession, empathizing but not offering the $30 that would get her through the weekend? Or seeing her as a fellow human in need, and not as a patient/client, do I offer her the money?

The bottom line? Because perplexing and uncomfortable questions just keep coming at me, being "all in" requires me to be steadfastly thoughtful, disciplined, emotionally brave, and accountable.

Needless to say, there are many times when I fall short. When that happens, however, I remember what life was like back then when I was a harried, ambitious lawyer trying to have it both ways – and compare that life with the one I have now. Doing so, I am sustained by the accumulating evidence that Radical Decency is worth pursuing, not because it's easy, but because its rewards are commensurate with its demands.

PART 2

THE PROBLEM AND THE CURE

If you want to get somewhere, you need to know where the journey begins – the "Here." Then, of course, you need to identify where you want that journey to take you – the "There." In the Chapters that follow, we explore both:

The "Here:" The deeply embedded processes that keep us rooted in our current "compete- to-win" ways and their deep historical roots (Chapter 4), as well as their debilitating impact on our lives (Chapter 5); and

The "There:" A vision of what a life, lived in a radically decent way, might look like (Chapter 6).

These discussions set the stage for the third part of the book, which addresses the most vital question of all: Knowing where we are and where we want to go, how exactly do we get from Here to There?

But first things first. Let's look at where we are now – whether or not we like it – and, if we don't, where we wish we could be.

CHAPTER 4

The "Here:" The Disease that Ails Us

As we seek to craft more decent lives, we need to understand precisely what makes this seemingly straightforward goal so difficult.

For starters, let's consider the mainstream culture's compete and win, dominate and control values and my belief that, because they are so wildly oversold, we need to decisively diverge from them. Does that mean that these values are the fundamental problem? No.

In fact, properly managed, they can be quite valuable. A competitive spirit in appropriate circumstances sharpens our wits, motivates us to higher levels of performance, and creates an intimate bond with co-competitors. Likewise, domination and control can, at times, be lifesaving. Overpowering a would-be attacker, for example, is an entirely healthy use of our aggressive instincts.

Reform efforts that focus on specific manifestations of the culture's indecency also miss the mark. Why? Because notwithstanding their self-evident importance, they fail to confront the underlying greed that's the system's main driver. As a result, instead of being a catalyst for additional reforms, they more often have the opposite effect, galvanizing fierce and unrelenting efforts on the part of those with power to reinstate their privilege.

The fate of Dodd-Frank, the financial legislation passed in the aftermath of the 2008 financial meltdown, offers a prime example of this process at work. Immediately upon its passage, virtually all the political momentum shifted to the industry's massive effort to undo it – with results that speak for themselves.

Through heavy lobbying and the constant pressure of lawsuits directed toward the agencies charged with Dodd-Frank's implementation, more than 30% of the law's mandated rules still had not been implemented, seven years after its passage. And as memories of the financial meltdown have faded, the policy initiatives have all been in the direction of laws and regulations that soften and reverse its reforms.

Campaign finance reform offers another example of this boomerang effect at work. In the aftermath of Watergate, public financing of Presidential campaigns became a reality. And for a while, it worked. But instead of building momentum for additional reforms, its success provoked a sustained counterattack. As a result, public financing is now defunct with just two fringe candidate, Martin O'Malley and Jill Stein, using it in 2016. Once again, the political system is dominated by big donors, with Super PACs raising over $1 billion in the 2016 election cycle – with 74% of that money coming from just 257 donors.

Finally, there is the history of racial injustice in America. As Michelle Alexander describes in her 2010 book, *The New Jim Crow: Mass Incarceration in the Age of Colorblindness*, each period of racial progress has been quickly followed by a renewal of institutional racism by other means. Thus, the end of slavery provoked the Jim Crow laws of the 1880s and 1890s. In an analogous way, the advances of the 1960s quickly led to the "War on Crime," an initiative that led to a 26-fold increase in the rate of imprisonment for African American men between 1983 and 2000; the cumulative effect being that, by 2008, almost 40% of Black men were either in jail or on probation or parole.

So if the fundamental issue isn't the culture's dominant values nor specific, indecent aspects of the current system, what *is* the crux of the problem? It's a process by which the culture's values ooze silently and unseen into virtually every aspect of our existence.

Broadly speaking, this process unfolds in two ways. The first is a relatively straightforward process that rewards us for playing by the culture's compete-to-win rules and penalizes us if we don't: Seduction, pressure and marginalization. The second – more subtle and pernicious – is the process by which these same values insinuate themselves into our psyches, powerfully molding our thoughts, emotions and taken-for-granted ways of being in the world: Infiltration and infection.

Note, importantly, that these processes operate gradually and in a piecemeal fashion. As a result, they are largely invisible. And this fact greatly complicates the challenge we face since its far harder to undo things that are unseen and unacknowledged.

And make no mistake about it. As mechanisms for derailing efforts to alter the status quo, these two processes are chillingly effective.

SEDUCED, PRESSURED AND MARGINALIZED

We live in a world in which most of us, as well as virtually all of our businesses and institutions, are: (1) *seduced* by the promise of success to compete relentlessly for "wins;" and (2) *pressured* by fear of failure to avoid any meaningful divergence from these values. The end result? Our larger life goals are forever pushed to the *margins* of our lives.

In her deeply insightful and passionate 2013 book, *This Changes Everything: Capitalism vs. The Climate*, Naomi Klein, the Canadian author, social activist, and filmmaker offers a stark example of this process at work. She begins by detailing the extent to which many of the environmental movement's largest organizations – the Environmental Defense Fund, the Nature Conservancy, the Conservation Fund, the World Wildlife Fund,

Conservation International, and the World Resources Institute – are funded by contributions from companies such as Monsanto, Shell, Exxon-Mobil, FedEx, GM, Toyota and McDonalds.

Then, as the example set forth below illustrates, she describes how the siren song of large contributions and "the ever-powerful desire to be seen as serious" by the economy's biggest players, has deeply altered the trajectory of the environmental movement.

> The Environmental Defense Fund insists it does not take donations from the companies . . . that "would undermine our independence and integrity." And it's true that Walmart doesn't donate to the EDF directly. However . . . the Walton Family Foundation, entirely controlled by Walmart's founding family, gave it $65 million between 2009 and 2013, and accounted for nearly 15 percent of its funding in 2011. EDF [also] claims that it "holds Walmart to the same standards we would any other company" which, judging by Walmart's rather dismal environmental record . . . is not a very high standard at all.

Klein then notes that the problem goes beyond specific environmental groups pulling their punches when it comes to big donors:

> The 1990s was the key decade when the contours of the climate battle were being drawn. It was also the period when Big Green [pushed by large corporate donors] became most enthusiastically pro-corporate. Global warming was not defined as a crisis being fueled by over-consumption, or by high emissions industrial agriculture, or by the car culture, or by a trade system that insists that vast geographical distances don't matter — root causes that would have demanded changes in how we live . . . but, instead, as a narrow technical problem with no end of profitable [win-win] solutions within the market system."

The lesson to be drawn from Klein's brilliant reporting could not be clearer: **Seduced** by the seemingly irresistible allure of big dollars and a place at the table with the economy's biggest players and, equally, **pressured** by the fear of losing these perks, the very groups to which we look for leadership in the crucial fight for the future of our planet have been deeply **marginalized**.

This same seamless and invisible process infects most every other key area of the culture as well. Thus, consider academia. This is an area that many of us would like to think is largely immune from this process; that at least at the most august of our institutions of higher learning, a commitment to seeking the truth prevails. But here, too, the good work that is done by many individual academics is embedded, to a disturbing degree, in a larger system that has been seduced, pressured and marginalized.

In *Inside Job*, the documentary about the financial meltdown of 2008, Glenn Hubbard, Dean of Columbia's School of Business, agreed that scholars should "disclose if they have a financial conflict," even though his school had no policy to that effect. And yet, when asked if the majority of his outside activities were on behalf of the financial services industry, his response was "not to my knowledge," followed by "possibly" and finally, with his friendly, aw-shucks demeanor suddenly replaced by icy disdain: "This isn't a deposition; you have three more minutes."

In fact, Hubbard, who as the Chairman of the Council of Economic Advisors under George W. Bush was a cheerleader for financial deregulation, served on a least six boards of major financial institutions, including: Capmark, a major commercial mortgage lender; KKR, one of the world's largest hedge funds; and Met Life where his annual compensation was $250,000. Hubbard undoubtedly received substantial fees from directorships at these other companies as well, and also received $100,000 as an expert witness defending Bear Stearns hedge fund managers from charges of fraud.

Sadly, Hubbard is not an aberration. In the same movie, John Campbell, Chairman of Harvard University's Economics Department, was asked if Harvard required faculty disclosure of compensation received for outside activities. He said, "no, I don't see why we should."

The interviewer then posed this hypothetical: "A medical researcher writes an article saying that to treat this disease, you should prescribe this drug, and it turns out the doctor makes 80% of his personal income from the drug's manufacture. Doesn't that bother you?" Campbell, with a pinched and vaguely suspicious look on his face, responded as follows: "It's certainly important to disclose the ummm . . . the ummm." Then, after a four-second pause, he shifted course, saying, "Well, I think that's different from the cases we're talking about here."

But, of course, it isn't.

In fact, some of Harvard's most renowned faculty members have gotten rich through huge sums received from the financial sector. The list includes Martin Feldstein, one of its best-known economics professors and the Chairman of President Reagan's Council of Economic Advisers. Feldstein received millions from 1988 through 2009 as a board member of AIG, the notorious insurance company that imploded in 2008 and nearly brought the global economy down with it. It also includes Larry Somers, once Harvard's president, who made much of his fortune, reported by him at between $16 and $38 million, from consulting and speaking fees from hedge funds and investment banks.

When asked about these payments – and many others like them – Campbell said they were "basically irrelevant."

What's so depressing about these examples is that we're talking not about ravenous capitalists, but instead about organizations that we instinctively look to as watchdogs of the system. The disturbing truth is that the seductive allure of wealth and status, and the fear of failure, are at work everywhere, infecting politics, higher education, the media, our religious institutions, the entertainment industry – indeed, most every sector of the culture that seeks to influence the choices that, cumulatively, will mold our future.

This same process is deeply influential in our individual lives as well. People like Hubbard and Campbell didn't start life thinking they wanted to be shills for big finance. Exceedingly bright and curious, most started out with the goal of becoming serious scholars. Similarly, entirely commendable aspirations motivate most of the people who choose careers as environmental activists, teachers, clergymen, social workers – even politicians.

But then "reality" sets in. After all, these are people with families and household bills to pay. In addition, they live in a culture in which success and status are defined by money. As a result, it's hard to resist the seductive pull of the many compromises that allow them (or so they tell themselves) to continue to be people of integrity and, at the same time, to participate in the American dream.

Sadly – but understandably – this process of seduction, pressure and marginalization even affects that group of truly admirable people that are activists, dedicated to making things different. Far too often, the culture's powerful incentives – and relentless unforgiving penalties for deviance – push them toward:

- A softening of their message to make it palatable to the more mainstream people who write the checks that pay their salary, fund their organizations, and pay for their consulting gigs;

- "Smart" strategic choices – to ensure more money, access to those in power, and media attention – such as jumping on the current hot issue even though it's only tenuously related to their mission, or staying on the sidelines when a truly important issue might alienate key allies;

- Self-protective strategies that, instead of whole-heartedly supporting others who share their goals, keep these "competitors" at arm's length, to prevent them from gaining access to their proprietary know-how and products, and donors.

Consider, as well, the choices made by the many good people who while not explicitly seeing themselves as activists chose their careers out of a sincere desire to serve others:

- The teacher who, in order to stay in the good graces of the school's administration, puts aside his passion to inspire students in order to drill them on how to take the standardized tests that determine his school's funding level; or

- The psychiatrist who, like more than 90% of her colleagues, abandons psychotherapy for a practice limited to prescribing drugs – in order to maintain an income comparable to her colleagues in other medical specialties.

And, of course, there are the many decent people who want to do better but feel compelled to put up with their boss' many indignities and then, far too often, pass them on to others in order to fit in and get by; as, for example, the mid-level manager who silently endures the sting of the boss's angry outburst and, then, insists that his subordinates work late, not to get vital work done, but to placate his superior.

Taken in isolation, most all of the choices outlined above seem relatively inconsequential and, indeed, defensible as concessions to life's practicalities. But that is precisely why they are so devastatingly effective when it comes to rooting us in the status quo. A heightened understanding of this process of seduction, pressure and marginalization – leading, hopefully, to concrete steps to counteract it – is vitally important if we hope to create better lives and a more decent and humane world.

INFILTRATED AND INFECTED

My wife and I started couples' therapy in the mid-1990s, after 10 years of marriage. In our first session Sunny Shulkin, our gifted therapist, casually described the way in which couples typically fight. It goes this way: The woman speaks and the man listens – but in a special way. He is carefully sifting her words for ammunition so that, when her lips finally stop moving, he can fire back. And as he counterattacks, she, in turn, is busy collecting her own ammunition so that, when he stops talking, she can return the fire.

Boy, did Sunny's words hit home! Even though Dale and I loved and respected each other, that's exactly how we fought! When we really got into it, our attacks and counterattacks were swift, relentless and without remorse.

Now, after working with hundreds of couples as a therapist, for 20 years, I understand that Sunny wasn't a mind reader. To the contrary, based on long years of experience, she understood one of our world's sad realities. The culture's habitual compete-to-win ways have thoroughly infected even our most intimate relationships. Indeed, the pattern she described is so common that many couples think it's inevitable and "normal." They can't even imagine another way. And if compete-to-win mindsets have so thoroughly infected our marriages, it's hard to imagine any area of living that is beyond its influence.

To illustrate the depth and breadth of "infiltration and infection" consider two of our most private and, seemingly, benign human activities: Humor and reason.

Calling attention to this process, in these areas, doesn't mean that either quality is bad. To the contrary, humor, skillfully used, offers highly effective, cut-to-the-bone social commentary – as well as good fun. Meanwhile, logical thought, and the ideas it fosters, are indispensable tools as we seek to create better lives and a better world. But precisely because humor and reason are so valuable, we need to be alert to the mainstream

culture's remarkable ability to twist even them into mechanisms that perpetuate and expand the reach of its compete-to-win values.

The (Mis)uses of Humor

Jokes, quips, irony, and sarcasm are deeply woven into the fabric of
our lives and, with the little jolt of pleasure they evoke, a welcome compan-
ion as we tend to our daily chores. Much of our humor is also gentle and
genuinely connecting, but by no means all of it. And if we hope to fully
realize our potential as agents of Radical Decency, we cannot uncritically
give ourselves over to humor's darker side – teasing, sarcasm and ridicule.

To fully understand this aspect of humor, we need to understand
something about anger. Anger is an integral part of our fight-or-flight brain
and is specifically designed to overpower someone else's will. Given the
culture's emphasis on domination and control, it is no surprise that anger
and aggression are endemic. But direct expressions of anger risk unwanted
consequences: The alienation of people important to us; a socially disabling
reputation as someone who is unpleasant and overly aggressive; and, of
course, retaliation.

One of humor's unstated but important roles is to offer an acceptable
social cover for anger. A joke or teasing comment can be utterly benign –
even warm and loving. But the same comment, made with different intent
and timing, can morph into a searing putdown. Thus, when Stan's buddies
call him "Piggy" as he shovels popcorn into his mouth as they watch a
football game, it's all in good fun. Not so, however, when, in the presence
of an attractive new woman, one of those buddies – annoyed by Stan's bid
for her attention – uses the nickname to call attention to the breadcrumbs
and wine stains that have found their way onto his shirt.

The sinister genius of this sort of humor is that it provides a double cloak of non-accountability for anger and aggression. First, it is often

difficult to gauge the joke- teller's intent. Is this an attack? It certainly feels that way. But how can I be sure?

In addition, even when the intent is clear, effective countermeasures are difficult. If you try to confront your grinning put-down artist, you're likely to be greeted with one of these all-too-familiar, accountability-denying responses: "Just kidding" or "What's the matter, can't you take a joke?" Often, you as the victim might even be recast as the problem: "Get over it! You're too sensitive!"

In the form of ridicule, humor is also frequently used as a direct mode of attack. Done well, it is devastatingly effective. Recall, for example, Winston Churchill's withering response when confronted on his drunkenness by his indignant hostess: "Lady, you're ugly. And in the morning, I'll be sober." Or, consider author Tom Clancy's "humorous" description of President Clinton as "a man who thinks that international affairs means dating a girl from out of town."

Many of us, me included, tend to be disarmed by the cleverness of these sorts of comments and, thus, to excuse their searing, dismissive aggressiveness. But we shouldn't. Fueled by the mainstream culture's endemic compete-to-win mindset, they diminish and can even supplant our ability to interact with others in ways that acknowledge and respect difference and seek common ground. Committed to an across-the-board decency practice, we can't indulge our taste for ridicule, aggressive teasing, and other forms of "indecent" humor.

The Limits of Reason

Many of us consider reason to be an unalloyed good. Seeing our emotions as frequently unreliable and potentially damaging, we view our ability to think calmly and logically as a mature, stabilizing force; a way to get those unruly emotions under control.

But however reassuring it is, this view ignores our biological reality. Our emotional brain is, actually, far more powerful than our thinking brain. In fact, all data initially enters our brain through its emotion command center, a structure called the amygdala. Why? So we can go after the really good stuff we crave and, at all costs, avoid the risk of injury or death.

The brain is forever scanning for one of these two situations. So, for example, at the least hint of danger, a powerful jolt of emotion – commonly called "fight or flight" – floods our brain. Only after it is seized by this strong emotion does the data begin to migrate into our thinking brain.

In his 2012 book, *The Righteous Mind: Why Good People are Divided by Politics and Religion*, Jonathan Haidt describes our thinking brain as a rider, sitting atop an elephant that is our emotional brain. Why an elephant and not a horse? Because it's a lot bigger and a lot more powerful. Haidt also points out that, while we like to think of our rider as an impartial judge, carefully sifting the evidence offered by the elephant, it is actually more like a defense lawyer, busily rationalizing and justifying the actions toward which our emotional brain impels us.

The fact that we view our reasoning ability as cool and objective – when, in fact, it's anything but – means that it is ripe for infiltration and infection by the culture's mainstream values. We wind up weaving webs of logic that our thinking brain assures us are true. But on issues that engage our strongest emotions, they are far too often cover stories for our aggressive and manipulative behaviors. In this chilling quote, the psychologist and social theorist Jordan Peterson describes the deadly extremes to which this process can go:

> I understand and having understood, I impose [a rational] order on reality. That's what every ideologue and utopian does. It's convincing and serves as a mask that covers up their tendency to atrocity with the appearance of virtue. Most utopian thinking is of that sort even though the mask can be very well argued.

While this description is, perhaps, a bit overheated and overstated, evidence that supports Peterson's cautionary comments is all around us. At its worst, it has led to political choices that have led to the death of millions, from the Russian purges of the 1930s and the Holocaust, to the Rwandan and Bosnian massacres of the 1990s, to today's ongoing genocide of the Yazidis in Northern Iraq and Syria. Less dramatically, the fiction of all-powerful rationality has shredded one intimate relationship after another as friends and lovers battle about who is "right," certain that their disagreement can be resolved if only "he" (or "she") would just accept the compelling logic of "my" position.

A SHORT HISTORY OF INDECENCY

So here is the situation we face: Against all good sense, we've managed to create a culture that fails to support us in being decent to ourselves, to others, or to our planet.

In this section, I explore the origins of this unfortunate state of affairs. But before doing so, I want to emphasize two points. The first is a hopeful one. Since historical events have created the situation in which we find ourselves, it's within our power to create a different reality. The second point, much more sobering, is the depth of the challenge we face as we seek to unravel patterns of behavior that, as described below, have been 10,000 years in the making.

Throughout nearly all of our 300,000-year history as Homo sapiens, the rhythm of our lives was dictated by the physical world. To feed ourselves, we foraged and hunted. We sought warmth and shelter in the winter, shade in the summer. Daily chores mostly started at sunup and ended at sundown.

But as Jared Diamond points out in his 1997 book, *Guns, Germs, and Steel: The Fates of Human Societies,* a dramatic turning point occurred about 10,000 years ago with the domestication of crops and animals. Our history since then is a direct outgrowth of two powerful trends jumpstarted and fueled by the exponential increase in food and population that these innovations made possible:

1. The ability of one group of people, those who control the food supply, to dominate others. This, in turn, has led to the creation of ever-larger nations, empires, religious movements, and other complex, hierarchical – and typically authoritarian – organizations; and

2. An accelerating ability to harness nature to our purposes, from the plow and sailing ship in ancient Egypt and Mesopotamia to nuclear power, antibiotics, and the airplane in our time.

Given this extraordinary turning point in our history, major shifts in the ways in which we Homo sapiens lived were inevitable. But because the change catalysts were technological and organizational – and not moral or ethical – the ways in which they affected the world and our lives was entirely up for grabs. And, sadly, their overall direction has not been wise and humane. While material advances have, of course, created physical ease and utilitarian benefits far beyond anything our ancient forebears could have imagined, they have not been used to meet our emotional and spiritual needs. Instead, we have moved in the opposite direction, subordinating the essence of our humanness to the demands of the increasingly powerful authoritarian organizations that these processes have spawned. Moreover, while this spirit-deadening, exploitative way of living has been with us for millennia, its reach and impact has grown exponentially since the last years of the 19th century; a deeply consequential development I discuss in Chapter 1.

●●●●●

One of the most concerning aspects of these developments is their potential for deeply distorting the way in which our brain functions. As discussed in Chapter 2, Homo sapiens evolved over 300,000 years to be affiliative beings, profoundly dependent on ongoing, intimate contact with one another for our emotional and intellectual growth, and continued vitality. Thus, you may remember – from that Chapter – leading neuroscientists describing us humans as "only existing in connection with one another" (Daniel Siegel) and as animals that, absent intimate brain to brain connection, "will shrink and eventually die" (Louis Cozolino).

But nature has also equipped us with our rapid-response fight-or-flight brain. Designed to deal with danger, it's fast – 10 times faster than our thinking brain – and very powerful. Energy chemicals (cortisol, adrenaline and noradrenaline) are pumped into our system, blood rushes to our large muscle groups, and the activity of the thinking brain shrinks – all to avoid weakness and indecision at a time of crisis. Faced with a potentially life-threatening emergency, we are ready to act quickly and forcefully.

When the natural world dictated the rhythm of our lives, a comfortable balance was maintained between our fight-or-flight and affiliative brains. Most of our hours and days were spent in nonreactive emotional states as we went about the highly routinized chores of daily living. Working side-by-side, as we tended to crops or did the wash at a nearby stream, we'd quietly and steadily interact with one another. Then, occasionally, danger arrived on the scene – a predatory animal, human enemy, or natural disaster – that would activate our fight-or-flight brain. When the crisis ended, we would return to our normal, more relaxed and comfortably social state of mind.

But in today's world, after 150 years of momentous technological change, everything is different. Groomed to be competitors and pushed by an endless stream of cultural cues to always be a winner, we're "on" more or less constantly, always pushing to make more money, to look sexier and more youthful, to have more friends on Facebook and followers on Twitter. And, on the flip side, we're forever scanning for danger lest we lose our competitive edge.

The result: We run the risk of making fight or flight, designed by nature to be an auxiliary system to deal with isolated moments of danger, our baseline, neurological operating system.

When fight-or-flight is in control, our emotional brain's very purpose is to negate the affiliative side of our brain, replacing it – for that moment – with a single goal: To neutralize or "annihilate" a perceived threat either through aggressive force (fight) or withdrawal (flight). As an occasional, emergency mechanism, this process makes complete sense. But when our fight-or-flight brain is in a continual state of activation, or near-activation, the effect is very different. Never fully reverting to our affiliative state of mind, our ability to interact with one another with empathy and curiosity is deeply diminished. And, indeed, the effects of this corrosive process are all around us:

- The many couples and families that are locked in an endless cycle of criticism, countercriticism and withdrawal;

- Our tendency toward harsh self-judgment whenever we fall short – a classic case of fight-or-fight turned inward;

- The combative and attacking behaviors that dominate the political realm as never before.

So here we are, immersed in what seems to be an ever-accelerating, anti-relational way of living, 10,000 years in the making. And to make matters worse, the processes described earlier in this Chapter – seduction, pressure and marginalization on the one side, and infiltration and infection on the other – are steadily reinforcing its effects. It's enough to discourage even the hardiest among us.

But the future is inherently uncertain. And while these anti-relational ways of operating have grown exponentially, so too has our awareness of the price we pay. Perhaps the increasing psychological pain of our treadmill-like existence – together with the twin risks of environmental devastation and algorithmic subjugation (described in Chapter 1) – will spur a shift in our direction. And that, to be sure, is our hope.

In the meantime, we need to do our part, advocating and modeling the values-based approach to living that Radical Decency promotes; trusting that doing so is both an effective, and life-affirming, response.

CHAPTER 5

The Price We Pay

We live with an enormous amount of self-inflicted pain. In that regard, let me remind you of a few statistics I first shared with you in Chapter 2:

- 44% of American teenagers feel "a lot" or "overwhelming" pressure to succeed in school;

- Nearly 9 out of 10 college students report more mental distress than that experienced by their average 1930's counterparts; and

- Stress about money is reported by 72% of American adults, with 25% rating it as "extreme."

In this Chapter, I explore the central role played by our self-absorbed, materialistic ways in producing these sorts of outcomes, focusing on four of its most serious psychological consequences: Perfectionism, the passivity bred by consumerism, our obsessive denial of aging and dying, and money's vise-like grip on our lives.

Before getting into the specifics of each, however, I want to highlight an important point. One largely hidden, but extremely effective way in which the mainstream culture keeps us stuck in our compete-to-win behaviors is by obscuring its negative effects. Not content to simply ignore the pain that our current modus operandi inflicts on so many of us, the culture takes this process of obfuscation a step further by creating cover stories – endlessly told and retold – that cast the system's painful byproducts as highly desirable virtues.

Take perfectionism, for example. At some level, most of us get it. Yes, we feel relentless pressure to get an A on our next paper, or to nab that promotion, or to maintain our ideal weight and blemish-free complexion. And when we don't, we're all too aware of the jolt of pain and shame that is caused by our "failure."

But instead of forthrightly acknowledging this dark side of our drive for perfection, the mainstream culture endlessly celebrates "winners" and, equally, those special "losers" who tirelessly strive to turn a loss into a win and finally, against all odds, prevail. Consider, for example, the iconic status of the movie character, Rocky, who morphs from a washed-up pug into heavyweight champion, or those pesky rebels in the Star Wars movies who are forever overcoming impossible odds to defeat the evil Empire.

Similarly, money and the things it buys are cast as unalloyed virtues. The more money you make the more valuable you are, a status reinforced and magnified by our use of money to buy bright, shiny objects – the fancy car, the exotic vacation, the $2,400 Louis Vuitton handbag.

In an ad that is typical of the laudatory messages that bombard us, we feast on a series of images of a chiseled, square-jawed young man as he sprints through woods and then gazes out at the horizon from a penthouse balcony, a stunningly beautiful woman at his side. Then, fast cut, we watch him drive fast and free in a gleaming sports car on winding mountain roads. As we watch, a rich baritone voice authoritatively tells us what is means to be a winner:

> How do you want to live? As a decent person, not a bad
> guy, a good friend? Is that it? Good? Of course not! King of the
> hill? Better! Top of your game! Win! All powerful, like a boss,

like a standard bearer, like a pro. We couldn't agree more. We are professional grade. GMC.

Surrounded by such noisy and insistent affirmations, the price we pay for our immersion in the culture's compete-to-win mindsets is deeply obscured. Most of us are left, at best, with a vague sense that something is seriously out of whack. But what, exactly, is it?

Sadly, remarkably, even the people whose job it is to heal our psychic wounds are deeply implicated in this process of obfuscation. Thus, the Diagnostic and Statistical Manual (the DSM), designed by psychotherapy's best minds to comprehensively catalog all of our psychological ills, has 22 categories and subcategories for depression and another 20 for anxiety. Yet, there isn't a single diagnostic option for perfectionism, our denial of our own aging and death, or our obsession with money – each of which, as we shall see, are triggers for so much of our troubled psychic state.

THE PERILS OF PERFECTIONISM

Merriam-Webster defines perfectionism as:

A disposition to regard anything short of perfection as unacceptable; especially, the setting of unrealistically demanding goals accompanied by a disposition to regard failure to achieve them as unacceptable and a sign of personal worthlessness.

In our culture, this mindset finds its archetypal expression in the constant reminder that "you can do anything, if you just try hard enough," a pervasive cultural rallying cry that studiously omits its inevitable corollary: "And if you don't accomplish your goals, there is something wrong with *you*."

"You can do anything" is, of course, demonstrably false. Largely consigned to subpar, financially starved ghetto schools, the high school drop-out rate for African Americans is twice the rate of whites (45% vs. 22%), and even those that graduate perform on average four academic years below their white counterparts. Given these realities, the odds of a poor black child going to an Ivy League college – even if he "just tries hard enough" – are astronomically small. Similarly, if you work in a dying industry, such as textile manufacturing or printing, you may not find any work at all, let alone the position of your dreams.

The primary reason for most of our "failures" is not a lack of effort. Instead, it's all about life's thorny, unforgiving and unavoidable realities:

1. *The game is fixed.* Those with money and connections have a long head start. Thus, according to a 2015 Pew Research Center study, children with parents in the 90th percentile of wage earners ($120,000 per year) will make, on average, 3 times more than those born to parents in the 10th percentile ($40,000 per year); a differential that gets ever steeper as parental income grows.

2. *So much in life is arbitrary.* However determined we may be we'll fail if the boss doesn't like us, the company is downsized, or an illness or injury undermines our health.

3. *We are all limited, flawed beings.* The simple truth is that we can't do everything to which we set our minds, no matter how hard we try. Thus, despite my intense love of music, the quality of my voice and tenuous ability to stay on key meant that I never got to sing in my school's choir – or in my good buddy Billy's rock band.

While in theory we recognize these limiting realities, we so often fail to follow through on their implications when it comes to our own strivings. Falling short of perfection, our automatic response is "I am the problem" and the solution is to "man up." I need to take responsibility, redouble my efforts, do better next time, and never succumb to the weak, wimpy temptation to blame my situation on circumstances beyond my control.

In my psychotherapy practice, I continually confront this mindset. Take Shana, for example, a single mom committed to living in a small, tight-knit community in Philadelphia's exurbs, with an excellent public-school system. When she came to me, she was fortunate enough to have a well-paying job, at a tech company, within minutes of her home. However, after several years of relative stability, her company began outsourcing its services to cheaper overseas locations. Early on, she trusted her boss's reassurances that she was safe. But after two years of alarming attrition, her fears steadily increased. Then, in a fourth round of cuts, her job was eliminated.

When Shana got the news, she was crushed. Despite all the evidence to the contrary, she was, in her eyes, a failure. "If I'd done my job right, they wouldn't have fired me," she said. In addition, she blamed herself for being far too passive in the years leading up to her dismissal – never mind that she had had every reason to hang onto one of the few jobs in her field that allowed her to remain in the rural community that meant so much to her and her kids. "What was *wrong* with me?" she wailed. "I should have been out looking for my next job, instead of leaving my fate in the company's hands."

A second story, involving another client, illustrates the fact that even success does not inoculate you against the searing self-judgment that perfectionism breeds. A poor, working-class kid with a community college degree, Rob was a natural when it came to assessing risk in complex business environments. Thus, despite the absence of a blue chip, MBA pedigree, he had, by the age of 35, become a highly valued senior executive at a major insurance company.

But Rob had an Achilles heel. Formal presentations triggered severe anxiety. And while his aversion to public speaking had never seriously interfered with his job performance, his superiors kept pushing him to conquer his fear – to just get over it. "You're on the fast track career-wise," they told him, "but you'll never realize your potential if you're unable to make smooth, confident, professional public presentations."

When Rob and I began working together, he had internalized this relentless hectoring – and its underlying message: *You're defective and need to be fixed*. Only after months of hard work in therapy was he able, finally, to cultivate a different, less perfectionist outlook, delivering this message to his boss:

> Look, I'm never going to be a comfortable, confident public speaker. I need a role that uses my analytical skills but avoids those situations. And if that means I don't get promoted to the company's highest levels, so be it.

Even at this point however, while Rob was far more comfortable in his own skin, the feeling that he was flawed and "less than" never fully left him.

Finally, there is the poignant example of the couples I see from time to time, where the man is having sexual performance issues. With tragic regularity, his partner's immediate, ego-piercing reaction is that, since a "good" wife – that is, a perfect one – is able to sexually arouse and satisfy her husband, *she* is the problem and is woefully imperfect.

As these examples illustrate, our perfectionist tendencies show up in an endless variety of situations, wreaking emotional havoc in many forms:

- Ashamed of whatever deficiency we see in ourselves, we withdraw from others and become depressed.

- Reflexively judging and doubting ourselves, we become anxious, cautious, indecisive, and/or defensive.

- Unable to shake the sense than we are "defective, "less than," or "a fraud," we stop taking on challenges that seems awkward, confusing, or potentially embarrassing – and simply go through the motions.

So while the mainstream culture's rhetoric is all about the "thrill of victory" and "achieving great things," our resulting perfectionism more commonly moves us in the opposite direction, creating a pandemic of spirit-sapping beliefs and behaviors.

Another unfortunate aspect of our obsession with individual perfection is that it obscures the systemic factors that so powerfully contribute to what ails us. For example, millions of people were financially leveled by the 2008 economic crisis. Yet, remarkably, no meaningful effort was made to correct the many systemic defects that triggered the crisis. Instead, the people who "recklessly" took out the crisis-precipitating subprime home loan mortgages were left to shoulder the blame.

On the systemic side of this equation were the rating agencies – Moody's, Fitch's, Standard and Poor's – whose job was to assess the quality of these mortgages. Since these entities were paid by the investment banks whose mortgages they were evaluating, it was absolutely obvious, in retrospect, that the Triple A ratings they uncritically bestowed on these mortgages were a prime cause of the crisis. And yet, nothing was ever been done to eliminate this obvious conflict of interest.

On the other hand, there was no shortage of voices arguing that the millions of ordinary people who were victimized by the crisis needed to shoulder their "fair share" of the blame, the theory being that if they got financial relief, they'd only be encouraged to make similarly unwise financial investments in the future. The end result? Millions of individual borrowers who lost their homes and savings were punished because they didn't have the intestinal fortitude to "do the right thing" by "just saying no" to home loans that the banks so aggressively, and irresponsibly, urged them to accept.

Another appalling example of how perfectionism obscures systematic causes centers on the torturing of prisoners in Iraq, in the early 2000's. In its aftermath, a handful of low-level "bad actors" were prosecuted but no meaningful effort was made to look at the macro factors that led the United

States to adopt these unspeakably cruel policies. Instead, the implicit message was that these brutal outcomes were all about individual choice. The responsibility lay with the ordinary soldiers in the field who "should have known better" and "done the right thing."

●●●●●

What, then, is the bottom line about perfectionism? When it comes reinforcing our compete-to-win ways of living, it does double duty. First, instead of energizing us, it far more typically triggers spirit-deflating states of mind that deeply discourage change initiatives. Second, with its extreme emphasis on personal accountability, it steers us away from the systemic issues that so urgently need to be addressed if we hope to create better lives and a more decent and humane world.

THE BUYING GAME

Consumerism stands side by side with economic success as one of the twin pillars of a mainstream life. From infancy, our children are so inundated with video games and store-bought toys that simple pleasures such as skipping a rock, kicking a can down the street, or tree climbing – staples of my childhood – have become lost arts. Throughout our lives, we are bombarded with endless opportunities to shop, promoted by nonstop ads and the culture's uncritical celebration of the latest ingenious gadgets, and the newest and fanciest cars and clothes.

On its face, this consumer mindset may seem relatively benign. What's wrong, after all, with buying and enjoying all the marvelous products that are available to those of us lucky enough to live in the 21st century? But this isn't the full story. We urgently need to understand and counteract the debilitating effect consumerism has on our ability to be active agents in our lives.

Several years ago, I participated in a service trip to Cuernavaca, Mexico. Early one morning, we traveled in open-air trucks to an organic farm where we helped to plant crops. Finishing just before noon, we returned to our guesthouse to a simple lunch of macaroni salad and bologna-and-cheese sandwiches. As I ate my lunch and participated in the group's spirited conversation, I noticed how good I felt. My body ached – in a good way – from the morning's work and my spirit was energized by the shared experience and solidarity I felt with my companions. Even my bologna-and-cheese sandwich seemed tasty!

Our group consisted of people like me, privileged North Americans thoroughly habituated to a consumer-oriented way of living. As eager and expert consumers, we had – in an ironic and entirely unconscious expression of our taken-for-granted sense of entitlement – planned a dinner that night at the fanciest restaurant in Cuernavaca. Drinks were served on a gorgeous lawn where peacocks quietly grazed. When a sudden downpour erupted, waiters magically appeared with oversized umbrellas to escort us to our tables. The place settings were elegant in every detail, the food perfectly presented and delicious, the service superb.

The stark juxtaposition of lunch and dinner stunned me. Sitting at dinner I realized that its seductive beauty had lulled me into a state of passivity. That morning and at lunch, I was an active participant in creating my experience. At dinner, I reverted to the habitual consumer posture I knew so well. I was the docile recipient of something someone else had created. In my body, a soothing numbness replaced the vibrant feeling of aliveness I'd felt that morning. I was inert, infantilized.

This posture of passivity flows almost inevitably out of our ingrained consumer habits. Our implicit expectation is that most everything we need has been prepared by others and is purchasable. Our only job is to choose "this" product or "that" one.

Applied to the purchase of clothes, cars and electronics, this mindset is not necessarily a problem. What is problematic, however, is the extent to which it has seeped into virtually every area of our lives.

Off-the-Shelf, Ready-to-Wear Communities

In *Bowling Alone: The Collapse and Revival of American Community,* Robert Putnam comprehensively documents the decline in our communal involvements in the last half of the 20th century. Earlier, in a 1996 *American Spectator* article, "The Strange Disappearance of Civic America," Putnam summarized the exhaustive research upon which the book is based:

> Surveys of average Americans in which they recorded every single activity during a day indicate that, since 1965, time spent socializing and visiting is down by 25%, and time devoted to clubs and organizations is down even more sharply (by roughly half). Membership in such diverse organizations as the PTA, the Elks, the League of Women Voters, the Red Cross, labor unions, and even bowling leagues show a decline of roughly 25% to 50%. Surveys also show sharp declines in many measures of collective political participation, including attending a rally or speech (off 36% between 1973 and 1993), attending a meeting on town or school affairs (off 39%), or working for a political party (off 56%).

While many factors have contributed to this trend, consumerism is a key culprit. When it comes to our communal organizations, most of us are like shoppers pushing a cart down the Acme aisle. In an ironic twist on President Kennedy's "ask not what your country can do for you, ask what you can do for your country," the question we now instinctively ask is: What can this organization do for *me*?

In politics, for example, we sit back, listen to each candidate's sales pitch and, then, buy the person who offers the best product. As evidence of this trend, consider the emergence of political polling. This industry barely existed in 1940s. But now its findings are headline news, day in and day out, chronicling in excruciating detail the "marketability" of the "products" being "sold" to us by our politicians.

Our focus, now, is the product's "success" in the political marketplace and far less on substance. Thus, Obamacare was commonly viewed as a "failure" when the polls showed a majority of Americans in opposition. Then, it magically morphed into a success when the poll numbers reversed – even though the underlying law hadn't changed one iota. Similarly, bad poll numbers influence a candidate's reputation far more heavily than flawed policies. Recall, for example, the precipitous fall from grace of Jeb Bush, the Republicans' early frontrunner in 2016, as his poll numbers dramatically sank, ultimately to single digits.

What is lost in this process is our instinct to get actively involved in the political and communal organizations with which we identify. As consumers of the products being sold we feel little, if any, obligation to show up for meetings or to volunteer for the many necessary but thankless jobs that keep these organizations alive and vibrant. And when, as is inevitable, problems arise, we're all too ready to jump ship. Instead of working to fix what might be broken within the organization, we simply walk away from the now flawed product and look for a new, shinier one.

This mindset comes at a great cost. Active involvement in our communal/political lives fosters a sense of contribution to, and control over, our destiny. When our candidate loses, for example, we're empowered to get to work promoting alternative policies, political movements, and candidates. But when we are passive consumers, an electoral defeat leaves us feeling helpless – and, in turn, more prone to depression, anger, insecurity and despair. All we can do is rail against the new incumbent, something we now do, liberals and conservatives alike, with ever-increasing stridency.

Ironically, things aren't all that much better when our guy or gal wins. Once in office, her actual performance will almost inevitably fall far short of the overblown product she sold us. So once again, the likely outcome is not empowerment but, instead, frustration, disappointment, and a sense of helplessness.

Consumers of Love

Properly conceived, romance is all about intimacy. At first, of course, we're awash in "back-of-the-brain" love chemicals, the giddy, dizzying stuff that brings two people together in the first place. But then, ideally, the relationship evolves. We share ourselves with this person, lovingly expressing our vulnerabilities and needs and, equally, seeking to understand our partner's needs and desires.

The norm that exists in our consumer-oriented culture is, however, very different. Choosing a partner has largely become an exercise in comparative shopping, not unlike a search for the right car or laundry detergent. Looking for a partner? Sign on to the popular Tinder dating site where, with a swipe of your thumb on a person's picture, left or right, you can "buy" a potential mate or move on to a "better deal," leaving that person on the shelf.

For some, this supermarket approach to dating leads to a meaningful and lasting relationship. But the trend is in the opposite direction. Far too often, the consumer mindset that brought the couple together carries over into the relationship itself, with partners continually assessing the value of the product. Then, when the other person's emotional complexities show up – as is inevitable – they are all too ready to move on to a new potential mate who, expertly marketed via flattering pictures and a carefully crafted online profile, promises uncomplicated love and fulfillment.

People who take this approach think they're taking charge of their life. But this belief is illusory. Like me, sitting at a banquet prepared by others, their stance is passive. As consumers, their options are actually quite limited: Either take what is being offered or leave it.

What is lost, of course, is any opportunity to struggle, learn, grow and evolve. Instead of doing the hard work of relationship, our instinct is to move on, trusting that the marketplace for love will surely offer a better deal. Walking this murky path, a mutually cooperative and enduring connection with an intimate partner is, for far too many, perpetually beyond our reach.

Disposable Workers

Finally, consider the extent to which this consumer mindset has taken root in the workplace. In the same half-century that Robert Putnam chronicled in *Bowling Alone,* unions and workers' rights were in steep decline, thanks in part to our pervasive consumer mindsets. We now live in a world in which workers, too, are seen as mere products to be bought in the marketplace – and, then, like an old kitchen appliance or iPhone, to be discarded when their usefulness is at an end. And what is truly astonishing, and disturbing, is the extent to which so many workers, steeped in consumerism, passively accept this perspective about who they are and what their value is.

Recall, in this regard, my client Shana whose story I shared earlier in this Chapter. Even before she was fired from her job, she endured years of spirit-crushing anxiety as she watched her co-workers disappear, wondering if and when her turn would come. And yet, the idea that she and her coworkers could fight back never occurred to her.

Then, there is the all-too-typical case of my client, Barry. Employed for 29 years as a security guard for a public agency, he has shown up each day, played by the rules, and persevered through an endless stream of supervisors, some good and others bullying and nitpicking. After all these years, you'd think his job would be secure.

Not so. Through seniority, he's now one of the highest-paid guards in an agency being pressured to save money. As a result, he's become a target.

His requests for vacation and personal leave are now being questioned and often denied. He's also being given lousy assignments, such as manning the small, badly heated booth at the back of the loading dock. And if he's even a minute late for morning roll call, he gets written up.

No one at the agency is saying so, but Barry and I both believe it's trying to push him out or, failing that, to document a case to justify his dismissal. And, with a toothless union and a toadying human resources department as his only recourses – an increasingly common reality into-day's work world – he feels helpless to do anything about it.

Sadly, the stories of Shana and Barry are all too typical. Millions of workers are being treated like disposable products. And with their con-sumer-steeped mindsets, they are doing far too little to counteract it.

ILLUSIONS OF IMMORTALITY

Two key events mark and define our lives: Birth and death. The first just happens, without our anticipation or awareness. Dying, however, is a different story. Consciousness of our mortality is always with us and how we deal with it vitally affects our quality of life.

Unfortunately, the culture's predominant values deeply marginalize this reality. If asked, we agree that death is inevitable. But the ways in which we compose our lives reflect a very different reality.

Thoroughly interwoven into our compete, win, dominate and con-trol mindsets is the implicit belief that, through shrewd choices and sheer force of will, we can make ourselves invulnerable to the effects of time. The right combination of food, supplements, exercise, and stretching will allow us to always feel great and never get sick.

This fantasy of invincibility is, moreover, reinforced by the image we present to the world. So many of us dye our hair; surgically alter our faces, breasts, and thighs; inject Botox; and/or consume Viagra – all strategies designed to maintain the illusion of everlasting youth, both for others and for ourselves.

The illusion of perpetual life is also baked into the outlook of those most conversant with death, our mainstream medical professionals. Doctors talk boldly about finding "cures" for virtually every disease that ails us, from cancer to heart disease to Alzheimer's, and aggressively fight to save the lives of patients who are irreversibly dying. For many medical professionals, death isn't life's natural endpoint. It is, instead, an enemy to be defeated.

Note, also, how thoroughly money is implicated in this strident denial of mortality. Many rich people obsessively pamper their bodies to mask the reality of aging. In addition, they surround themselves with things that, being big and beautiful, seem ageless and indestructible: Art and fine wine collections; clothes and accessories by Chanel and Hermes; living spaces filled with furniture designed by Roche Bobois or perfectly arranged, for hundreds of thousands of dollars, by Philippe Starck.

And beyond that is the obsessive accumulation of money itself, which as Charles Eisenstein points out in *Sacred Economics: Money, Gift, and Society in the Age of Transition,* personifies the immortality we so vainly seek:

> The one thing that most closely resembles the divine is money. It is an invisible, immortal force that steers all things, omnipotent and limitless, an 'invisible hand' . . . far removed from materiality and exempt from nature's most important laws, for it does not decay and return to the soil as all other things do. Instead, it bears the properties of eternal preservation and everlasting increase.

Getting more and more of this "magical" stuff, the rich feed the delusion that they, too, will somehow endure forever. And even for those of us who aren't super-rich, life's taken-for-granted goal is, far too often, to make more and more money, the implicit belief being that if we accumulate enough, we can join that hallowed priesthood of ultra-rich humans who seem exempt from life's grim existential realities.

Getting regular exercise, eating a sensible diet and obtaining good medical care are, of course, positive behaviors. But the underlying mindset they reinforce is not. We act as though death is and will forever be 10, 20 or 30 years down the road from wherever we are now. Somewhere on this journey we do, of course, die. But by virtue of this cognitive sleight of hand, it is always premature – a stroke of bad fortune rather than an inevitable part of our experience.

The price we pay for this chronic state of denial is far too high. There is a natural rhythm to life and, fully embraced, each stage brims with its own special rewards and challenges. But all that is swept aside when we reflexively seek to freeze time, struggling to maintain the ambition and sexual allure of a 30-year-old into our 60s and beyond. Instead of gracefully leaving center stage to the next generation, we strive to remain competitive with younger people, both professionally and socially.

But the strategy never works. Even Hugh Hefner, the super-rich founder of *Playboy* and notorious Casanova, eventually became a pathetic caricature; a doddering old man in pajamas surrounded by bizarrely coquettish women, young enough to be his granddaughters.

In this regard, I remember a story related to me by a fellow attorney – let's call him James – who, in his 40s, was elected Chancellor of the Philadelphia Bar Association, our profession's most prestigious local position. Shortly after his election, a group of older attorneys requested a meeting. All in their 70s, they had been leading attorneys at powerful, local law firms but, now, they were at the end of their careers. James kicked the meeting off with a few, carefully considered remarks:

> I am so pleased to be here with you. Walking across
> City Hall Plaza to join you on this beautiful spring afternoon,
> I thought about how proud you must be. You represent all that

is best in our profession and have been role models for me and so many other young attorneys. If anyone has earned the right to relax and smell the roses, it's you.

As James tells the story, he never laid a bigger egg in his life! Staring at him with sour and stony disbelief, these old warhorses revealed their agenda: We've lost our power and want it back! Entirely absent was any sense of receding with grace to a position of elder statesman, mentoring a new generation of attorneys. Since James couldn't turn back time, they left the meeting frustrated and angry.

In the 30 years since that meeting, James became one of Philadelphia's premier attorneys and power brokers. Now in his 70s himself, I wonder if he's "relaxing and smelling the roses." Knowing how driven he always was, I have my doubts.

Chronic denial of aging also leaves us woefully unprepared when our life's natural end point becomes imminent. So many of us react to a terminal diagnosis with disbelief which, when you think about it, is pretty funny. Did we really think it wasn't going to happen to us? What is less funny is our lack of preparation when we're faced with life's final challenge. The result? Too many of us die badly, railing against our fate and filled with complaints because our body no longer works as it's "supposed to."

But it doesn't have to be this way. It's possible to embrace aging, dying and death with grace and equanimity. For me, this reality came into focus several years ago as I listened to an interview with the Irish memoirist Nuala O'Faolain, then 68. Living with a terminal cancer diagnosis, she was struggling with the fact that all of her accumulated wisdom would die with her.

Hearing her anguish, I remembered a story that my dear friend Barbara Fenhagen told me about a friend in California whose home in Berkeley Hills burned down in the 1980s, destroying all of her possessions. Shortly after that event, people started contacting her. Years earlier, she had sent copies of her favorite recipes to a friend. That friend called to say that she was recopying them and sending them back to her. Her children also called to say they were making copies of the family photos she'd faithfully sent to them over the years. As these calls continued, this wise woman came to a realization: The only thing that is safely mine is what I give away.

For me, this second story answers O'Faolain's dilemma. I now look at the rhythm of our years as consisting of two interwoven but distinct paths. The first, an acquisitive one, starts at an intensely high level, exemplified by the infant who is constantly exploring, touching, experimenting, testing, grabbing and learning. This remains our dominant preoccupation into young adulthood as we hone our social and romantic skills, build careers, and establish homes, families and places in our communities.

Since effective adults are skilled at loving others, we are always aware of life's second path – offering our love and wisdom back to others. But while this may be a somewhat muted subtext in the earlier years of life, we need to increasingly embrace it as we age into our middle years and beyond; becoming mentors and cheerleaders for those in the upcoming generation. Doing so, our later years cease to be a doomed attempt to stay forever young. Instead, recognizing that we are in a sweet race against time to "give it away," we are infused with a spirit-affirming purpose.

This outlook on life can support us in dying well. Tough as it is likely to be, our impending death will be vitally important to everyone who loves us, not only because they will miss us (we hope), but also because our death is a vivid reminder that they, too, will face this moment. What greater gift to our loved ones, then, than to handle this last great mystery with equanimity, acceptance and, even, curiosity and a sense of anticipation? Approached in this way, our decline and death – instead of being a dreaded event to be ignored and denied – can become a final, ennobling act of giving it away.

THE VISE OF MONEY

When it comes to money, our anxieties and fears are massive. For many, they show up as a grim, daily struggle to simply pay the bills – and God forbid a car accident or illness blows a hole in our budget. Thus, according to a recent Federal Reserve survey, more than a third of all Americans, if faced with an emergency expense of just $400, would have to sell something or get a loan.

And more money doesn't remove these concerns. To the contrary, most all of us live with an incessant foreboding about the future: How can I pay for the kids' college educations? How can I possibly provide for my retirement? Today's norm is a deflating sense that we can never really get ahead and will be forever indentured to jobs for which we feel little or no passion. And so, the precious years of our lives slip away.

What is so ironic and sad about all of this is that, when you really think about it, it's almost impossible to win the money game. To begin with, because moneymaking is such an intensely competitive sport, there is no place of rest, no moment in which victory can be declared.

In this regard, consider the experience of my good friend and law partner, Spencer Franck, who regularly served on our firm's committee that determined each partner's percentage share of the profits and, hence, his or her income for the coming year. According to Spencer, on the day percentages were announced, no one ever pounded the table for an additional $20,000. On the other hand, a steady stream of partners would inevitably arrive at his office to complain bitterly that partner X's share was half a percent point higher than his – and this from a group of people whose incomes, even at the low end of the partnership scale, were well into six figures.

To the same point is the hilarious but telling episode of the TV series *Silicon Valley* in which a deal, financed by a super-rich investor, suddenly collapses. Witnessing the investor's searing pain, we assume he's lost his fortune. But, as the story unfolds, we learn that he hasn't gone broke at all. Instead, he's "lost a comma." With his net worth slipping below $1 billion – hence the lost comma – he felt totally humiliated in the eyes of his peers.

And even if we somehow escape this comparative trap, a win in the money game is still a rarity since, as Art Rooney, the late owner of the Pittsburgh Steelers, once observed, "people live up to their means." Thus, in the 1980s novel, *Bonfire of the Vanities,* Tom Wolfe explained how a bond broker making $900,000 a year was just getting by what with the expense of private schools, a Park Avenue condo, and a summer home in the Hamptons.

Closer to home, I always remember a particularly difficult conversation I had in the 1990s with Jonathon, a friend and fellow board member at a local nonprofit. A pleasant, soft-spoken and entirely prudent man in his late 30s, Jonathon supported his wife, a stay-at-home mom, and two kids on his salary as a software developer. And yet, when I approached him for a contribution to our annual fundraising drive, he earnestly explained to me – with averted eyes– that he was "broke" and could give nothing. His annual income: $80,000 (an amount whose purchasing power, in 1995, would be equivalent to $130,000 today).

•••••

As unrelenting as these more obvious money pressures are, they fail to tell the full story. It's also important to understand the pervasive meanings and taboos that surround money and dramatically ratchet up its influence in our lives. In particular:

1. *Money cuts to our emotional core.* It intensely judges who we are. Hence Jonathon's searing self-judgment when he admitted to me that he was "broke" and my shame when Spencer's committee cut my share of the firm's profits by 10%.

2. *Money's judgments are stark and brutal.* So easy to measure, the arithmetic is all too simple: If you make more, you're worth more; if you make less, you're worth less.

3. *We suffer alone.* With most every other detail of people's lives broadcast to the world via Facebook and Instagram, we somehow "just know" that how much people make, spend, or have stashed in the bank are taboo subjects.

It's Personal!

There have been times and places in which wealth was far more a communal matter than it is today. In socialist countries and on Israeli kibbutzim, for example, the wealth of the collective plays a far greater role in people's overall sense of well-being. Remember as well that as hunter/gatherers – our way of living for most of our 300,000 years of existence as Homo sapiens – a communal outlook was a given. Living in groups of 40 to 160 people and working hard simply to survive, there was no meaningful connection between what we produced and what we received or "owned."

In the world as it now exists, however, wealth is intensely personal. It's about each of us individually, standing alone before the world. And walking hand-in-hand with this mindset is money's fierce power to judge our value as a person.

This point was brought home to me several years ago, as I facilitated a discussion of money in one of my men's groups. Understanding that most people are reluctant to reveal the particulars of their finances, I asked each man to write his annual income, net worth, and yearly expenses on a slip of paper. Then I asked them to fold the paper so the contents were hidden and to place it on the table in front them. My intent was to use the act of writing these numbers down as an emotional prompt, trusting that this act alone would jumpstart a more intimate conversation about money.

And so it did – but in a totally unexpected way. To my surprise, one of the participants simply blurted out his financial particulars and the other men followed suit. The conversation that followed, after a stunned silence, was eye opening. Financially undressed, every man confessed to an area of marked shame or fear. One talked about the great pain he felt around his spending habits, and his fear about how he'd be able to manage in the years ahead. Another revealed for the first time, after years in the group, that he felt like a failure because his (low six-figure) income didn't measure up to the incomes of his fellow University of Pennsylvania law school grads. Still another was living with intense remorse about unwise investment decisions, confessing that he felt like he'd failed his wife and children.

Sadly, what these men revealed that day has been told to me over and over again by my therapy clients. The number of people who live in their own private purgatory when it comes to money has stunned me. Our felt value as human beings – or, more typically, our felt lack of value – is, to a truly extraordinary extent, measured and confirmed by the ways in which we make and manage our money.

The Numbers Never Lie

Growing up in a New York City suburb in the 1950s, I was a big-time Yankees fan. In 1956, to the delight of 10-year-old Jeff, Mickey Mantle was the undisputed king of baseball, winning the Triple Crown with 53 home runs, 130 RBIs, and a .353 batting average. In 1961, a somewhat older Mickey was still really good, logging 54 home runs and hitting .321. But, eclipsed by Roger Maris's 61 homers, he was no longer the top dog. And by 1967, Mickey was a forlorn figure, a shadow of his former self with a .237 batting average and a measly 18 homers.

When it comes to judging a ball player, notice how visible, definitive, and unforgiving these numbers are. There is no room for doubt. A winner in 1956, Mickey Mantle was a dead loser in everyone's eyes just 10 years later. But while measuring the value of ball players in this way makes some sense, it makes no sense at all when it is applied to our lives. And to a disturbing extent, that is exactly what we do – with our income and net worth, like a ball player's batting average and home run total, being the all-important statistics.

One sneaky, scary, and easily overlooked aspect of money, exemplified by this process, is how definitive and quantifiable it is. A $90,000 a year income is unquestionably more than a $60,000 income, and $3 million in the bank feels a whole lot better than a $20,000 rainy day account. For us, just like Mickey, there is no avoiding the harsh implication of our numbers.

Money is moreover a wonderfully adaptable, universally applicable measuring stick that judges all of us without regard to our interests, passions or dispositions. Just like business people, the success of artists, academics, and religious leaders is typically judged by their ability to "sell the product;" by commanding a high price for their books and art works or filling an auditorium or church with paying customers/congregants. And despite decades of effort by women's rights advocates, we still judge the work of a stay-at-home parent – still more typically a woman – as less important than that of her income-producing partner because she isn't paid for it.

Moreover, this "you're only as good as your numbers" outlook is, if anything, intensifying. It used to be that income and net worth were the defining numbers. But, now, our FICO credit score has assumed an outsized role in our lives. With our ability to get a loan, job, or apartment increasingly dependent on that number, it should come as no surprise that a 2013 study of 8400 young adults, by the National Institutes of Health, reported that a high level of debt relative to assets – and, thus, a low credit rating – was strongly associated with higher depression and anxiety, and worse health. In addition, since we're now, mostly, on our own when it comes to our retirement, still another number has emerged that remorselessly measures our effectiveness in life: The amount of money in our 401(k) or IRA.

The upshot? Since almost no one bats .340 and hits 40 home runs, year in and year out – and since the numbers never lie – it's hard for most of us to avoid the belief that, in the "game" of life, we are at best utility infielders.

Secrecy; Locking in the Pain

Some years ago, Madonna had a filmmaker record her life. She told him that everything was fair game. He could film her having sex. He could film her going to her bathroom. But when she met with her financial advisors, no cameras. And in an updated version of the same story, Donald Trump, in preparation for his 2011 celebrity roast on Comedy Central, specifically ok'ed jokes that referenced his hair, weight, and sexual attraction to daughter Ivanka. However, he ruled out any joke about not being as wealthy as he claimed to be.

In our "tell-all" world, ask yourself this question: How many people do you know who tell all about their finances?

In an experiment I used to run with groups, I would ask participants to reflect on two sets of questions.

1. Who do you have sex with? How often? How do you do it?

2. How much money do you make? How much do you spend? What is your net worth?

After group members silently contemplated their answers for a minute or so, I would then ask which set of questions caused greater anxiety as they thought about sharing their responses. Typically, 80-90 percent of participants chose the money questions.

What lessons can we take from the attitudes of Madonna, Trump, and my group participants when it comes to money? Here are two:

- Don't ask: Its rude and inappropriate; and

- Don't tell: It's bragging – or shameful and humiliating.

And note, importantly, that these social taboos are not about good manners. To the contrary, they have a deadly serious, highly consequential purpose.

At a macro level, here's the shell game they make possible. First, we have progressively shrunk governmental programs for the disadvantaged and increasingly look to volunteerism and individual initiative to fill the void. But then, by throwing this cloak of anonymity around our uses of money, the financing of vast parts of the social safety net is left to the whims of individuals who – shielded by this fierce "don't ask, don't tell" norm – feel virtually no social pressure to step up to the plate.

The results are predictable. Wealthy people, who in theory would take the lead in these voluntary efforts, invest a grotesquely tiny proportion of their resources in programs for the needy. In 2011, the top 20% of earners contributed just 1.3% of their income to charity; meaning that the average person making $1 million a year donated $13,000 or more accurately, after the likely tax deduction, less than $9,000. In addition, when it comes to the truly needy, even this meager amount overstates the situation since, again using 2011 as our example, only one-third of all charitable contributions were targeted for the poor.

In truth, this cone of silence around money is a prescription for an unraveling of society. It invites the wealthy to quietly retreat into their gated communities, private clubs, and first-class cabins – and the less privileged to narrow their focus to family, job and their immediate circle. And, indeed, each of these is happening every day, seemingly at an accelerating pace.

Our secrecy around money also extracts an unacceptably high price in our personal lives. Intimate sharing is an essential part of healing. If someone close to us dies or we're struggling in a difficult relationship, we are far better served if we seek out a friend, or possibly a therapist, for perspective and emotional support.

The same is also true when we seek to heal from culturally inflicted pain. Prior to the 1960s, for example, our assumptions about women, like our current mindsets about money, were seldom discussed or challenged; the result being that we were frozen, largely unawares, in deeply painful, sexist behaviors. Since then, however, there has been a dramatic shift in our attitudes about gender nurtured and sustained, very significantly, by honest, intense, ongoing discussions about patriarchy and sexism.

Open and honest sharing is life's Miracle-Gro. As we struggle with its many challenges, we desperately need the soothing, empathic presence of others who, because they, too, are flawed, struggling humans – just like us – can understand what we're going through. Together, we're able to sustain one another and find new, more creative ways. Alone and isolated, our fears and anxieties are far more likely to rage unchecked, deeply diminishing our ability to find relief.

If we hope to live differently and better, our discussions about money need to mirror the conversations we've been having in recent years about gender. In the media, in our living rooms, and in the bedroom before the light goes out, we need to be in frank and open dialogue about:

- The insecurities and fears that money triggers;

- The hopes and dreams that fuel our drive to get more and more of it;

- The judgments we have about those who have it and those who don't; and

- The many ways in which money worries flatten our spirit and straitjacket our lives.

Then, crucially, we need to start making choices that increasingly challenge our taken-for-granted, money-driven ways. This may mean cutting back on our work hours to spend more time with our 10-year-old son or aging mother, and/or increasing our charitable commitments beyond a place of comfortable tokenism. It may also mean considering a less prestigious, lower-paying job at a place where the mission and ways of operating more fully reflect our values.

None of this is easy, of course. Diverging from ways of living that are so heavily reinforced by the culture's compete-to-win norms is apt to be uncomfortable, even scary. But to paraphrase one of my important teachers, while we can act our way into thinking differently, we are seldom able to think our way into acting differently. The inescapable truth is this: If we hope to loosen money's vise-like grip on our lives, it's the only way.

CHAPTER 6

The "There:" A Radically Decent Life

If our current "here," with all the debilitating consequences described in the last Chapter, has created a failed culture, what is the "there" we should be aiming for?

Needless to say, a soul-satisfying life varies greatly from one person to another. One of my clients, Vicki, when asked in kindergarten what she wanted to be when she grew up, said "entomologist." At 28, unhappy in her safe corporate job, she left that company to pursue her lifelong dream of studying insects. Brady, on the other hand, is an exuberant financial planner who feels enormous satisfaction helping middle-class people make wiser choices with their money. And then there is Nick, who moved to a small town in Alaska where he enjoys hiking, working on improvements to his cabin, smoking weed, and hanging with his neighbors at the local pool hall.

There are many paths our lives might take, if we feel free to craft them in our own idiosyncratic way. Recognizing this variability, the essence of the "there" I suggest is a process, not a destination. Thus, I begin the Chapter with a vision of happiness not as a static, "happily-ever-after" end place but, instead, as an ever-unfolding journey that, based on Radical

Decency's 7 Values, can best sustain us in finding our own personal sweet spot in life.

HAPPINESS

In today's world, one encouraging reality is that we haven't given up on happiness. According to a Nielsen survey, the goal for 45 percent of Americans is "to enjoy life to the fullest." And our actions reflect these hopes. A recent Gallup Poll reported that fully half of all Americans have bet on the chance for "the good life" by buying a lottery ticket. In addition, millions tune into TV's perennially top-rated "The Bachelor," each Monday night, to watch contestants pursue their happily-ever-after fantasy of marrying a stunningly attractive bachelor or bachelorette – who they just met.

But while we long to be happy, most of us give remarkably little thought to what this means in the context of a culture that relentlessly pushes us to make its competitive goals our highest priority. When it comes to pornography, former Supreme Court Justice Potter Stewart famously said, "I can't define it, but know it when I see it." And that is our (deeply mistaken) belief about happiness.

This glib, unreflective approach to happiness has serious consequences. Because we live in a compete-to-win culture, this "I just know what it is" approach results in choices that provide the short-term adrenaline highs that are its key emotional payoffs: Better toys, trips to exotic new places, the hit offered by alcohol and drugs. What's often neglected in the process are the more lasting rewards offered by long term, mutually nourishing engagements with family, friends, and community.

For most of us, vacation means time on the ski slopes or at the beach, and not a retreat devoted to a more in-depth understanding of our chosen religious/wisdom tradition, or a service trip to Guatemala to live and work with indigenous villagers. Similarly, for many of my Millennial clients, dating is an endless stream of encounters between strangers – at bars or on

Internet dating sites – with each person evaluating the hit of romantic love the other evokes and, then, his or her ability to maintain the other person's interest through scintillating conversation and mind blowing sex.

There is nothing wrong with these sorts of experiences. To the contrary, viewed in isolation they are often adventuresome and fun. But when we make them the primary focus in our quest for a happy life, they are bound to disappoint. The reason? The initial, powerful jolt of pleasure provided by that new car, experiential adventure, or latest sex partner inevitably diminishes with time. And so, caught up in a never-ending search for new ways to recreate that initial high, our quest for happiness is never-ending – and never fulfilled.

So is there a more productive path to a happy life? The answer is, I think, yes. The key is to understand our basic biological and psychological processes and then to craft an approach to living that, while respecting these realities, nurtures our better nature. In this model, happiness is not the goal. It is, instead, a byproduct of the choices we make.

Life's Sweet Spot

Three well known psychological theorists – psychiatrist Daniel Siegel, psychologist and social theorist Jordan Peterson, and the legendary family therapist Virginia Satir – describe the starting place for this journey toward happiness. What is so interesting is that, while they differ dramatically from one another in other respects, these thinkers share a common vision of the path to a nourishing and productive life.

Speaking at the Psychotherapy Networker Symposium several years ago, Siegel offered the metaphor of life as a river with one bank representing safety and the other aliveness, the challenge being to creatively integrate and balance them. An adequate level of safety and predictability is vital to avoid feeling chaotic and out of control. Equally, however, we need healthy levels of novelty lest we wash up on the river's other shore, consigned to a drab, risk-free life.

Jordan Peterson, speaking as part of the Canadian podcast series "Big Ideas" offers another version of the same concept:

> The optimally meaningful life is to be found on the border between [chaos and order]. You're secure enough to be confident, but not so secure that you're bored. You're interested enough to be awake, but not so interested that you're terrified. . . Time slips by and you're no longer self-conscious.

He then goes on to offer this day-by-day practice to guide us:

> You'll take some tentative steps in [a] direction, get a little way, and think "no, that's wrong." Then your life's meaning will appear over there, and you'll take a few steps in that direction and see that that's wrong too. But you keep chasing it, moving forward, doing things. And because you're honest with yourself, you learn from your mistakes and get wiser and wiser.

Finally, to the same point, is this from Virginia Satir:

> My growth exists in new territory, step by step. One step ahead, see what's there, to the right or left, whatever seems to have the most space. Does it fit for me? I cannot map it out ahead of time. That's how it is in the unknown. Take a step, then see where I can go, keeping in mind where I might like to end up. I may end up somewhere else; maybe at a place better than what I thought of. But that is the way, step by step.

A Values-Based Journey

Note that the process each of these thinkers describe makes no reference to values. In theory, then, it could lead to drugs, compulsive sexual conquests, or the endless pursuit of wealth and privilege. But my gut has always told me that this isn't – couldn't – be true. And in another lecture, "The Necessity of Virtue," Peterson explains why. In this podcast, Peterson begins his analysis with one of Buddhism's fundamental premises: That life is suffering. He then references Cain, who railed against God for favoring his brother Abel and, then, killed him.

What is Peterson's understanding of the Biblical story? Cain screwed up. He failed to accept the fact that, living in an indifferent universe, the suffering that came his way was inevitable. Instead, he committed the cardinal Buddhist mistake of inflicting additional pain on himself, and others, in his vain attempt to deny and reverse that reality.

For Peterson, this parable is foundational. When we emerged into self-consciousness – the very quality that makes our species unique – the first thing we became aware of was our own vulnerability and, with it, the inevitability of suffering. Understanding this, our immediate and instinctual move, like Eve in the Garden of Eden, was to recoil from it, cover up, hide and deny it.

The problem with this approach? When we deny our vulnerability and believe we can control our destiny, we no longer view another's good fortune or our bad luck as happenstance, to be accepted with equanimity. Instead, we envy the other's fate and curse our own: "I can, and **should**, have what he has!"

This mindset leads inexorably toward inner states of frustration and anger and to behaviors that are insensitive, manipulative and, at their worst, cruel and murderous as we seek to take what this other person has or to destroy fate's favored child. In addition, it twists and diminishes our emotional world as we vainly seek to suppress the fear, confusion, and sadness that so inconveniently remind us of our vulnerability. Needless to say, these states of mind and ways of acting tear at the very fabric of our humanity. This is, decidedly, not happiness.

Unfortunately, Cain's outlook is the narrative that predominates in our culture. In our compete-to-win world, we are pushed incessantly to deny our vulnerability and to view fate as an enemy to be defeated, rather than as an unalterable reality to be understood and accepted. And the predictable outcome is, sadly, the bad feelings described in the last Chapter.

For this reason, the title of second Peterson's lecture, "The Necessity of Virtue," is well chosen. If we unthinkingly conform to the culture's mainstream values, their temporary adrenaline highs notwithstanding, we consign ourselves to a Cain-like existence. And, on the flip side, if we hope to craft more nourishing and generative lives, "virtue" – that is, values that decisively challenge our compete-to-win mindsets – is a "necessity."

So, yes, drawing on the good ideas of the thinkers quoted above, each of us needs to steer our own unique path in life, discovering that combination of vocation and passion that, for us, best integrates safety and aliveness. We need to be on a journey that leads us to that sweet spot where, in Peterson's words, we're "secure enough to be confident but not so secure that we're bored" and "interested enough to be awake but not so interested that we're terrified." But – and this is an all-important but –if we hope to create a sustainably happy life, the choices we make need to be steadily guided by a set of virtues that protects us from the allure of the mainstream culture's seductive but unsustainable highs.

Radical Decency is not, to be sure, the only available values-based approach to living. But it's a good one. While it offers a roadmap for living a valued life, it also accounts for the real-life pressures and enticements that get in its way. In addition, as I'm fond of reminding my readers, Radical Decency's life-altering rewards come our way wholly apart from our ability to realize our "real world" social and career-based aspirations, bringing in its wake:

- A here-and-now focus that shrinks future fears and past regrets;

- A decisive shift away from self-judgment and toward self-love and understanding; and

- A greater clarity of purpose.

●●●●●

In the opening pages of this book, I describe the life I led in my 30s and 40s. As a big firm lawyer, was I success in the eyes of the world? Yes. But was I happy? Not in the least.

Many things have changed in my life since then. A key catalyst was a personal growth workshop – the Essential Experience – that I took in my late 40s as well as the supportive and caring community I became a part of when it ended. In the workshop, I was challenged to create a "contract" – a personal mission statement – to support me to move more effectively toward my own sweet spot in life.

Today, I hardly remember the contract that I wrote when I first participated in the workshop. But as I developed my thinking about Radical Decency, I found myself creating a new, more compelling contract. Guided by Decency's 7 Values, it has allowed me to more fully inhabit that place of safety and nourishing stimulation that is the hallmark of a happy life.

MY PERSONAL GUIDE TO LIVING

Letting go of outcomes and attending to each moment's endless possibilities for offering and accepting love, I am embracing my living and dying with compassion, curiosity, zest, and a deepening sense of acceptance and celebration.

That's it. That's the contract I created.

My challenge, then and now, is of course to live it day by day. What follows are some reflections on how that journey has gone so far; its rewards, pitfalls, and lessons learned.

My starting point was the contract's second phrase: "Attending to each moment's endless possibilities for offering and accepting love." And my initial belief was that, while it would be tricky in its practical application, it was emotionally uncomplicated. But, as I quickly discovered, it was anything but.

Far too often, my longed-for generosity of spirit was diminished by anger, judgment, annoyance, or jealousy; a fear of losing, getting less, or being left out. So, for example, when my dear friend Eric took over as leader of the workshop I was, to my chagrin, jealous of his success, even though I had no interest whatsoever in actually running it. And on many other occasions as well, a critical word or look would shift my attitude to one of self-criticism ("how could I say something so stupid!") or sour judgment ("why should I listen to you?").

As I moved forward with my contract, I also came to the uncomfortable realization that it was really hard to make good on its very first goal as well, "letting go of outcomes." Confronting life's many challenges, large and small – landing a new client, making a compelling presentation at an upcoming court hearing, even getting through rush-hour traffic – I wanted to be the guy who took his best shot and, then, accepted the outcome with equanimity. But it was so hard. I was still hanging on to my ingrained need to win.

Over time, I realized that the common thread underlying both of these uncomfortable realizations was the gnawing belief that people really didn't care about me; that I didn't matter. Unable to let go of that mindset, I couldn't let go of the need to prove my worth by winning, or my frustration, annoyance and jealousy when I fell short.

Struggling to work through this issue led me to this life-changing realization: We humans are deeply and unalterably connected to one another by the grim, existential realities that define our existence.

- We are here on earth through no choice of our own.

- We will all leave at a time that is not of our choosing. Our physical decline and death, and that of everyone we love, are certainties.

- Despite the pronouncements of an endless stream of gurus throughout history, we don't understand why we're here or what we're supposed to do while we are.

In addition – and this is an all-important point – we are, to the best of our knowledge, the only species that is aware of these realities.

Whether we consciously acknowledge it or not, these stark and unforgiving truths are with us every day of our lives. And, for this reason, they fundamentally mold our relationships with one another. Knowing that we can never overcome them, we are like the World War I soldiers who, sharing a foxhole in a never-ending, unwinnable war, develop an intense and enduring sense of solidarity with, and love for, our comrades in arms; that is, our fellow humans.

As my awareness of this reality has grown, my distorted beliefs about my unlovability have dramatically receded. I am now able to see, more and more, that I am literally surrounded by beings that are eager to connect with me out of a shared comradeship that is – quite literally – my birthright as a human. And I don't have to do anything to be its beneficiary.

This is the point Henri Nouwen, the Catholic brother and theologian, so beautifully illustrates in his 2002 book, *Life of the Beloved: Spiritual Living in a Secular World*. In it, he tells the story of a profoundly mentally challenged woman who lived with him in his cloistered community. Unable to talk, she spent her days wandering about the grounds, smiling at others, becoming in this way dearly beloved by all. What I now realize is that, when all my extra IQ points don't get in the way, I am no different than her.

Needless to say, this does not mean everyone loves me. Like everyone else, I regularly run into people who aren't interested in me. But recognizing our shared humanity has freed me, more and more, from the need to prove that I matter. As a result, I am, in the beginning words of my contract, far better able to "let go of outcomes" and, as a result "attend to each moment's endless possibilities for offering and accepting love."

•••••

Notice that my contract focuses on possibility and choice, and not on loving everyone all the time. Why? Because loving another increases our level of intimacy and, with that, our vulnerability. So before I act on the many "possibilities" available to me, I first make sure I'm not unduly compromising my physical or emotional safety. So, for example, if someone is verbally aggressive with me, I am now far more likely to say nothing and simply move on, rather than getting sucked into what is likely to be an unhealthy, emotionally draining tit-for-tat exchange.

In addition, because my energy is finite, I am always making choices. Do I invest in this person or situation? Or, given the many other possibilities and responsibilities that fill my life, do I make a different choice? Thus, there might be a Saturday afternoon when I simply veg out on the couch, watching a dumb TV show. Why? Because I'm physically and emotionally drained and decency to self seems paramount. At other times, however, I'll choose to go to a predictably dreary business meeting, knowing that by showing up I'm helping a charitable organization I care about.

These qualifications, however, operate in the context of a larger reality. When we are pre-occupied with our own, ego-driven ambitions, it's far too easy to overlook the many loving options that are always staring us right in the face. Thus, my central challenge is not to limit my loving acts through carefully considered choices but, instead, to make them my consistent priority.

Living this way isn't easy. It requires a lot of moment-by-moment awareness in the face of choices that are regularly ambiguous and perplexing. So, for example:

- Do I put aside the work I was hoping to get done today to attend to a sad and distracted co-worker?

- Do I skip the NFL game I was looking forward to watching to spend time with a friend, still in the hospital recovering from his recent operation?

- Recognizing my granddaughter's desire/demand for undivided attention, do I play dolls with her – an activity I decidedly don't understand (and don't particularly enjoy) – until *she's* ready to move on?

- Do I stifle my annoyance and remain courteous with my harried and distracted waiter, or do I share my irritation with his abrupt behavior and slow service?

Because these sorts of choices are constant and never-ending, it's easy to lose focus and drift back to a life on autopilot. And that's precisely where the second half of my contract comes in. Acting in these ways, "I embrace my living and dying with compassion, curiosity, zest, and a deepening sense of acceptance and celebration." Trusting that this is true – even when I am feeling confusion or annoyance in the moment – I am inspired to keep working my contract, day by day, moment by moment.

Doing so, one trap I work hard to avoid is to see this state of mind as a deserved reward for my good behavior – as in, "IF I attend to each moment's endless possibilities, THEN all these good feelings will come my way." The problem with this approach is that when my loving choices don't lead to these lofty states of heart and mind, I'm far too ready to drop the whole project, slipping back to my old compete-to-win ways.

The alternative, the one I've embraced, is to trust that my new way of being in the world *is itself* generative and nourishing. Then, the hoped-for states of mind in the second half of my contract are transformed from an implicit judgment on its effectiveness into a moment by moment reminder of where its greatest challenges lie. Operating from this mindset, I resist the temptation to treat a slide-back into my old snarky, judgmental mindsets as confirmation that my contract just isn't working – and to set it aside. Instead, I treat it as a signal to go in the opposite direction, doubling down on my loving intentions.

Viewed from this mindset, the second half of my contract is working really well. Its immediate, visceral feedback on how I'm doing is a constant reminder, and incentive, to find more effective strategies for implementing its goals. Indeed, the on-the-ground strategies for jumpstarting the process that have emerged, as a result, are one of my contract's most unexpected and positive payoffs.

Here is one example, a long ago gift from my law school mentor, memorably named Fairfax Leary, Jr. Hanging out with "Fax" one day, he told me in his sweet, enthusiastic way that his wife, Sarah, instead of habitually countering another's idea with "why," would consistently say, "why not?" I've always remembered that story with warmth and affection for both Fax and Sarah and have often retold it over the years. But now it's consistently there, in the forefront of my brain, inspiring many of my choices in life.

So when my wife, Dale, asks me if I'd like to try the new Thai restaurant, or make the five-hour trip to Pittsburgh for her cousin's birthday, or check out the roller derby tournament that's in town, my response, more and more, is to say, "why not?" This doesn't mean that we do everything she suggests. But cultivating this frame of mind fosters my "curiosity" and "zest," two hallmarks of the nourishing and generative life contemplated by the second half of my contract.

Another example involves a story told by Rabbi Dayle Friedman, author of the 2015 book, *Jewish Wisdom for Growing Older: Finding Your Grit and Grace Beyond Midlife.* Working as a hospice chaplain, she was tending to a bedridden and dying 98-year-old patient, also a rabbi, who motioned her to come near so they could talk. Leaning over him, her ear almost touching his lips so she could hear him, he said simply: "Isn't life beautiful?"

Our time on earth is limited and we can resist that reality, pushing it off into an indeterminate future. Or we can embrace it, understanding that each moment is a precious opportunity to leave a legacy of caring and love. Striving to walk this second path, the inspiring words of that 98-year-old rabbi are there to support me. Regularly invoking them brings me closer to an outlook on life that, in my contract's words, "embraces my living and dying" with "a deepening sense of acceptance and celebration." I practice my contract not despite, but **because of**, the inevitability of my decline and death.

●●●●●

Radical Decency is very much about our individual journey. However, the hard truth is that – with the exception of the few saints among us – we'll never be able to find our way to life's sweet spot if we fail to challenge the cultural mindsets that so relentlessly pushing us toward "Cain-like" lives. Failing to bring our decency values to our workplaces and communities, its compete-to-win mindsets will, almost inevitably, infiltrate and infect the small islands of decency we seek to carve out with family and friends.

With this in mind, I end the Chapter with a hopeful – and entirely realistic – "bedtime story" about a group of people who jumpstarted the radically decent life of their dreams by creating a radically decent business.

DREAMING A "POSSIBLE" DREAM: A STORY

Once upon a time . . .

A group of friends stumbled on *Beyond Civilization: Humanity's Next Great Adventure*, a book written in 1999 by the iconoclastic writer Daniel Quinn. In it, Quinn tells the story of a newspaper in rural New Mexico that he started in the 1980s with his wife and two friends. While the paper was only a modest financial success, they soon realized that a higher priority was their pleasure in working together. Looking back on the experience, years later, Quinn saw the newspaper as the model for a new kind of "tribe," based not on traditional notions of kinship and physical proximity but, instead, on work environments that offered a shared sense of mission and community.

To the group that read the book, Quinn's vision made a lot of sense. Since work dominated the best hours of most of their days and the lion's share of their energy, why not make it a primary place of friendship, belonging and emotional sustenance? Instead of being an unfortunate exception to their most deeply held values, why couldn't work be a place where their deepest aspirations could find vital expression, in concert with people they liked, admired, and trusted?

So they decided to go into business together. The type of business didn't really matter. It could have been a financial planning firm, a computer software company, a chiropractic office or, even, a farm. What was important is that, having spent years at typical mainstream companies, they were determined to operate differently.

Like any other business, profitability was essential. So they made it Priority 1A, really important but nevertheless – and this was key to their vision – clearly subordinated to Priority 1: A commitment to Radical Decency in every aspect of their business and lives.

It's easy to embrace Radical Decency in theory but a lot harder to apply day-to-day, especially in the pressured-packed environment of a profit-making business. So in the beginning they went slowly; exploring their fundamental ideas in detail, allowing the group to evolve organically. Eventually, a core group of people emerged that understood the philosophy and were eager to organize their work lives around it.

Getting the company off the ground was wrenchingly difficult. In addition to all the problems that a new business must face, the organizers had to figure out what it meant to actually run a radically decent business. From day one, big, really complicated questions had to be answered:

- Who "owns" the company and what rights are associated with ownership?

- Who should participate in the firm's profits – and risk of loss?

- How do you price products when the goal is fairness both to the company and its customers, and not simply to charge whatever the market will bear?

- How do you compensate owners and workers alike in ways that reflect Decency's 6th and 7th Values – fairness and justice?

- How do you make decisions in an environment where collegiality is not just a hoped-for result, but is at the very heart of the company's mission?

- How do you effectively follow through on a commitment to be truly decent in the larger world?

What also became apparent, early on, was that "little" things mattered. Virtually everyone involved had long experience working at "business-as-usual" companies. As a result, mainstream ways of operating were what they knew, and what they instinctually fell back upon in times of stress. And on the flip side, there were no manuals to guide them as they worked to create a radically decent business. So many things were new, complicated, and perplexing.

One ever-present danger was that day-to-day pressures would drag them back to mainstream ways of operating, one small compromise at a time:

- Overpromising what they could deliver, in order to make a much-needed sale;

- Overlooking small indecencies when the person in question – say, a top salesperson – was making a major contribution to the bottom line;

- In the face of pressure to get things done quickly and efficiently, allowing top-down, authoritarian attitudes to erode their commitment to collegiality and cooperative decision-making;

- Pulling back on contributions to the larger community when profits dipped.

The group found that the best antidote to these sorts of temptations was intense and detailed – even obsessive – attention to the company's mission in all things, large and small. So in the early days, participants spent a lot of time figuring out what Radical Decency had to teach them about running meetings, talking to each other (and to customers, vendors, and competitors), dealing with co-worker conflict, and even how to keep the lunchroom and bathrooms clean.

These seemingly endless conversations were a frequent source of frustration since "important" work had to get done. But it was time well spent. Eventually, it all became easier. Like a baseball player obsessively practicing an improved swing, these new, more decent ways of operating eventually became the group's ingrained, taken for granted business practices. And, with that, their sure-footedness in putting Radical Decency into practice grew, month by month, year by year.

As this process unfolded, good things started to happen at an accelerating pace. Word began to spread among potential employees. This is a place where talk about worker well-being isn't just a lot of empty words; where a fair living wage and good benefits, open and collegial decision-making, and work/life balance are authentic priorities. As a result, the company was able to attract an unusually capable, imaginative and loyal group of employees.

Similarly, customers came to understand that they could rely on the company to be open and honest about what it could (and could not) do for them and to always deliver a quality product at a fair price, fully disclosed in advance. The result: An ever-expanding group of customers were powerfully drawn to the company as a place where people were decent in word and deed, and operated with unusual sensitivity, thoughtfulness, and thoroughness.

To their great pleasure and surprise, the group of friends also found their success extending beyond the four walls of their company. Following through on their across-the-board decency commitment, the partners worked hard to find suppliers, lawyers, accountants, marketing experts, and other consultants who had a similar commitment to decency. Before long, they found themselves at the center of a growing group of collaborators who not only "got it," but also were eager to recast their own businesses in values-based ways.

At an income-generating level, this emerging network of radically decent businesses worked really well. Because their relationships were anchored in a shared set of values, referrals occurred far more frequently than they do in typical marketing networks, based solely in economic self-interest. In addition, their philosophical compatibility meant that referrals turned into customers on a much more regular basis.

And the network's success didn't end there. It grew to include new, creative contributions to the larger community as well. Acting alone, the social justice initiatives of the network's individual companies tended to be isolated and intermittent. But bound together by a full-throttled commitment to Radical Decency, the change initiatives of these diverse businesses – retailers, manufacturers, schools, entrepreneurial start-ups, mission-driven nonprofits, health care entities, legal and accounting firms – became far more imaginative and far-reaching. Before long:

- Landlords were collaborating with trauma specialists to offer respite housing to victims of abuse;

- People with employment challenges were being placed at radically decent businesses by like-minded career and business consultants; and

- Investors were funding new Radical Decency initiatives that, because they drew on the diverse experiences and skills of network participants, were both financially sound and unusually creative and effective in their impact.

In time, a wide variety of articles and seminars also started to appear reflecting on lessons learned and additional steps that might be taken to craft even more effective ways to implement Radical Decency, not just in business but in every area of living.

And the original group of friends? Well, things evolved and changed. Some stayed at their widget company, the business that got the whole thing started. Others, intrigued with other aspects of this ever-growing network, moved on. But bound together by their shared values and supportive community, they maintained the intimate connection they'd forged in their early years; brothers and sisters, warmly supporting one another as they each crafted their unique journey through life.

And they each lived – ever after – with an ennobling purpose and energizing sense of possibility.

PART 3

GETTING FROM "HERE" TO "THERE"

Monday morning is the place where dreams die.

Like Fiona – whose story I shared in Chapter 1 – we go to a weekend spiritual retreat, personal growth workshop, or romantic getaway and, by Sunday night, our excitement about life's possibilities is high. Then, Monday morning arrives. We're jarred awake by the alarm and, just like that, we're pulled back into the life we left behind. With the insistent demands of the "real" world reasserting themselves, we recede into the spiritually and emotionally blunted existence demanded by our compete-to-win world.

When I took the Essential Experience Workshop – the weekend work-shop that inspired my "contract for living," discussed in the last Chapter – I awakened to new possibilities and directions I could take in life. But my real "Eureka moment" didn't arrive until a year later. Re-experiencing the workshop as a part of the team that assists in creating the experience for others, a realization came to me like a sharp slap to the side of the head: "I can't just do this work at an occasional weekend retreat. If I hope to live differently and better, I have to do it every day of my life."

Understanding the "Here," the problematic world in which we live, is vitally important. So, too, is a clear vision of the "There," the more nourishing and generative life to which we aspire. But, in the end, the single most important issue is an intensely practical one: What do we need to do, day by day, to get from "Here" to "There?"

We grapple with this vital question in the next four Chapters.

Chapter 8 explains how Decency's 7 Values, radically applied, can fundamentally alter our relationships, with special emphasis on our committed intimate partnerships. Then, in Chapters 9, and 10, we explore similar possibilities at work and in politics. But I begin, in Chapter 7, with a discussion of three guidelines for being radically decent, day by day, that are key to getting from "Here" to "There."

CHAPTER 7

Practice Pointers

Radical Decency is, ultimately, wonderfully rewarding. But putting it into practice is very challenging. Why? Because it regularly requires choices that go against the compete-to-win mindsets that have so deeply infiltrated and infected our ways of being.

Coming to grips with this inconvenient but unavoidable reality, I've developed a series of specific guidelines – practice pointers – to support me in making these less easy, less instinctual choices. One simple example is a phrase I frequently repeat to myself when, once again, I'm challenged to change my old, habitual ways: "I'm comfortable being uncomfortable."

Do I really mean this? Of course not. But moments of choice, both large and small, just keep coming up, challenging me:

- To acknowledge my failure to call a sick friend rather than letting the oversight slide;

- To forego a business opportunity when someone else is more qualified; or, even,

- To remain behind that excruciatingly slow driver in front of me instead of swerving around and in front of him.

In situations such as these, quietly reminding myself of this phrase helps me to be the person I want to be.

What follows is a discussion of three practice pointers that are, in my view, key to a successful Radical Decency practice.

MAKE WISDOM STRETCHING A WAY OF LIFE

One element that makes Radical Decency less intuitive and, thus, far more perplexing is this: Even as it decisively pulls us away from the culture's self-absorbed ways, it emphatically rejects its opposite. From Radical Decency's perspective, a life given over to altruistic self-sacrifice – neglecting decency to self in the process – is just as problematic. What it calls for, instead, is a both/and approach: Be decent to yourself as well as to others and to the larger world – and do so at all times.

But because this approach continually confronts us with situations in which our needs and the needs of others conflict, being "both/and" regularly requires us to make uncomfortable and confusing choices. Here are a few examples:

- Planning a family outing, do I conveniently "forget" to invite my needy cousin who, while always grateful to be included, is predictably socially inept and annoying?

- When a co-worker's project is going badly, do I sit quietly on the sidelines and let it happen? Or do I jump in and help out even though by doing so, I too might become identified, in the boss' mind, with this failed project?

- As a person who is childless and always scraping for money, do I vote for the county council candidate who's pushing for a cut in property taxes or the one who's advocating for a larger investment in the local school system?

In a world that doesn't embrace a "both/and" outlook, our instinct in these situations is either: (1) To automatically put our needs and desires first; or (2) feeling uncomfortable with this "selfish" approach, to defer to the needs and desires of others. As I describe below, a key element in operationalizing Radical Decency is to let go of this "either/or" mindset; adopting, instead, a "wisdom-stretching" approach.

•••••

Using the co-worker scenario, just described, as our example, here's where "either/or" thinking all too typically leads. Reacting to my coworker's dilemma, I might quickly and instinctually rationalize my self-serving silence:

"Hey, business is business. Why should I stick my neck out? If she's hurt by her own incompetence, that's her problem."

Or, alternatively, instinctually judging my self-protective instincts as "unworthy and selfish," I might jump in to help; defending her choices to the boss and even, perhaps, taking over parts of the project.

At first blush, these choices might seem to be dramatically different. But, in one very important respect, they are simply two sides of the same coin. With each, I am avoiding the ambiguity and discomfort I would feel if I attempted, in a serious and sustained way, to balance and integrate decency to myself, to my co-worker, to my boss, and to the larger organization and society of which I am a part.

From Radical Decency's perspective, the "right" answer to this dilemma, and so many others like it, lies less in the choices made than in the process itself. Instead of avoiding the conflicting decency considerations inherent in these situations, we need to embrace them. Doing so, wisdom is transformed from a noun – as in "am I wise?" – into a verb – as in "I am regularly exercising and, thus, strengthening my 'wisdom-ing' muscles."

This wisdom-stretching approach is regularly confusing and uncomfortable. But it's well worth the effort since, consistently practiced, it makes us smarter and wiser, cultivating each of the following qualities:

Thoughtfulness: Open-mindedness, tolerance of uncertainty and ambiguity, and an ability to consider life's deepest dilemmas.

Analytic Skill: The ability to more fully understand the diverse factors at play in each situation, and to see underlying patterns and themes.

Intuitive Awareness: Body and sensory attunement, sensitivity to nonverbal cues, and the ability to be more fully present in each moment.

Creativity: The ability to imagine and put into practice more expansive, multi-dimensional choices.

Prudence: Self-regulation, humility, and patience.

Courage: The ability to act in the face of uncertainty, discomfort and risk.

Walking the Walk

So how does wisdom-stretching work in practice? As an example, let's take a situation that most of us have encountered: What do you do when a stranger asks for money?

Faced with this situation, most of us start with an instinctual conclusion, either yes or no, that we then bolster with a handy rationale; e.g. "Bad idea. She'll use the money to buy drugs" or, alternatively, "Poor guy, down on his luck. I'll give him some loose change." Wisdom-stretching, however, challenges us to reflect instead on the situation's many implications for ourselves, others, and the larger world.

Here's how that process might look.

In most cases, only a person in extreme need would beg. Therefore, giving him money has merit. Indeed, focusing solely on decency to this person, I might even offer to buy him a meal. On the other hand, giving him money would encourage public begging, an act that inevitably violates other people's space (and, thus, decency to others). In addition, a donation to an appropriate agency, if I took the time to make one, would certainly be more strategic (decency to the world). But, on the flip side, making a charitable donation would negate a more public, immediate act of caring (promoting decency to the world) and the good feeling I would derive from a spontaneous act of generosity (decency to self).

You can already see the complexity. But, thinking about this situation in radically decent terms, there's more. Being approached for money without permission disrespects me (decency to self). On the other hand, fairness and justice – two of Decency's 7 core values – nudge me to consider my own privilege. While the mainstream system has allowed me to lead a comfortable life, it has, in all likelihood, severely penalized this person who is, after all, reduced to begging on the street. So perhaps this reality should trump his rudeness.

I could go on.

Given the compromised values, and sheer complexity of the world in which we live, our decisions in wisdom-stretching moments such as this one are seldom fully satisfactory. In my own life, for example, I continue to "ad hoc" it with panhandlers, giving at times, demurring at others. But my wisdom-stretching mindset has changed me. When this situation comes up, my old instinctive reaction – eyes to the ground, quickened pace to avoid contact – has given way to a more nuanced approach.

Absent a street person's aggressive belligerence, I now seek to acknowledge his or her humanity with eye contact and, perhaps, a sympathetic smile. I also make a quick mental calculation, as best I can. Does this person seem physically disabled or emotionally impaired? Or, does she seem to be stoned? Is he depressed and helpless, or manipulative and calculating? And I also allow my mood in the moment to influence my choice. If I am busy and preoccupied, I will sometimes allow myself to simply walk by.

Finally, attempting to make good on my Radical Decency commitment in this and similar situations, I've changed my approach to charitable giving. I no longer make significant contributions to my (warmly remembered) alma maters, Johns Hopkins University and the University of Pennsylvania, since both of them are already bursting with multi-billion dollar, tax-exempt endowments. Instead, I focus on organizations that more directly confront and seek to mitigate the vast amount of suffering that our indecent culture inflicts on the world.

•••••

Another example of wisdom stretching involved an interaction I had, several years ago, with a long-time client. Calling me at 2 a.m., he told me he'd been mugged. Bloody and dazed from a blow to the head, he was sitting alone in a local hospital's Emergency Room and, clearly very upset, wanted me to join him.

In this situation, my profession's ethics are clear: This was an inappropriate boundary cross. The "right" response was to enforce a "healthy" boundary, offering a firm though empathetic *no* and directing him to "more appropriate" sources of support, such as family and friends.

But, in that moment, I could see that factors beyond professional boundaries were also at play. This man, with no family or close friends in the area, was shaken to his core and turned to me as the person who, he thought, could best comfort him in this moment of crisis. So I made the "wrong" choice. I spent the night with him at the hospital, choosing to believe that the exchange that unfolded – his reaching out to me in a vulnerable moment, my caring response, his gratitude – was the wiser, more decent choice.

In this instance, things went well. Our therapeutic relationship was strengthened by his increased trust in me as a caring person. And he never made a similar request. But things didn't have to go that way. He could have become confused about the nature of our relationship, expecting similar acts of friendship in the future. Then, feeling hurt when they didn't occur, our more limited therapist/client relationship might have soured into still another relationship that left him feeling disappointed and rejected.

I am always eager to reflect on and to learn from my choices in wisdom-stretching situations such as this one. In this case, I consulted with a fellow therapist before acting – my wife, who was lying beside me in bed when I got the call. But for me, the story's key take away is not about whether the choice was good or bad, right or wrong. It lies, instead, in my willingness to move beyond the mainstream culture's prescribed ways of acting, embodied in my profession's code of ethics, and to embrace the moment's wisdom-stretching challenge in all of its complexity.

I like, and aspire to be, the person I was that night.

EMBRACE DIFFERENCE – YOURS AND OTHERS

When we're fully committed to Radical Decency, our goal is to approach each and every interaction with understanding, empathy and appreciation – three of Decency's 7 values. This challenge leads to a second key "practice pointer:" We need to cultivate ways of relating that, instead of flattening and stereotyping other people, recognize and honor their uniqueness. And, importantly, we need to bring this same insight and generosity to the ways we see ourselves as well.

Working as a therapist over the years, one thing I've come to deeply appreciate is how gloriously different we are from one another. Sitting one afternoon with Lila, a graphic designer, and her engineer husband, Josh, the session's initial banter drifted to my office décor. When I pressed the matter, Lila sheepishly admitted that the arrangement of mementos and bric-a-brac on my desk and bookcase was "all wrong." Josh and I were stunned. What was she talking about? We didn't get it.

Digging deeper, we realized how different the worlds we inhabited really were. Lila exists in a far more visual environment. Walking into my office she saw and experienced volumes, space, color and line. But for Josh and me, our first moments together were all about words and facial expressions. These additional elements, so vividly experienced by Lila, were only vague background for us, with barely any impact on our consciousness.

A similar, more dramatic moment took place with another client, Claire, when she told me that in certain moments of high intensity all forms – furniture, wall hangings, me – dissolved into energetic resonances. While this might seem weird to some, it isn't. Karen, whom you first met in Chapter 3, regularly tells me about the "bodily vibrations" she experiences when someone in her presence is sad or scared. Consider as well the testimony of the Harvard neuro-anatomist Jill Bolte Taylor in her 2009 book, *My Stroke of Insight*. The victim of a stroke that destroyed her analytical, left-brain function, she had no idea if someone was with in her hospital room unless that person was in a heightened emotional state. Only then did her unimpaired, energetically attuned right brain register that person's presence

One reality of the compete-to-win world in which we live is that it grievously flattens these sorts of differences. Instead, it relentlessly pushes us to conform to a very specific idea of what a human being should be: Logical, focused, goal-oriented, organized, efficient and, of course, relentlessly driven to be a winner.

One of the key ways in which this ideal is promoted and reinforced is through the practice of labeling others – and ourselves. We live in a world in which we are literally drenched in, and defined by, labels. I am/you are:

- White, Black, or Hispanic;

- Catholic, Muslim, Protestant, Evangelical Christian, or Jewish;

- Liberal, progressive, conservative, or libertarian;

- Cool or uncool;

- A jock, nerd, or slut:

- A success or failure;

- Soft and sensitive, or hard and determined.

And that's just a sample. The list is almost endless.

By giving us a head start on understanding who a person is, labels can play a useful role. But instead of being the beginning place for further exploration, they are too often the end point, short-circuiting our ability to see others in their unique complexity. Since you're a married, church-going businessman who lives in a suburb of Houston, votes Republican, and loves to play golf, I (rightly or wrongly) "know" who you are. And if you doubt the power of these sorts of labels, take a moment to mentally alter a few of these attributes – Manhattan for Houston, Democrat for Republican, yoga for golf, female for male – and notice how quickly your image of this person changes with it.

To understand the power labeling has in molding our perception of others, consider a political discussion with a new person. Early on, each of you will inevitably tip your hand about your feelings on a hot-button issue – abortion or gun control, for example. From that point forward, you'll each now "know" with whom you're dealing – a conservative, liberal, or libertarian – and instinctually treat him or her as a stereotypical person who fits that label.

In most cases, moreover, what we do to this other person we also do to our self. Thus, if the person you're dealing with is on the "other" side politically, you'll typically feel compelled to push your side's party line, lest you somehow irretrievably concede some of your key points. On the other hand, if you're in the same partisan camp, you'll likely stick to your shared outlook since deviating in any serious way runs the risk of being seen as suspect and unreliable – a traitor to the cause. In either case, what is deeply diminished is any instinct to share or even be aware of:

- Any ambiguities that might color your support for your side's positions; or

- Any sympathies you might feel for the values underlying the other person's positions, even if you don't agree with how they're expressed.

Needless to say, labeling and self-labeling are not limited to political discussions. Imagine a married couple: She wants to clean up to prepare for guests and he wants to watch the ball game. Think how quickly he can become a selfish jerk (in her eyes) and she a control freak (in his). And, all too often, these labels – through sheer repetition – are internalized, becoming part of how the husband and wife view themselves as well.

This same process shows up with special poignancy in my psychotherapy practice. It's amazing how often people will tell me, in our first session, that they are an "obsessive-compulsive," an "abused spouse," or a "manic depressive."

With this self-labeling, my new "social misfit" client (for example) reduces himself to a symptom, spending far more psychic energy noticing behaviors that confirm his self-diagnosis than on those that contradict it. Thus, he'll be exquisitely aware of how his emotional sensitivity contributes to his social anxiety, harshly judging himself in the process. However, he'll ignore the fact that this same quality has made him an especially attuned and loving father and spouse.

Drop the Labels and See the Person

To resist and counteract this endemic labeling requires a fundamental re-orientation in how we view others and ourselves. Instead of pigeon-holing individuals as "this" or "that" kind of person, we need to begin to see them, and us, as the wonderfully complex, multi-faceted beings we actually are.

So, yes, the fact that a person you just met is an elementary school teacher of Asian descent might offer early clues about who she is. But we need to resist the temptation to use these attributes to simply fill in the blanks; e.g., she's demure and soft spoken, warm and nurturing. Far better to listen with an open mind and heart – with special attunement to what might be unique and different about her – and to actively cultivate this process by, for example:

- Asking genuinely curious questions: "What's the most fun you've had in the last week?" or "What do you feel passionate about in life?" (Saving for later: "Where do you live?" or "What kind of work do you do?"); and

- Offering insight into your own idiosyncratic sides, trusting that doing so will support her in doing the same. (For me, perhaps, a reference to my love of 50s rock 'n roll or addiction to the earnest silliness of sports talk radio).

Interacting this way, with this new person, is far more likely to uncover unique aspects of her being; aspects that even she – instinctually internalizing the qualities the culture associates with female, Asian-American, third grade teachers – might not be fully aware of.

As an example of this approach's rich rewards, consider my friendship with William. Warm and thoughtful, with a thoroughly engaging sense of humor, he was trained to be a biologist at the best schools, Harvard and Duke, and had all the necessary, left-brained skills to be a successful researcher or applied scientist. But conventional success has never happened for William. Instead, he bounced from job to job, never finding a comfortable fit and, with that, constantly judging himself as flawed and less than. And, sadly, I regularly judged him as well, glibly offering advice on how he might "fix" himself so he could get on with his life.

What I finally came to realize is that William is not, and will never be, a mainstream, career-building kind of a guy. To the contrary, his core is tactile and sensing, not logical and achievement oriented. He loves to milk goats and did so for five years, rising each morning at 5 a.m., even in the dead of winter! He's also tracked animals, participated in archeological digs, led bicycle trips, and worked on farms. He's now working, on a part-time basis, as a pediatric home care nurse and spends much of his remaining time on general home maintenance and repair projects.

The unique sensibilities that led William to make these choices, far from being unfortunate character flaws, are the very qualities that make him such a special and fascinating person. And as this understanding has grown, I have come to see William as more than a dear friend. He is also one of my important teachers, helping me to appreciate aspects of living that otherwise would have been beyond my ability to imagine, as a guy who has long walked a far more mainstream path in life. I also like to think that my now unabashed appreciation for William has helped him to let go of the harsh self-judgment with which he suffered for so long.

Opening ourselves up to the very different and rewarding worlds that people like William, Lila, and Claire have to offer – and to our own unique qualities as well – is an essential aspect of Radical Decency. It's the fertile ground from which the intimate interactions and relationships, so central to its soul nourishing possibilities, can flower and grow. If we hope to realize its transformative potential, we need to steadily cultivate openness to, and endless curiosity about, who we and others really are.

BE A VALUES-INFUSED LOVER

The last of Radical Decency's foundational "practice pointers" involves the vital matter of love.

When it comes to love, we are dealing with a deeply complex concept. The term is used to describe many different kinds of relationships: Friendship; sibling and parental love; self-love; love for activities such as listening to jazz or climbing rocks; love of God; and, of course, sexually infused romantic love. Further complicating the matter is the power of the word. Because "love" is so deeply evocative, its use can provoke strong and, sometimes, very uncomfortable feelings. One example is when it's used to describe sexual attraction to someone very young. The word may also distress us when used to describe the rapturous embrace of an unhinged but highly charismatic leader.

As we seek to live a more radically decent life, a key question is how we can best handle the many feelings that receive the love label. The sensible starting place? The distinction between love the "noun" and love the "verb."

When used as a noun, love describes all of the feelings noted above and more. And like all feelings, they are emotional states, deeply resistant to logic and reason. I have "that feeling" about this person or thing – and that's that. Love, the verb, on the other hand, is action based and is quintessentially a choice. Loving my spouse, Jesus, or my comrades in arms, I might (for example) make my wife's morning cup of coffee, volunteer to run the church's fundraising raffle, or risk my life to save a fellow soldier pinned down by enemy fire.

Note, importantly, that love the noun is not a values-driven state of mind. To the contrary, we all have friends who have fallen in love with a person who is cruel or selfish and, against all good reason, stays in the relationship. (At some point, perhaps you've found yourself in such a relationship as well.) And countless millions of people, throughout history, have perpetrated or excused even the most heinous crimes as a result of their loving devotion to God, country, ethnicity, or ideology – the Spanish Inquisition, Stalinism, Fascism and, more recently, the religious wars in Northern Ireland and Hutu mass slaughter of Tutsi in Rwanda – to name just a few.

One of life's great joys, the emotional hit we get from love is, at its most fundamental level, a deeply visceral response to the existential realities that haunt our existence: (1) Being here through no choice of our own; (2) our inevitable decline and death; and (3) the need to navigate this capricious journey essentially alone, making up our own meaning along the way. Given these grim, unalterable facts, we long for the psychic relief we feel when we wholeheartedly claim another – and are claimed in return. That is what love, the noun, provides. It's one of our greatest and most readily accessible sources of salvation.

So, yes, while love, the noun can lead to truly horrible choices, the best response to its dark undercurrent isn't to tamp down its wonderful, life affirming passion. Instead, using love's other vital element – love, the verb – we need to make choices that allow us to love unreservedly while, at the same time, staying true to our values.

Saying "No" to Love

Striving to put this idea into practice, I often think about a workshop I attended several years ago in which Esther Perel, the well-known couples' therapist and author, described trust as a leap of faith. "We believe in it," she said, "all the while knowing it may not be true."

As I see it, this mindset applies to love as well. While we wholeheartedly commit ourselves to "this" person or "that" cause, we also know that unforeseen circumstances may sever this passionately felt "forever" feeling (when, for example, our lover proves to be an abuser). So, going in, our leap of faith is passionate and unqualified. But we're still able to make the painful decision – if we must – to end the relationship if a failure of "love, the verb" goes beyond a point of no return.

Making this choice is never easy. The pain is all too real. And it's exacerbated by the fact that, living in a compete-to-win world, many of us wind up navigating these waters with a flawed moral compass. Infected by the culture's "I can make anything work, if I try hard enough" mentality, we persist in loving people, ideas, institutions, and movements long after they've proven to be deeply flawed or, even, physically dangerous.

Radical Decency offers the moral guidance we need when faced with these wrenchingly difficult life choices. We strive, always, to make values-based choices with the object of our love. But we also insist on love that goes both ways. I treat you with respect, empathy, appreciation, acceptance, and so on (decency to others) and expect similar acts in return (decency to self).

Managing our day-by-day choices in this radically decent way, we grow our ability to choose loving relationships based not just on passion, but also on trust, shared values, and a mutually nourishing interweaving of our lives. That, in turn, cultivates the clarity of mind and emotional fortitude we need to resist our fierce instinct to go with "that feeling" in situations that do violence to our core values.

When Love Gets Tough

These choice points come up in life more often than we might think. So, for example, I walk into a room and find myself captivated by the look, smile, energy, and wit of a woman I've never met before. Just like that, with no forethought and little volition, I experience a momentary, but very real surge of a "love" feeling. But cherishing the intimacy my wife and I have cultivated through many acts of love over the years, I understand that the wise – though, in the moment, far less enjoyable – choice is to avoid even a muted, seemingly harmless expression of that feeling.

Needless to say, the need to temper our love feelings with values-based choices also comes up in far more consequential situations. Consider, for example, the dilemma of Emil, a client who had recently moved to Philadelphia from South Africa in order to marry Jackie, a woman he'd met a year earlier at a business conference.

Emil sought me out because his 12-year-old daughter, Hannah, hurt by his sudden departure from their home had, in an emotionally fraught phone call, called her new stepmom a "selfish bitch." Deeply hurt, Jackie insisted that Emil, as a loyal husband, send the following email to his daughter: "Your treatment of Jackie is unacceptable. We're not going to talk with you until you get on the phone and offer her a full apology."

The resulting cut-off of contact with his daughter, now well into its second month, was deeply painful for Emil. But this period of separation had a silver lining. He began to realize that placating his wife and hoping for the best wasn't enough. And so, in the middle of still another agonizing, hand wringing therapy session, I presented him with the following question:

> "Look Emil, I know how much you love your wife and
> want to be loyal to her. But here's the thing. If this standoff lasts
> for several more months, or even years, are you be willing to
> live with that outcome?

"No," was his immediate heartfelt response, "losing my relationship with Hannah would be a deal breaker with Jackie" – to which he added after a brief painful pause, "if, God forbid, it ever came to that." With his values and priorities now vividly clarified, Emil understood that – however scary it was – he needed to make choices that, while continuing to love and honor his wife, also tended to his relationship with his daughter.

Over the next few weeks, dramatic changes took place. Speaking to Jackie, Emil told her that, while he loved her very much, he'd be calling his daughter. And he stuck to his guns, even when she reacted with explosive anger – "why are you choosing her over *me?*" – and, to his shock and dismay, walked out, returning to her family home in Atlanta.

Emil then called his daughter and, instead of defending Jackie, told her how much he loved his "little girl." And then when Hannah, through her tears, said how sorry she was for hurting Jackie, he praised her bravery, a response that evoked the words he so longed to hear: "I love you too, Daddy."

In the end, after taking a few days to cool down, Jackie got back in touch, reaffirming her commitment to the marriage. Returning to their home in Philadelphia, a highly emotional reunion ensued in which, through tears, she told Emil she loved him and very much wanted to support his efforts to mend his relationship with his daughter.

In this case, the love story had a happy ending. Emil, Jackie and Hannah all wound up in a better place. But often things don't go that way. And that, sadly, was the case with Lydia, a friend and regular reader of my blog. Driven by religious zealotry, her parents and siblings had turned cold, angry and judgmental when she challenged their beliefs and prejudices. Forced, finally, to sever all ties with her family of origin, she sent me the following email, describing her pain:

> While I'm not perfect I live the values you write about pretty well. But nothing – not my religion, not Radical Decency, NOTHING – has prepared me for this. The loss, anxiety, and sleepless nights are unbearable. I might not make it. How do you live these principles when your family becomes a microcosm of hell? I feel I have no family. I cannot deal with the stress of being there, where decency is not valued and the abuse is constant.

Putting these two examples together, here is the reality with which we must deal: Loving in this values-based way is a highly uncertain enterprise.

Its immediate aftermath may be a happy ending, as it was for Emil. Or it may result in the searing, seemingly unbearable pain that Lydia experienced.

In the end, however, values-based loving has a redemptive promise that transcends even the pain we feel when we lose a deeply cherished relationship. And so it was for Lydia. After taking time to heal from her family rift and to accept it, as best she could, she was able to create a network of friends whose love and support was far healthier and more nourishing than any she'd been offered by her parents and siblings.

•••••

In closing this discussion of love, I offer the following thought. While we need to apply this values-based approach to our intimate relationships, we also desperately need to apply it to our love of country, religion, and ethnicity. Without it, as history shows, these relationships will far too regularly invite – indeed even demand – unspeakable cruelties, inflicted on both nonconformists within and nonbelievers without.

If we hope to create a more decent world, love of God, country and ethnicity will continue to be a vital part of living, of course. But these relationships, like our relationships with friends and family, will no longer be automatic and forever. They, too, will be grounded in, and guided by, our most deeply held values.

CHAPTER 8

Relationship – Ending the Dance of Dominance

Twenty-five years ago, I was an attorney managing a busy bankruptcy practice. My secretary, Elaine, was a charming, gray-haired women, ten years my senior, with a relaxed manner and mischievous sense of humor. After three years of working together, our relationship was warm and friendly. And yet, in an utterly typical exchange, I would rush from my office and, passing Elaine's desk, bark: "I'm late for court, where's the Famco file?"

Back then, both Elaine and I viewed this interaction as entirely unexceptional and more-or-less benign. But it wasn't. What I understand now, all these years later, is that the very ordinariness of this exchange – and so many others like it – masks something very widespread and deeply corrosive.

WHERE DO "I" END AND "YOU" BEGIN?

One of our most critical unnamed challenges we face as we seek to create more decent lives and a more humane world is a massive, culture-wide epidemic of boundary confusion. Simply put, we live in a world in which most of us are strikingly unaware, in our day-to-day choices, of where "I" end and other people begin. And, because this flawed way of interacting is so pervasive, it is thoroughly baked into the background of "just the way things are," hiding out in plain sight.

Here's how the process works.

In a world in which compete-to-win values are so pervasive, the default relationship between two people is an authoritarian one in which one person is dominant and the other controlled. At times, this pattern is explicit, apparent to the people involved (and everyone else); for example, an angry parent or spouse, or a coach berating an inattentive player.

But far more often, it lurks below the surface, showing up in more subtle ways – an aggressive remark, a look of disdain – bursting to the surface only occasionally, if ever, as an explicit assertion of power. This subtler authoritarian mindset suffuses an astonishing number of interactions: In the workplace, with friends and neighbors and, even, in our intimate relationships.

In this environment, boundary crossing is an almost irresistible tactic for the person seeking to dominate. Why? Because unlike straightforward persuasion, skillful boundary crossing keeps other people in line without any need to enlist their cooperation and, very often, with no or just a vague awareness on their part (or yours) of what is happening

The interaction between Elaine and I, described above, is a good example of what I mean. As I approached her desk, I was already understandably anxious. To get to the courthouse on time, I needed to find a cab and also hope that traffic would cooperate. And my mind was already swimming with all the problems that might arise as I presented my case. But instead of handling my anxiety on my own, my aggressive, dictatorial words were an implicit but, at an emotional level, clearly-understood demand that Elaine take my anxiety on – something that Elaine, sitting innocently at her desk, had in no way invited or consented to. Quite simply, I had crossed her boundaries.

And the tactic worked. Elaine didn't remain neutral. Immediately, she took on my anxiety. With her blood pressure spiking, she frantically scurried around, throwing open file cabinet drawers to find the Famco file so that our now shared anxiety – anxiety that properly belonged to me – could be relieved.

ON-THE-JOB INVASIONS

While boundary crossing shows up everywhere, it shows up with particular virulence at work. To understand how it works, consider the situation at Kim Roberts & Co., a company I worked with as a consultant several years ago.

Kim, its founder, is an intense, extremely hardworking woman in her late 40s who built the firm based on her reputation as a relentless, "whatever it takes to succeed" marketing consultant. While the firm now has 5 partners and 7 other professionals on staff, Kim generates 75% of the business and is unquestionably in charge.

The people who work there, Kim included, are chronically overworked, anxious, and unhappy. And yet because the money is good and the job market uncertain, they are reluctant to leave. Like so many others in the workplace, they feel trapped. When asked about their situation, their typical response is: "What can I do? Sure, things are unpleasant here. But that's just the way things are in the competitive, dog-eat-dog business we're in."

But the problem faced by the folks at Kim Roberts & Co. *isn't* something inherent in the workplace or competitive market. It is, instead, a problem that is entirely fixable: An epidemic of boundary confusion.

It begins with Kim's understandable anxiety when something doesn't go right. But because she's the boss and can get away with it, she regularly crosses coworkers' boundaries as she struggles to deal with her difficult feelings. This pattern regularly comes up, for example, when she receives work product that doesn't meet her standards. A typical Kim Roberts response? To throw a report back across the desk with a dismissive "this stinks."

And the boundary invasions don't end there. Kim regularly vents her frustration and anxiety with her more senior people, including Martin, her chief of staff: "What's wrong with Terry [a junior staff member]. Her work is sloppy and she isn't here when I need her." Martin, internalizing Kim's tense, judgmental state of mind (boundary cross #1), then passes her feelings along to the more junior people, along with his own emotionally charged feelings stirred up by Kim's sharp comments (boundary cross #2): "Don't you get it, Terry? Not working through the weekend and making excuses won't cut it. We need committed professionals."

Since Kim's employees are themselves products of the culture's win/lose mindsets, these verbal potshots fall on fertile soil. Unschooled in the art of managing these sorts of boundary-crossing attacks, they allow these harsh words to invade their psyches. Feeling that they somehow did something wrong, they are suffused with self-judgment, anxiety, and self-doubt.

And what goes around comes around. Not knowing how to handle their difficult feelings any better than Kim, they cope with them by engaging in boundary crosses of their own, directed back at Kim. With them, however, it shows up as sarcasm, sullenness, and/or water cooler gossip; responses that, because they're indirect, are less likely to invite retaliation. Thus, the sad, ironic outcome when it comes to authoritarian boundary crossing relationships is that everyone loses – even the dominant person who, in addition to her original upset, now has to deal with her subordinates' inevitable blowback.

GETTING PERSONAL

When we look beyond the workplace, these same boundary crossing ways are also endemic – even in our friendships and most intimate relationships. Consider the case of Chuck and Craig. Business colleagues and friends, the two men regularly get together to banter about politics and sports. Having agreed to meet for lunch several weeks earlier, Chuck is a no show. But Craig's call from the restaurant, where he is waiting, isn't a simple "What happened?" Instead, he snaps: "Where are you? I arranged my entire day around our get together!" – pushing his annoyance back on Chuck. And Chuck responds similarly, seeking to shift the blame back onto Craig: "Give me a break. You never called to confirm. I thought you'd cancelled."

Look as well at the situation involving 14-year-old Mark and his mom. Mark's parents, seeking me out for family therapy, made it clear from the outset that my job was to "fix" Mark who, from an early age, had bullied his peers and been combative with authority figures. But our early therapy sessions revealed far more. With Mark about to start high school, his increasingly frantic mother was resorting more and more to deeply wounding, boundary-crossing language. "You'll never get into a good college," she'd railed at him. Or, she'd warn, "Girls don't like boys who act this way" or simply spit out "What's *wrong* with you?" Sadly and predictably, my efforts to introduce this boundary-crossing pattern into our work were met with defensiveness and incomprehension from Mark's mom ("What am I supposed to do, sit by and watch him ruin his life?") and, even worse, from him ("Mom's right, I'm a bad kid").

Let me move now to my most important relationship – with Dale, my wife of 30-plus years. A bright-eyed, witty, five-foot bundle of energy, I love her deeply. Not long ago we hosted a dinner party for another couple. As we discussed the upcoming election, Dale really got into it, passionately elaborating on an idea that was important to her. As she continued to hold forth, I became increasingly uncomfortable, feeling she was going on too long, being too strident. So I interjected a sarcastic remark that, evoking laughter, silenced her in mid-sentence. With this act of boundary-crossing aggression masked as humor – so commonplace that it passed unremarked upon by our guests – I "won," relieving my own discomfort at the expense of the person I love most in life.

Sadly, this same epidemic of boundary confusion has even infiltrated to the core of the mating dance we call romantic love, a place where most of us like to think we do better. Take Jack and Susan, for example. For them, the romance was there from the start. When Jack saw her walking up the path to the restaurant for their first date, his heart leapt and a warm jolt of energy surged. A little later, as they waited for dessert and coffee, Susan – captured by his warm eyes, the gap in his front teeth, and slightly goofy manner – was suddenly hit by this realization: "This could really be the guy I'm looking for!"

What happened that evening for Susan and Jack was, of course, that strong visceral/sexual "in love" attraction we all relish – and rightly so. It is, after all, one of life's great joys. The problem, however, is the prevailing belief that "happily ever after" will just naturally unfold from this transformed, dopamine-fueled state. And with so little attention being paid to how couples actually relate to one another, our ingrained, boundary-crossing ways of behaving all too typically become our default way of dealing with our romantic partner.

So it was for Jack and Susan.

Since Susan was perfect, in his eyes, any self-doubt she might express was forcefully pushed aside by Jack: "How can you be insecure? That's ridiculous. Everybody loves you." In our culture, words such as these pass for love. But can you feel its dark, boundary-crossing underside? With Jack insistently silencing any part of Susan that contradicted his fantasy, she quickly learned to suffer her insecurities alone. And, of course, the same thing was happening in reverse. Relishing her image of him as a confident, up-and-coming businessman, Susan would brush aside his work anxieties with a breezy, "Oh, I'm sure you'll figure it out." And Jack, in turn, felt compelled to minimize and hide his very real professional insecurities and fears.

With this boundary obliterating, "in love" fantasy dance firmly in place, the next chapter for Jack and Susan was sadly predictable. As the drug of first love faded, the real Jack began to intrude on Susan's fantasy world, and vice versa. But instead of respecting their differences and getting to know one another, they fought back. Susan responded to this now unvarnished version of Jack with disbelief, anger, and a demand for a return of the old Jack: "You're always pre-occupied and distracted. I'm sick to death of your blank stares and one-word responses." With Jack responding in kind, they became locked in a demoralizing, win/lose power struggle.

All too often, this is the point at which a relationship, originally so full of promise, ends – or sinks into an enduring state of confusion, disappointment and hurt.

But this isn't inevitable. Couples can change. And that, happily, has been the case for Susan and Jack.

In a typical, pre-therapy interaction, Susan's edgy, boundary-crossing "Why didn't you make the bed," was greeted with disgruntled counter-aggression: "Give me a break, I'm busy getting the kids ready for school." But now, when they re-play this interaction, Jack acknowledges her frustration and moves immediately into positive problem solving: "You're right, I didn't get to it. I'll be sure to take care of it before I leave." Then, later that day, with this initial interaction fully behind them, he completes the cycle of intimacy, gently telling Susan that he was unsettled by her tone and asking her to pay attention to that in the future; feedback she warmly acknowledges.

With this more relational, boundary-*honoring* way of interacting becoming more and more habitual, Jack and Susan are now, increasingly, realizing the initial promise of their relationship.

PATRIARCHY: BOUNDARY-CROSSING'S EPICENTER

As I see it, patriarchy stands at the very center of our efforts to end our debilitating, boundary-crossing ways, a perspective driven by three factors:

(1) Patriarchy – social arrangements in which men have familial and political power, control the wealth, and enjoy unquestioned moral authority and social privilege – has been with us for millennia. Its roots are deep and enduring.

(2) How we deal with the "other" sex is always there – right in front of us – needing to be dealt with right now; and

(3) Our male/female challenges go to the very core of our being, affecting relationships between mothers and sons, fathers and daughters, wives and husbands, brothers and sisters.

If we can develop the skills needed to heal and grow in this vitally important and fiercely unforgiving relational crucible, we'll be empowered to confront our boundary-crossing ways in every other area of life as well. Patriarchy is, in short, a uniquely promising point of leverage as we seek to create better lives and a more humane and decent world.

•••••

When it comes to gender relations, feminism's second wave, beginning in the 1960s, has unquestionably brought important, life-changing progress. The enduring sexual myths and stereotypes that so profoundly disrespect – and cancel out essential parts of – women, are being challenged as never before: Their assumed lack of physical capability; the sexually shackling Madonna/whore dichotomy; and, more generally, the view that they are overly emotional and irrational.

One need only compare the women presented in 1950s TV shows such as *Father Knows Best* and *I Love Lucy*, with the women in *The Good Wife*, *Scandal*, and *Sex in the City* to be reminded of the progress we've made. In addition, women's employment opportunities have dramatically expanded, with their numbers increasing, since the 1960s, from 10% to 35% for lawyers, 5% to 34% for doctors, 1% to 29% for engineers, and even 2% to 13% for law enforcement professionals.

As a result of these developments, there are now many more couples in which the woman is working at a job that is just as demanding as that of her male partner – or more so. And, in these situations, household and childrearing responsibilities are often being divided up on a much more equitable basis. Pointing to these relationships, a number of Millennials have confidently told me that their generation has, mostly, made our old patriarchal ways a thing of the past.

But the deeper truth is that traditional gender roles – our ways of interacting since, literally, Biblical times – persist with bedeviling persistence. Women still earn 20% less on average than men, the rate of intimate partner violence for woman remains at 1 in 4 (as compared to only 1 in 9 for men), and the #MeToo movement laid bare an alarming pattern of sexual harassment, not by women, but by privileged men. As with racism, a confident declaration of patriarchy's end just doesn't jibe with the facts.

Indeed, how could it be otherwise? After all, we still live in a culture in which our boys and girls are indoctrinated into traditional gender roles through an endless variety of subtle, and not so subtle, cues and sanctions. Thus, to cite just a few examples, these roles are thoroughly baked into so many of our (deservedly) treasured religious/historical stories and traditions; endless ads and sitcoms plots; the very different ways in which we habitually compliment our girls and boys; and peer pressure that continues to push them (despite our best efforts) to replicate these traditional roles.

Needless to say, we should celebrate the evolving outlooks of these more co-equal Millennial couples. But we also need to understand that while, for them, gender equality is on the rise, a lot of work remains. Thus, a recent study of highly educated, economically privileged couples reports that on a typical weekend day "women do a lot more housework and childcare – 222 versus 170 minutes – while he leisures." And when tensions rise, many of these new age men still instinctually revert to the authoritative, dismissive tone that is a hallmark of patriarchy.

Moreover, in too many of these new age relationships, boundary-crossing, dominance/submissive patterns still persist, the only difference be that she is now on top – or, at least, is going toe-to-toe with him in a never-ending power struggle. What is needed, however, is not a reshuffling of the win/lose deck but, instead, new ways of interacting across the gender divide, that are more equal, mutually nourishing and respectful of each partner's individuality.

In the sections that follow, I offer a description of how our ingrained patriarchal patterns elaborate themselves in our lives and, then, what we can do about them – first for women and then for men.

WOMEN: PLAYING NICE AND FEELING ROTTEN

When I write about men's lives, I do so with some confidence. I am one, after all, and ran men's groups for two decades. Writing about women, however, is different. In key areas I lack the "gut knowing" that comes from shared experience. But assuming an unbridgeable gap in understanding the opposite sex would defeat our larger purposes. So here goes.

The ideas that follow are gleaned, first of all, from my journey of healing, growth, and discovery with my wife, Dale, my teacher and partner in every sense. I have also learned a tremendous amount from the many courageous and thoughtful women I have encountered in my therapy practice and in life, including my daughters, female friends, work associates, and a number of life-changing teachers. So, with humility and a certain amount of trepidation, here are some of my insights about being a woman in this culture.

●●●●●

Women are, without question, pushed by the culture toward care-taking dispositions. To illustrate this point, psychologists Terence Real and Carol Gilligan, in their work as co-therapists, tell the following story: Ask an 8-year-old girl what kind of pizza she wants and she'll tell you. Ask an 11-year-old girl and she'll say, "I'm not sure." Ask a 13-year-old girl – now fully socialized to her assigned gender role – and her answer is likely to be, "What do *you* want?"

Thirteen-year-old girls, and women of all ages, don't stop wanting their pizza with mushrooms and onions. But ingrained in a woman's psyche is a reflexive instinct to compromise her own needs to the needs of others. So when it comes to setting appropriate boundaries, and forthrightly asking for what they want, a heightened conflict exists between her needs and the needs of others. And to further complicate the situation, women – from their teenage years forward – have to deal with men who, groomed by the culture to be aggressive, are pushing for sex, often in forceful and demanding ways.

Here, then, is the situation women face as they emerge into adulthood. Even as they struggle to manage their insistent sexuality, they are required to set appropriate boundaries with their male peers, and to do so in the face of a powerful internalized voice telling them to accommodate to their demands. This is a prescription for confusion and pain for any girl – or woman – if she hasn't cultivated the emotional tools needed to put these deeply embedded caretaking habits to one side when that is the better choice.

Note, moreover, that this painful pattern plays out, not just in the bedroom, but also in a wide variety of taken-for-granted ways: An unwanted sexualized look; mansplaining; a rat-a-tat-tat of sarcastic comments that put the woman "in her place"; a fart followed by a smirking laugh.

So, to cite just one example, I meet a friend for lunch who tells me about a man she passed on the street, on the way to the restaurant, who stared just a little too long and too directly and said, as he brushed by, "you should smile." My instinctual reaction – felt but thankfully unsaid – was "so what?" Only after a moment's reflection was I able to get in touch with the yucky feeling this interaction evoked in her as a woman who routinely deals with these sorts of boundary crosses in a world still deeply in the grip of patriarchy.

A Tricky Balancing Act

So what's a woman to do?

To truly heal and grow, we all, men and women alike, need to fully disengage from the boundary-crossing, dominance/submission pattern inherent in patriarchy. For women, this means letting go of their habitual caretaking ways while, at the same time, feeling free to express them in situations where that is her preferred choice. They should be able to warmly respond to their partners' needs and longings and just as capably say no – to unwanted sex or to a pepperoni pizza.

In doing this work, women need to deal with a fundamental asymmetry in the way in which men and women assert themselves. In any given moment, many women express their needs with commendable clarity – and do so a second or even a third time. But then, too often, their entrenched caretaking instincts creep back in and they back off. By contrast, a typical man will push for what he wants again, and again, and again. Like the tide, his assertiveness is relentless and unremitting.

If a woman asserts her needs 75% of the time and the man asserts his 100% of the time, the net effect is an inherently out of balance negotiation that drifts back toward dominance by him and complicity by her. Understanding this, she needs to cultivate habits of assertiveness that are as comfortably and persistently assertive as his.

Doing so is very challenging. In this regard, I think of my client, Brenda, a woman in her late 40s. When she walked into my office for the first time, her eyes danced with discernment and an ironic, humor-filled take on life. Exuding an innate dynamism, she jumped right in, expressing her thoughts, feelings, hopes, and frustrations with ease and directness.

Our initial work focused on Brenda's efforts to deal with a demanding male boss and a distant, judgmental father. Noticing a theme, I would, from time to time, inquire about her relationship with another key man in her life; her long-time husband, Max. Her invariable response: "Nothing to talk about there. We're fine."

As Brenda's self-awareness grew, however, this perspective shifted. She began to realize that Max, while kindhearted and still endearingly infatuated with her, was deeply withdrawn. Brenda was the family's go-to person: Running the household, organizing the social calendar, handling most every emotional crisis. Max, meanwhile, pitched in when asked, but otherwise did his own thing. He spent long hours at work, enjoyed his daily runs, and religiously participated in weekend golf outings. Max was also the guy in the den watching football at family events.

Brenda began to see with painful clarity that, her dynamic personality notwithstanding, she'd nonetheless been inducted into a caretaker role that, while more subtle, was very much like that of her similarly powerful, but sad and frustrated mother. Ultimately, she told Max that if he couldn't commit to a more equal relationship, she would leave the marriage.

Brenda's journey from that point forward illustrates just how difficult it is to shed entrenched caretaking mindsets. Appalled at the thought of losing his wife, Max gamely came to couples sessions for months on end. But he never grew into the emotionally available partner she was seeking. Instead, the persistent, unacknowledged subtext of his behavior was this:

I want Brenda to be happy. So when she actively pushes, I'll do my best to respond. But this is weird. Hopefully, if I wait it out, she'll get over it and things will get back to "normal."

But "normal" was no longer an option for Brenda. Even as this reality set in, however, Brenda struggled for months to let go of the belief that she couldn't leave the marriage until Max understood why; still, in this way, taking care of Max.

Even after she worked through that issue, moreover, her caretaking habits continued. Still living together, Brenda moved into a separate room and ended all physical intimacy. But Max, still not getting it, responded with persistent boundary-eroding moves – uninvited hugs, unsolicited back rubs, late-night visits to her bedside, all designed to insinuate himself back into her bed. And more than once, she gave in to these unwanted advances. A final, emotional break only occurred when Brenda got her own apartment and fully separated from Max.

Clint and Mona were a very different couple struggling with the same dynamic. Gen X'ers, in their mid-30s, they were far more aware of their gender-based patterns and committed to doing better. Clint worked hard to make requests rather than boundary-crossing demands: "Do you know where the car keys are?" and not a peremptory "where are the keys?" In addition, he proactively took on primary responsibility for more of the housekeeping chores including, for example, food shopping and weekend vacuuming. And yet, as the dirty clothes accumulated in the hamper, Mona continued to struggle with a sense of being judged by him as, somehow, falling short as a wife and homemaker.

Why? Because, despite his explicit reassurances, his tone of voice and emotional energy, when they discussed household chores, regularly communicated far more impatience than he thought. And she, in turn, primed to amplify whatever tone of insistence and judgment she perceived in his words, reflexively reverted to her old, caretaking mindset: "My job is to tend to my husband and home, and he's telling me I'm falling short."

Finally, there is the case of my own wife, Dale, as she put plans in place to spend Saturday with her girlfriend, a day usually reserved for us. Not at my self-aware best, I slipped into male, boundary-crossing behaviors: Annoyance and pouting. "Why do you need to so spend time with her! When will you be getting home!?"

When Dale is on her emotional game, she comfortably and lovingly maintains her autonomy and integrity, leaving me with a hug and these reassuring words: "It's nice to know I'll be missed, that I'm loved so much." But on this occasion, my boundary pushing triggered her knee-jerk need to take care of me. Feeling guilty about putting herself first, she responded with defensiveness and anger: "What do you want from me! Give me a break. I just want to spend the afternoon with my friend."

As these stories illustrate, the work involved in balancing and integrating deeply rooted caretaking instincts with newfound assertiveness is regularly confusing, frustrating, and uncomfortable. But if we hope to create better lives and a more decent and humane world, dismantling them is a must.

•••••

Needless to say, ending our patriarchal ways requires imagination and leadership from men as well. Before turning to the that side of the equation, let's take a look at the exemplary way in which Dana has overcome her care-taking ways in her relationship with her partner, Jake.

The turning point for Dana came when she made the difficult choice to relocate from her longtime home in the Northeast to rural Wisconsin to accommodate her husband's career as area manager for a large, heavy equipment firm. When, consumed by the new job's demands, Jake became preoccupied and emotionally withdrawn, Dana's first reaction was to accuse and complain: "Dammit Jake, with all I've given up for us, how can you treat me this way?"

But with time and support, she found her power – and self-assertive voice – telling Jake that, absent change, she'd leave the relationship. Since then, Dana has been clear and persistent, asking for what she wants and needs from Jake and spelling out the consequences of an inadequate response. At the same time, she's regularly expressing appreciation for his good faith efforts.

Jake's initial response has been positive. However, a point that can't be over-emphasized is this: Because Dana is persisting in this new pattern of relating, a return to their old, patriarchal ways is impossible. For Dana (and, thus, for Jake), the old status quo needs to be null and void.

WE MEN ARE NOT EMOTIONAL PYGMIES

Into my 40s, I did what a lot of men do. I kept my feelings mostly to myself, except with my wife. And even when I did share with Dale, I wasn't very skillful, to say the least. I was able to express anger and annoyance, no problem there. But sadly for Dale – and for me – I voiced my more vulnerable fears and longings in equally reactive ways. "Why can't you get off the freakin phone?" (I would say), instead of "I'm missing you and hope we can spend some time together soon." I pretty much accepted the culture's derisive message that, as a man, I was an insensitive jerk, a victim of testosterone poisoning, hopelessly aggressive and far too focused on sex.

•••••

When we men get together, it's frequently at a bar or ballgame, or in the cushioning presence of our female partners; situations in which a re-thinking of our gender-based patterns is unnecessary. In my 40s however – to my great good fortune – I began to spend time in men's groups and other personal-growth forums, such as the Mankind Project; environments that encouraged frank and open discussions with other guys about life's challenges and what it means to deal with them as a man.

Through these experiences, I have learned three things that, as a man, have changed my life.

1. There is nothing wrong with us. We men make complete sense.

2. We are fully capable adults in every sense; as competent emotionally as we are in the practical realm; capable of being empathetic

as well as assertive. We too can play an active leadership role in ending our patriarchal ways.

3. The privilege that comes our way, as beneficiaries of patriarchy, is life's booby prize; a formula, not for a good life, but for a life suffused with shame, isolation, confusion and self-destructive behaviors.

MEN - WE MAKE COMPLETE SENSE!

As we seek to mount an effective response to our assigned gender role, we men need to remember that biology is not the issue. In her 2009 book, *Pink Brain, Blue Brain: How Small Differences Grow into Troublesome Gaps and What We Can Do About It,* Lise Eliot carefully reviews the evidence for gender-based biological differences. Her conclusion? While there are differences in our cognitive and emotional physiology, they are minor and, standing alone, do little to explain the differences between men and women.

So what is going on? As Clinton-era political commentator James Carville might have put it, "it's the culture, stupid."

We live in a world that accentuates these small genetic differences, pushing each sex toward certain capabilities and vulnerabilities and away from others. In the process, it shrinks the humanity of both.

Thus, Terence Real and Carol Gilligan offer the following bookend to the "girl ordering pizza" story, described earlier. In this case, a 3-year old boy falls down in the supermarket and his eyes fill with tears. The stereotypical response? An adult rushes in, telling him "Everything's fine, brush it off, be a little man." This response is, of course, very different from the cuddling and gentle stroking a 3-year old girl, in the same situation, would likely receive.

For us men, things have definitely gotten better in the last 40 years. Many parents, with heightened sensitivity to assigned gender roles, are working hard to change this pattern. But let's not kid ourselves. Our boys continue to be exposed to a torrent of messages – on TV, the Internet, and the playground – that reinforce the old messages: Suck it up, be tough, don't be needy, hide your fears and vulnerability. And never forget that intimate sharing and emotional comfort are unmanly; the province of girls and sissies.

This continuing, intense cultural conditioning makes sense of many male behaviors that women, often with withering judgment, find so perplexing. But it also means that, as learned behaviors, they can be changed. As the women's movement has so persuasively demonstrated, our culturally defined gender roles are not a life sentence.

●●●●●

In what follows, I offer a perspective on why some of our emblematic male ways of being do, indeed, make complete sense.

Our Sexual Behaviors

The Brauns are in the midst of a family therapy session. Alex, their 16-year-old son, is typically sullen, withdrawn, and monosyllabic. But, in this session, the mood unexpectedly shifts as Alex talks about an afternoon spent with his girlfriend and – sharing a warm, conspiratorial, smirking laugh with his dad – implies that, if he hasn't yet "scored," he's well on his way.

●●●●●

By the time we reach puberty, we boys are already emotionally isolated, having learned not to cry, seek physical comfort, or share our fears and vulnerabilities. But things are different when it comes to sex. Indeed, our emerging sexuality – at least insofar as it means scoring with girls – is seen as a badge of honor. So what we learn as boys is that hugging, strok-ing, and nurturance are not ok – except, that is, in the context of sex.

As a result, for men, far more than is the case for women, affection is deeply intertwined with intercourse. And for so many of us, this fusing of affection and sex – an unfortunate legacy from our upbringing – persists throughout life. Thus, we're preoccupied with sex, not because we're pigs, ready to "screw anything" but, instead, because the culture's relentless mes-sage is that this is the one area where we can get the physical and emotional nurturance for which we – like every other human – so deeply long.

Keeping it Light: How Men "Do" Intimacy

In the old joke, lame but telling, a couple comes home from a social evening with the wife describing, in vivid detail, the hostess' recent vaca-tion, her emotional struggles with her daughter, her plans to redecorate the back bedroom, and her latest sciatic attack. Seeking deeper connection, she then asks her husband about his time with their host. After a moment of confused silence, he says, "He got a new carburetor."

●●●●●

Because of the ways in which women are raised, intimate conversa-tion is a place of comfort for them. But for us men, it's an invitation into unfamiliar, emotionally unsafe territory. When our spouse says, "We need to talk," it signals the risk of feeling judged and shamed. Small wonder, then, that our instinct is to resist the invitation.

Our socialization also explains our typical male way of interacting with each other. Talking sports, cracking jokes, exchanging insults, or doing something side-by-side such as playing tennis or repairing a lawn-mower creates companionship at a distance that feels comfortable. We are, in effect, creating a space in which fear of our partner's shame-inducing judgment has been banished. In this environment, no one is humiliated, even when we get falling down drunk and vomit all over the bathroom floor.

But what is lost, sadly, is real intimacy. As Robert Garfield points out in *Breaking the Male Code: Unlocking the Power of Male Friendship* (2015): "Under the spell of the Male Code, men often feel too ashamed to expose their vulnerabilities to their buddies, even when their problems are spiraling out of control and they could really use the support."

Why Men Lash Out

In the United States, men account for 73% of all arrests, 80% of those arrested for violent crimes, 90% of those convicted of murder, 98% of those found guilty of mass murders, and 80% of drivers responsible for fatal accidents. Sadly, these statistics – as unbalanced as they are – don't seem all that surprising.

•••••

Men are markedly more aggressive than women. But the reason is cultural conditioning and not biological wiring. Given the ways in which we're socialized, we are far more conversant with aggressive emotions – anger, annoyance, and frustration – than we are with more vulnerable emotions such as hurt, sadness, fear, and confusion. But what is less obvious is how we use our aggressiveness to shield ourselves from these less familiar, less comfortable emotions

As the brilliant psychologist Steven Stosny points out in *Treating Attachment Abuse: A Compassionate Approach* (1995), anger is like a little hit of crack cocaine. Its negative consequences can be severe, but in the moment it actually feels better. Why? Because it shifts our body into action mode, pumping cortisol, adrenaline and noradrenaline into our system and blood into our large muscle groups, giving us a sudden jolt of physical energy. At the same time, anger shrinks the reasoning parts of the brain

– the parts that could engender uncertainty in a moment of crisis – leaving us with a heightened (and false) sense of clarity..

So a typical man, trained to be assertive but not open and vulnerable, predictably falls into this emotional trap: When vulnerable emotions come up, he "fast forwards" through this uncomfortable territory, seeking instead the short-term relief that annoyance or anger offers. Over time, this pattern becomes so automatic that many men are not even aware of the underlying hurt, fear or confusion that triggers it.

So in the realm of aggressive behavior, we are not perverse, inexplicable beings. Instead, what we are doing is a flawed, but perfectly understandable, adaptation to our assigned gender role. Knowing how this process works, the hopeful corollary is this: We are perfectly capable of doing things differently and better for "them" – and for us..

MEN'S ONGOING, NITTY-GRITTY WORK

Our culture offers a lot of rationales that allow men to avoid the hard, but necessary, emotional work they need to do. For example, side by side with the "men are inherently flawed" is the implicit but widespread believe that, when it comes to patriarchy, most all of the work is on the women's side. "If she could just be as assertive about her needs as I am," the thinking goes, our patterns of dominance and submission will go up in smoke. But this belief is simply wrong. In fact, the opposite is true.

The vital importance of men's work grows out of the deeply reciprocal nature of our gendered roles. As noted earlier, a woman who is being more assertive will frequently feel at risk of exploitation when she then re-engages with her nurturing instincts. Why? Because it's hard for a woman to be both nurturing of a male partner *and self-caring* if he just keeps expecting more.

To avoid this dilemma, we men need to treat her caring choices, not as deserved or taken for granted concessions, but rather as opportunities to reciprocate in the service of building a more co-equal and intimate relationship. When we do, her sense of facing an either-or choice – nurture him OR stand up for myself – will shrink dramatically. Trusting that he will be curious about and responsive to her needs, she'll more comfortably make choices in either direction.

As noted earlier, we also need to resist the idea that gender inequality has been solved in the last few decades. Despite heartening progress, we still have a heavy dose of what I call "equality with an asterisk." Yes, her job and career are as important as mine. But if someone needs to be at the teacher's conference, or at a sick relative's bedside, the default position is that "she will do it." And because men are the beneficiaries of this mindset, they have an especially important role to play in resisting this drift back toward patriarchy.

This gendered "asterisk" also shows up in what I call the "dutiful lieutenant syndrome." Far too often, we men believe that we're being good partners when we willingly do the tasks our partner assigns to us. But if we hope to overcome our legacy of male privilege, we need to be co-generals, fully understanding what needs to be done and, then, just doing it. We need to make the bed, clean the clothes, and re-stock the cupboard without being asked, and without the need for supervision or guidance. It is at this point, and this point only, that a there is a decisive turning away from our assigned gender role.

Another very important piece of our work, as men, lies in our habitual disposition and tone. Groomed to be aggressive, we too often talk in dismissive, authoritarian ways – often quite subtle – that put down and/or silence our partner.

- Her: I am thinking about buying a new car. Him: No way. It's not in our budget.

- Her: The movie seemed to be getting at X. Him: No, that's not what it meant.

- Her: I left my keys at my friend's house. Him: Why are you so disorganized?

Each of these seemingly casual, off-hand comments contains within it an assumption that the man has a right to judge and control his partner's thoughts and actions. They are implicit demands for agreement that, when she resists, often trigger his annoyance at being contradicted.

Still another challenge for us men grows out of our culturally groomed tendency to be thinkers and problem-solvers. This outlook, so useful in so many situations, encourages us to underestimate the depth of our ingrained sexist behaviors. "Hey, now that I get it, I'll stop doing it," we say to ourselves, sincerely believing that meaningful change will naturally flow from our new cognitive understanding.

But while intellectual insight can be extremely helpful, it's just the beginning. To truly move forward, we also need to enlist our emotions and heart wisdom in an ongoing effort to uncover our many layers of taken-for-granted male privilege and, then, to cultivate an ability to think, act, *and* feel differently.

As we do this work, women are our indispensable allies. Through long and unfortunate experience, they understand these gender-biased behaviors not just in their brains, but also in their very bones. For this reason, we need to look to them as our teachers and guides.

At the same time, however, we need to understand that, contrary to mainstream stereotypes, we aren't defective – not in the least – when it comes to relating in more egalitarian ways. It's just that we have less experience than they do. So while we're likely to be on a steeper learning curve, especially in the early stages, we are fully capable of being empowered partners in this challenging and vital work.

●●●●●

For us men, a key motivator for doing this work is to do the right thing by the women in our lives. But we also need to embrace its life-changing possibilities for us as well. Fully committing to it, our tense, "need to be in control" habits – byproducts of our compete-to-win culture – will be progressively replaced by the more intimate, relational ways of being that we, like all human beings, truly long for. We'll no longer have to settle for the thin emotional gruel to which our traditional male role consigns us.

BEYOND PATRIARCHY: SOLIDARITY AND HOPE

A wholehearted commitment to the possibilities that exist beyond patriarchy is a challenging and, often, frustrating and perplexing journey. But its outcome and greatest reward – for women and men alike – is a genuine sense of solidarity and mutual respect that can eclipse and replace the persistent disappointments and resentments to which our unexamined, gendered relationships otherwise consign us.

And, importantly, its promise is not limited to its effect on our differently sexed relationships. The skills we cultivate here, when translated into other areas of life – from work, to our communal involvements, to politics – are potentially transformative building blocks as we strive to create better lives and a more decent world. In the Chapters that follow, I discuss these hopeful possibilities.

BECOMING FULLY RELATIONAL: A STORY

With relationship, as with so many other areas of living, the shift toward Radical Decency will grow out of many small, moment-by-moment choices that more fully reflect its 7 Values. With that in mind, I end this Chapter with a story that inspires me not in spite of, but precisely because of, its seeming ordinariness. It comes from my colleague, Nancy Dreyfus, author of *Talk To Me Like I'm Someone You Love* (2013).

It begins with three-year-old Brett, sitting on his bedroom floor, happily absorbed with his blocks. His mother comes in, looks at her watch, and says, "Oh my God, we need to get to Grandma's." Brett, reacting to the tension in mom's voice, stiffens and says, "I don't want to. I don't like going there." With her own frustration spiking, mom then grabs his arm and impatiently pulls him toward the door.

Here, of course, is another example of our taken-for-granted, boundary-crossing ways: Mom pushing her anxiety onto Brett and her son resisting, in classic 3-year-old fashion.

But Dreyfus then re-tells the story in a very different, far more relational way. Coming into the room, Mom gets down on the floor, at eye level with Brett, and says:

> Wow, you're really working hard on that tower. I feel awful but Grandma is sick and we have to get to her place, now.

After a pause – to let Brett digest this news and react with a 3-year-old's typical frustrated protest – she continues:

> Of course you feel that way. There's no reason you should want to go. And I feel bad. But you're too little. I can't leave you here. Do you want to take the blocks with us? Or play with them when we get home?

Imagine how different our lives and world would be if this second story were greeted by readers with a ho-hum shrug. "Yeah, of course, what mom *wouldn't* handle the situation that way? That's how good mothers, and good people in every situation, treat one another."

This is the world we need to create: One in which we instinctually respect each other's boundaries and treat one other with respect, understanding, empathy, acceptance, appreciation, fairness and justice; a world, in other words, in which Radical Decency's 7 Values are the new norm in our relationships.

CHAPTER 9

Getting Down to Business

Work and business wield enormous influence in our lives. It's the place where most of us spend the best hours of the great majority of our days. It's also the epicenter of our culture's compete-to-win values; the place where they are most explicitly embraced and practiced, by so many and without restraint. If we hope to make any sustained progress toward creating a more decent world and more decent lives, changing things at work and in business is essential.

THE BIG PICTURE: TRIUMPHAL BUSINESS

The essence of power is the ability to amass large amounts of wealth and get lots of people to do your bidding. At the time of the Founding Fathers, government was the primary source of this sort of power, which prompted our forefathers to create a system of checks and balances designed primarily to limit governmental power. That system worked fairly well for the country's first 200 years. But we now live in a very different world. Today, we also need to come to grips with the outsized influence that businesses, and the people that own them, exert in our lives and in the world.

This seismic shift in the locus of power has been driven by technological advances that, since the 1960s, have revolutionized communications as well as our ability to analyze and manage vast amounts of complex material. There now exist hitherto unimaginable opportunities to create and keep track of ever more intricate and far-flung businesses and to aggregate and manage enormous sums of money. The result: An explosion in the capacity to create, maintain and expand vast accumulations of private wealth.

By way of example, from 1982 to 2016, the average annual earnings of the United States' five largest companies grew from $2.6 billion to $18.4 billion, a seven-fold increase. Meanwhile, the average net worth of Forbes' 400 wealthiest Americans grew from $285 million to $5.8 billion, a 20-fold increase. In the same time period, the earnings of the American family "in the middle" – that is, with half of families making more and half making less – barely doubled, from $24,600 to $59,000. And, according to a recent Hudson Institute study, that average family experienced almost no growth in its net worth at all, inching from $80,000 in 1983 to just $81,400 in 2013.

To put these numbers in context, suppose you decided to count your money, dollar by dollar, with each dollar counted consuming one second. For our "in the middle" family, the time needed to count a pile of money representing its total net worth has held steady at just over 22 hours in the last 25 years. On the other hand, the net worth count of the "in the middle" guy among Forbes' 400 wealthiest Americans, already requiring nine years in 1982, would now need 183 years. Yes, you read that right. *22 hours vs. 183 years!*

What has emerged as a result of this explosive growth is deeply consequential. In the last 40 years, business, and the people business has made rich, have used their massive wealth to buy off virtually every segment of society that could meaningfully limit its power. Today, business exercises unprecedented influence over both our public policies and the ways in which we live.

The most visible example is, of course, government. While, in theory, there is a clear philosophical divide between the two major parties, the deeper and more abiding trend is that both parties, fueled by business contributions, steadily support changes in the law that expand business' ability to make and keep their money. With striking bipartisan regularity, businesses and the wealthiest among us are the beneficiaries of tax breaks, regulatory protections, and massive financial bailouts that rarely find their way to our "in the middle" family.

In the last five decades, for example, Congress and the courts have expanded the monopoly power that patents confer, allowing them: (1) to cover, not just inventions, but also vaccines and other products drawn from nature; and (2) to be renewed based on insignificant product changes such as, in the case of Namenda (a widely used Alzheimer drug), the substitution of an extended release pill for the original. Similarly, copyright protection – increased just twice in our first 180 years, from 28 to 56 years – has been increased 11 times in the last 50 years, to a new minimum of 120 years.

Another example of politicians pandering to the rich is the increase in the Federal estate tax exemption from $675,000 in 2000 to $11.2 million in 2018, dropping the number of people subject to the tax, each year, from about 52,000 to just 1,800. To put this in context, even before these changes were made, wealthy people were already fully exempt from *any* capital gains tax at all on the large accumulations of stocks and bonds that for them – unlike our "in the middle" family – typically represent the great bulk of the assets they transfer to their heirs at death. Given this fact, there is only one plausible explanation for the steadily growing estate tax exemption for the rich: A bought-and-sold government.

Working in tandem with this explosion of laws, regulations and court rulings that benefit business has been an historic cutback in many of the system's most important checks and balances as they pertain to business:

- Antitrust laws, passed in the late 19th and early 20th centuries to limit business's size and monopoly power, have been effectively dismantled; a trend that, according to noted economist Robert Reich, has "unleashed a wave of mega-mergers that have allowed corporations to consolidate their market power and quash competition."

- Centuries-old, scripturally rooted (Exodus, 22:25; Luke, 6:34-35) state usury laws, that limit the amount of interest that can be charged on loans, have been thoroughly emasculated through federal exemptions for national banks, savings banks, installment lenders, and credit card companies.

- Regulations put in place in the 1930s to limit the size of banks and prohibit federally insured banks from making excessively risky investments, have been diluted or repealed outright.

- A new law, passed in 2005, excludes fully half of all Americans from bankruptcy's debt-free "fresh start" and makes it impossible for our children to get out from under their student loan debt, absent extraordinary circumstances.

- In the 1960s class actions emerged as a way for aggrieved consumers, investors, and employees to band together in a single, cost-effective lawsuit. But today, the effectiveness of class actions has been drastically curtailed by court decisions that impose onerous technical requirements on their use and uncritically enforce boilerplate arbitration clauses that prohibit not just class actions, but any recourse to the courts at all.

Stark as it is, business' power and influence does not end with our bought-and-sold politicians. Lest pressure for change come from other sources, our culture is organized so that almost every college, media outlet, nonprofit entity and religious organization of any size and enduring presence is also heavily dependent on investments, loans, and/or contributions from corporate America and the individuals it has made wealthy. And make no mistake about it: Business extracts its full measure of benefit in return for this largesse.

So, for example, consider the disheartening complicity of many of our largest academic institutions and nonprofit entities, exemplified by the choices made by the Environmental Defense Fund, Columbia's School of Business, and Harvard's Economics Department, described in Chapter 4. Each of these stories is a stark reminder of how eager even our most prestigious institutions can be to compromise their principles – so long as corporate dollars they get in return are large enough.

The enormous influence of business' money also explains why mainstream media outlets, with breathtaking consistency, flood us with stories about the latest scandals and the horse race aspects of politics, but barely mention the extraordinary series of new laws, regulatory decisions, and court rulings – such as those described above – that have so dramatically shifted power and privilege toward business.

LIVING IN A WORK-DRIVEN WORLD

The consequences of these trends are not abstract and theoretical. To the contrary, they have infiltrated and thoroughly infected our lives. Take Kent and Tammy, for example. This couple does things the right way. They work hard at their jobs, she as an occupational therapist for the local school district, he as a mid-level corporate executive. They are also attentive and loving parents to their three children and contribute to their community through volunteer work at their church and to the sports programs in which their kids participate.

But even though they'd be the first to acknowledge their many blessings, their lives are dominated by the unrestrained demands made on them by the businesses for which they work. For Kent, long, intense days at the office start early. He gets up at 5:30 am, takes the 7:10 train to Center City

Philadelphia, and is at his desk by 8:15. Tammy, meanwhile, rushes to get the kids ready so that, by 7:40, the older kids are on the school bus and she is on the way to their youngest daughter's school drop off – prelude to an equally intense day at work.

And the tyranny of work doesn't end when they get home. Like so many other professionals, Kent's nights and weekends are often interrupted by emails from co-workers or the need to prepare for the next day's meeting. Tammy, meanwhile, is expected to create and update the detailed treatment plans her employer requires in her "spare" time. With these pressures added to chores and the kids' seemingly endless round of extracurricular activities, there is far too little time for everything else – going to the gym, reading a book, giving their kids the relaxed, individualized time they crave or, even, getting a couple of hours of extra sleep to re-charge their batteries.

Tammy and Kent are fortunate in that they both have relatively interesting and well-paying jobs. But, even for them, work's rewards are eclipsed by its day-by-day realities. For Kent, every day is a spirit-draining grind, punctuated by arbitrary and time-consuming administrative procedures and endless meetings. And with just two occupational therapists serving the needs of the entire school district, too few resources, and the constant pressure to maintain up-to-date treatment plans, Tammy lives in a more-or-less constant state of low-level agitation.

Faced with these realities, we're deeply mistaken if we assume that these good people – and so many others like them – can simply put work aside and create a happy, fulfilling life in their "off hours." Work's presence is too pervasive and its effects far too powerful. Instead of taking the current realities of the workplace for granted and trying to work around them, we need change strategies that forthrightly deal with business' out of control power in and over our lives.

CREATING A MORE DECENT WORK WORLD: CAN WE DO IT?

Imagine how different things would be if Radical Decency became the new norm at our places of business. Think about the difference it would make in our lives and in the world if:

- Mainstream businesses, instead of seeing fair wages and good work conditions as bottom line costs to be minimized, treated them with the same priority concern now reserved for senior executive compensation and perks;

- Quality products at a fair price, truth in marketing, socially conscious purchasing and investing, and environmental prudence were taken-for-granted priorities;

- Kindness and respect were workplace norms; and

- The desire of conscientious employees – like Tammy and Kent – for a more sensible work/life balance, instead of being effectively ignored, was actively supported.

If business' prevailing mindset ever shifted in these ways so, too, would its expectations for the politicians, nonprofit organizations, universities, media outlets and religious institutions that depend so heavily on its largesse. One can only imagine, for example, how quickly mainstream politicians would shift their approach if their major funders expected them to craft laws that supported these kinds of policy shifts in the workplace. In short, a decisive shift toward decency in business would, inexorably, lead to greater decency in our lives and throughout the mainstream culture.

•••••

Given where we are today, a strategic decency initiative in the workplace will be extraordinarily difficult. But a number of factors make that effort more feasible than you might expect. To begin with, work is a lousy deal for everyone, even for bosses.

It's true, of course, that those at the top do make a lot more money – and that is no small thing. But as Kim Roberts' dilemma, discussed in the last Chapter, illustrates, no one gets a free ride when it comes to the joyless boundary-crossing relationships that pervade the workplace. To the contrary, subordinates almost always "get even" with their bosses, as Kim's employees did, through foot dragging, sullenness, deviousness, and so on. Thus, everyone – bosses and workers alike – have a real and abiding incentive to change business' current authoritarian ways of operating.

A second factor that makes a work-based decency initiative more feasible is, ironically, its authoritarian/hierarchical structure. Empowered and determined CEOs have the power to implement a broad array of radically decent policies.

And their potential interest in doing so is not some pie-in-the-sky dream. To begin with, enlightened bosses will understand that this approach will enhance the quality of their lives as well. In addition, a radically decent company would be well positioned to attract fiercely loyal customers and a highly talented, motivated team of employees. Imagine, for example, the commitment and creativity that would be unleashed if employees knew, without question, that their company was committed to fair pay, personnel policies grounded in dignity and respect, and a genuine interest in and appreciation for their contribution.

The central role our jobs play in our lives, as well as business' authoritarian structure, also makes a transition to Radical Decency more feasible at a practical level as well. A meeting to discuss the company's implementation of a decency initiative could be scheduled by the boss for 10 a.m. on a Tuesday and, since it would be part of the job, nearly everyone would show up on time and treat take-away assignments seriously. This may seem like a relatively trivial point, but it isn't. Imagine, by way of contrast, how hard it would be to schedule just one, let alone a series, of meetings of neighbors to take action against a local environmental hazard.

●●●●●

How, then, do we get from "here" to "there" in business? As I see, the initial inspiration and leadership will almost surely come from a pioneering group of owners and operators, intent on bringing Radical Decency to their businesses. But lasting success will also require better choices from mid-level managers and ordinary workers as well. In the next two sections, I describe the important work that people in these lower and mid-level positions can do – now – to move us in the direction of greater decency in the workplace. Then, in the final two sections, I discuss the challenges and immense rewards of running a radically decent business.

WORKERS: SETTING A TONE, LEADING FROM THE BOTTOM UP

The great majority of jobs don't require people to manage other people. Most employees show up at work each day, do their assigned tasks, and report to a boss. In the discussion that follows, I refer to these people as "workers" and the people they report to as "managers."

For workers intent on effectively contributing to a more decent work environment, a full understanding of their current, very difficult circumstances – the "here" from which their decency aspirations must necessarily begin – is an essential first step. Simply put, management has extraordinary power over their income, work conditions, and job security. In addition, their situation has gotten significantly more precarious in recent years with: (1) The continuing decline of unions; (2) the rise of employment contracts terminable at any time and without cause; and (3) the increasing use of independent contractors who are excluded from even the modest legal protections that full-time employees still retain.

Workers also need to recognize that, as things currently stand, they are operating in a thoroughly polluted interpersonal environment. At work, honesty, trust, and intimate sharing – all taken-for-granted building blocks in our closest relationships – can never be assumed. To the contrary, work is a place where insincerity, manipulation, backbiting, and outright lying are often condoned and, at times, even celebrated as smart tactics. Indeed, it's a telling, and depressing, commentary on where we are as a culture is that the smart guy line, "if you aren't cheating you aren't trying," instead of instantly evoking horror and disgust, is far more commonly accepted as a cynical but, nonetheless, honest acknowledgment of the way things are.

Recognizing these realities, workers need to accept the fact that trusting relationships, while not out of the question in the workplace, are the exception and not the rule – and tend to be unstable. While these relationships should be enjoyed and encouraged when they exist, they can quickly and capriciously disappear.

For me, this particular lesson in work's hard realities is a very personal one. Joining a large law firm in the 1980s, my department chair was a relaxed, live-and-let-live kind of a guy who spread the good cases around and trusted us to get good results. But then, just like that, he left the firm, replaced by a new boss who began keeping the best clients and cases for himself, and started sharpshooting any attorney, me included, who he viewed as a threat to his ambitions. Overnight, everything changed and there was nothing I could do about it. With the new boss regularly going behind my back to raise "concerns" about me with the firm's higher ups, I eventually felt compelled to leave.

As this story illustrates, the current reality at work is this: If your supervisor – call her Mother Teresa – makes her numbers and doesn't cause problems for her superiors, the company will happily accept her nurturing management style. But if she leaves and is replaced by Genghis Khan, the company will just as happily go along with his very different management style as well – so long as he, too, makes his numbers and doesn't cause any problems.

●●●●●

But things don't have to be this way. There was a time, not so long ago, when collective worker initiatives led to a dramatic improvement in work conditions resulting, for example, in minimum wage laws in the early years of the 20th century, and legislation safeguarding union organizing and establishing a 40-hour workweek in the 1930s. Needless to say, these sorts of effective, organized worker initiatives could happen again.

Even absent that, however, there are vitally important initiatives that individual workers can and need to take – now – if we hope to move the needle in the direction of Radical Decency. The four operational guidelines, set forth below, offer a roadmap for this work, highlighting its possibilities and, just as important, its realistic limitations.

Guideline 1: Create Firm Boundaries

A crucial point we always need to remember is that Radical Decency insists on decency, not just to others and the world, but to our self as well. Indeed, without this third aspect, the philosophy falls apart, receding into an idealistic but unsustainable platitude.

The workplace is the epicenter of the culture's indecent dog-eat-dog values and is, moreover, a place where owners, managers and supervisors have extraordinary power over workers' lives. For these reasons, decency to self leads to this key threshold guideline for a worker seeking to be an effective force for change: Absent a good reason for doing so, keep your emotions to yourself.

In other words, when it comes to the company's petty rules and procedures, or a clueless or nasty co-worker, spontaneous expressions of anger or frustration are an indulgence. So, too, are unfiltered expressions of your trenchant but slightly off-color brand of humor. The reason? You can never lose sight of the fact that an unsympathetic boss or competitive co-worker might seize on these sorts of behaviors to undercut you.

In the regard, Kyra's experience as a young therapist at a drug and alcohol facility is cautionary. A "tell it like it is" kind of person, her comments at staff meetings were direct and unsparing. If a co-worker said something that made no sense to her, she'd say so. Similarly, when the department head harped on one of the many pointless, ass-covering details that every therapist needed to include in their session notes, she would be unsparing in her criticism.

New to the world of work, Kyra assumed her comments, aggressive but smart and on point, would be appreciated. What she failed to understand, however, was that the boss' sensitivity to criticism and need to be in control were more important than her substantive contributions. So, when her coworkers began to complain about Kyra's acerbic style, her boss, already feeling uncomfortable due to her vocal impatience with the rules and procedures, was all too ready to listen. In the end, Kyra's position was irrevocably undermined. She was labeled a "difficult" employee, was subjected to repetitive meetings to discuss her "attitude problem," and was effectively excluded from the therapeutic team. Eventually, she had to leave the agency.

When you, as a worker, are provoked, there are practical strategies you can use to manage your anger, annoyance or disgust, such as remembering to breathe or simply to delay your response. Practicing these techniques in more routine interactions is very helpful since, later on, when powerful emotions suddenly spike in a more important situation, these calming practices will be more readily available to you. Remember, as well, what you're about. When you keep your feelings to yourself, you're not being a wimp. To the contrary, by creating a firm personal boundary in the face of inappropriate or provocative behavior, you're being wisely self-protective in a situation in which your ability to control consequences is limited.

Guideline 2: Being "That Person"

With this guideline we are entering the more hopeful realm of leadership from the bottom up. At well-run organizations, the people at the top already encourage honest, respectful, and empathic interactions. But here's the thing: Even if you're dealing with a soulless, indifferent boss, you can still move things in a positive direction.

One thing I've repeatedly noticed in many different work environments is the presence of "that person." My friend Bob is an excellent example. A quiet man with a world-weary air, he's been an adjustor at the local office of a large insurance company for many years. The challenges he and his co-workers face are unrelenting: Unreasonable monthly quotas; oppressive documentation; and a revolving door of supervisors who, browbeaten by the demands of their higher-ups, seem to forever berate and threaten their subordinates.

But Bob is treated differently. Everyone in the office – even each new boss, upon his or her arrival – somehow knows not to mess with him. Why? It has something to do with his professionalism. Bob does his job well. But there's more to it than that. Co-workers, and even bosses, readily share their complaints and frustrations with him, knowing he'll listen with patience and respect, affirming points of legitimate frustration but never fueling the fire with his own grievances.

Not a complainer himself, Bob will nevertheless speak up when the situation requires it. When he does, he does it firmly and quietly, conveying the unspoken message that "this is serious and demands attention." With all of Bob's actions reflecting integrity and respect both for himself and others, his co-workers and bosses alike listen when he speaks and take his ideas seriously.

Many workplaces have people like Bob. And while we may notice and admire them, we seldom take the time to understand what they're doing. But we should. These people are powerfully modeling bottom-up, values-based leadership.

What can we learn from Bob's example? It begins with good listening. When faced with an unreasonable boss, it's important not to give in to your natural, very human tendency to shut down or react with annoyance. Seek, instead, to reassure her that you're on her "side" – not through placating words or behaviors, but through patient attentiveness to her emotions even as you steer the conversation in a more reasoned direction. Then, as your reputation as "that person" grows, you may even be able to offer meaningful emotional support through understanding and empathy; the ground out of which growing influence over the company's ways of operating can flow.

Guideline 3: When Possible, Share Your Authentic Thoughts and Feelings

Guideline 2 speaks to what workers can reasonably do, at most workplaces. But keep in mind that with luck – nudged along, perhaps, by better choices made by you and your co-workers – yours may be a workplace where Decency's 7 Values really do matter to the people in charge. If that is the case, reinforce their better instincts by being more fully relational yourself, adding your own authentic thoughts and feelings into the ongoing conversation.

Doing so can be risky since you're still dealing with people who have arbitrary authority over your life and livelihood. So even as you speak up, do so with discretion, maintaining always civility, respect, understanding, and good listening skills. And never go to the opposite extreme: If a higher-up happens to have a warm, open style, don't use it as an opportunity to unload all you stored up resentments.

This guideline describes the role that Ann, a woman you first met in Chapter 2, played at the company for which she worked before making the life-altering changes described in that Chapter. As her company's COO, her official responsibilities were limited to day-to-day operations. But Colleen, the CEO and Ann's boss, was frustrated in her efforts to create a more decent corporate culture by her mercurial, bullying predecessor Ben, officially retired but still highly influential in his role as Board Chair. So Ann, a patient and empathic listener, quickly became Colleen's confidante.

But Ann offered far more than just a sympathetic ear. When Colleen, oppressed by Ben's latest outburst, wavered in her decency commitment, Ann would consistently challenge her to do the right thing. She was, moreover, equally authentic and direct with Ben, passionately expressing her opposition, for example, when he tried to bully a site manager into resigning so he could replace him with a favored business crony.

As COO, Ann was never able to fully solve the "Ben problem." But, to a remarkable degree, she became the company's moral compass, commanding the respect not just from co-workers but also from members of the company's board and, grudgingly, even from Ben himself. And she used this moral authority wisely, offering recourse for aggrieved and bullied workers and, at a policy level, forthrightly challenging Ben's excesses. So long as she was there, this was a significantly better, more decent company – and a far better place to work.

With regard to this third Guideline, remember finally this important point. If you're lucky enough to have bosses who really care about Radical Decency that in no way means that you should ease up on your own decency practice. To the contrary, even in these more fortunate situations, the choices you and your co-workers make will matter – a lot. If you, too, step up to the plate, Radical Decency's values are far more likely to take hold as the company's new norm. If you don't, the risk of reversion to business's mainstream ways will be much greater as well.

Guideline 4: Stand Up to Injustice

What goes on at work is serious business. Decisions made by companies and bosses have life-altering consequences for you, your co-workers, and society at large. So while job security is vitally important, there may come a time when you need to stand up to the company in order to maintain your integrity, or to be in solidarity with your co-workers or the larger community. That is what Ann did when she took on Ben and fought for the site manager's job. For others, this "moment of integrity" might involve speaking up about unsafe work conditions, an indefensibly cruel personnel policy, or a manufacturing process that endangers employee and public health.

The essential point to remember is this: We are people first and workers second. And when we turn away from our larger communal responsibilities, we are irreparably diminished. So be self-protective, of course. But don't let your fears stop you from speaking up when the situation requires it. Instead, be inspired by the many people throughout history – Jesus, Mandela, Martin Luther King – who have risked, not just jobs, but their very lives in order to confront injustice.

DECENCY: THE MANAGER'S ROLE

Because they are high up in the pecking order and have greater authority, things are often significantly better for supervisors and managers than they are for lower level workers. So for them, a key factor motivating them toward more decent choices is one to which I repeatedly return: In authoritarian relationships, no one wins.

For managers, the principles of civility, prudent management of emotions, and authenticity – discussed in Guidelines #1 through #3 with respect to workers – are, of course, just as applicable. Given their greater power, they also have heightened responsibility when it comes to standing up to injustice (Guideline #4). But because of their more pivotal organizational role, the opportunities supervisors and managers have for leadership in service of decency don't end there; a hopeful reality that Evan's story illustrates.

When Evan took over as his school's Special Education Director, morale was low after years of leaderless drift. But he brought with him a new leadership style, premised on this simple message: You're doing important work. If you do your job well, you'll have my respect, appreciation, and complete support. If not, you'll be held accountable.

For Evan, a decisive, culture-altering moment came early on when Corinne, a troubled seventh grader, returned to school after an extended absence. Most of her teachers understood her vulnerability and were firm but patient as she tried to re-integrate – but not Martha, her homeroom teacher. Embittered by years of administrative indifference, she responded to Corinne's acting out with demands for obedient silence. Even more troubling, given the student's history of physical abuse, Martha underscored her verbal demands by moving aggressively into Corinne's space, often stopping within inches of her face.

When Martha rebuffed Evan's attempts to discuss the situation, he didn't reprimand her or write her up. Instead, he seized the opportunity to set a new tone. First, he secured the backing of the school's Principal for his action plan, emphasizing the school's possible legal exposure to claims of abuse, absent an effective response. Then, he called a team meeting to discuss this troubled student's situation – a meeting that Martha, predictably, failed to attend.

In the small talk that preceded the "official" start of this meeting, Evan, leaning back in his chair, joked with his co-workers and shared war stories from his many years as special education classroom teacher. Then, building on this carefully cultivated mood of ease and collegiality, he led a discussion of Corinne's situation in which everyone's input, teachers and teacher aides alike, was encouraged and honored.

Based on his staff's ideas and feedback, Evan then put in place a series of new procedures – a revised lesson plan format, regular team meetings, and streamlined reporting mechanisms designed to ensure good follow-up and accountability; procedures that, from that point forward, became the department's new, standard ways of operating. In this way, without ever resorting to morale-deadening threats or punishments, Evan sent a clear message to Martha: Change your ways – or face serious consequences. And the message got through. Her aggressive approach with Colleen ended and, more generally, everyone else on staff clearly understood that Martha's sort of cynical, turned off attitude would no longer be tolerated.

For Evan and his department, these events were a turning point. Slowly but surely a new atmosphere took hold that was more professional and, at the same time, more relaxed and open. And with that, morale and productivity soared. Needless to say, if Evan's leadership style ever became the new norm for managers, the workplace – and, with it, our lives – would be profoundly altered.

RUNNING A RADICALLY DECENT BUSINESS

In the last two sections I made the case – persuasively I hope – for the vital contribution that both workers and managers can make to the effort to create a more radically decent ethos in business. I now turn to the many opportunities that enlightened owners and CEOs have to ignite, inspire, and propel this work.

In the summer of 2005, five years into my new career as a psychotherapist and brimming with confidence, I set out to create a radically decent business. With a group of colleagues and friends, I opened Eccoes Associates; a multi-disciplinary healing center that offered psychotherapy, life coaching, chiropractic, massage therapy, and financial planning. Turns out, creating a radically decent business is a lot more complicated than I thought back then!

Three years later, an unexpected rent increase combined with a career opportunity that our other senior psychotherapist just couldn't pass up, we closed our doors. Looking back, I am struck by how hard it was to live up to our ambitious decency goals in business' challenging environment. But while we weren't always successful, I'm also proud of what we accomplished and grateful for all I learned from the experience.

A number of key "lessons learned" are described below.

Lesson 1 (perhaps the most vital): Be clear and explicit about your goals from the outset and fully follow through on them.

We live in an environment in which "smart" business people say all the right things, masking the debris left behind by their singled-minded pursuit of profit and success with a self-justifying internal dialogue that goes something like this:

> Fundamentally, I'm a good guy/gal. Sure, I've done things I'm not proud of. At times, I've made promises I knew I couldn't keep to get a sale or an edge on the competition. I've also competed hard, sometimes in not so nice ways, for recognition and status. But work is tough and unforgiving. Who, in the end, hasn't done these things? Like it or not, this is just the way things are in business.

In order to resist the strong pull of this status quo mindset – and the ways of operating that result – our decency commitment needs to be deep, abiding, and across the board. It's not just about a more generous vacation and benefits policy. Nor is it only about a corporate charitable giving program, periodic community service days, or more open channels of communication. It's about all of these things and more. It challenges us to rethink virtually every aspect of our business.

Importantly, this doesn't mean self-immolation in the name of decency. To the contrary, since decency to self is integral to the philosophy, everything can't – and shouldn't – be changed at once. What is called for instead is an unqualified commitment to Decency's 7 Values and a determined, unwavering focus on finding ways to more and more fully realize that goal.

Because we're talking about business, making money will, of course, always be a central preoccupation: ***But not at the expense of decency***. Instead, profitability needs to be priority 1A, right next to – but clearly subordinate to – the goal of creating a radically decent enterprise. Eighty to

90 percent of the time, these two goals are fully compatible. But in that 10 to 20 percent zone, the temptation to compromise decency will be strong. And it is precisely in these moments when our decency practice will succeed or fail.

An excellent example of such a moment occurred during my tenure at Eccoes, when an ambulance company offered to steer a steady stream of chiropractic clients to us in return for a monthly fee. At first blush, it felt tacky. Did we really want to have ambulance drivers handing out our business cards at accident scenes?

On the other hand, we certainly could have used the business. And since we wouldn't be paying commissions based upon cases actually referred, we asked ourselves, fairly I think, if this was really any different than a monthly fee paid to a marketing firm to advertise our services. After all, we live in a world in which well-paid spokespeople – far cleverer and more convincing than most any ambulance driver – routinely urge potential patients to use medical practitioners they've never met.

In the end, concerned that the medical needs of potential clients would be unduly influenced by the ambulance company's financial incentive, we turned the offer down. Was this a good choice? To this day, I don't know. But the more important point is this: Thrown into that 10 to 20 percent zone of temptation, we didn't flinch. Instead of glossing over the decency issues raised by the proposed deal, we fully explored them and, then, used them to guide our decision.

Fully facing up to these moments of truth is vital. Failing to do so, your employees as well as the people you work with and depend upon – investors, vendors, referral sources, attorneys, and accountants – just won't get that Radical Decency really is your unwavering priority. As a result, their ways of operating will continue to reflect the sharp practices that are the marketplace's norms.

So for example, the smart, charming and persuasive advertising consultant you hire, as well as the streetwise business people on your staff and board, will insist on an ad campaign that tells potential customers only what they want to hear. And what of a radically decent ad campaign that forthrightly describes your product's value but doesn't oversell it? For these people it's a nonstarter, an approach that simply won't sell the product.

Similarly, when serious conflicts arise, your attorney, steeped in mainstream ways of thinking, will insist that you "have to" cut off all contact with your "adversary," admit nothing, and prepare the most aggressive possible counter attack. Then, when you suggest an honest and open discussion with the other side about what's gone wrong, she'll dismiss the suggestion as a lovely, but naïve, idea that she has learned – through long, hard experience in the "real" world – just won't work.

If you don't remain clearheaded and determined in your decency commitment in these situations, the game is lost. Choice by choice, inch by imperceptible inch, you'll slip back toward the cultural norm. In the end, you'll be running a business, perhaps even a profitable one. But it won't be radically decent.

At Eccoes, we highlighted our decency goals in a number of ways. We wrote them into our bylaws, co-created a list of 11 Radical Decency principles, and devoted one staff meeting per month to the intricacies of its application. In retrospect, we could have done more. For example, we could have added a detailed "decency" operating manual, an in-depth decency orientation for new employees, and regular staff seminars and retreats to inspire and maintain focus.

Failing to do so, our efforts to fully follow through on the challenge and potential rewards of this Lesson #1 fell short. Sure Radical Decency was on our minds and influenced our choices in many ways. But we weren't as unwavering in our commitment as we might have been – and needed to be. Over time, our drift back toward mainstream ways of operating was real. In the end, while I'm proud of all we accomplished, I am not sure that – if we hadn't not closed our doors for other reasons – we would have realized our goal of creating a radically decent business.

So what is the bottom line, Lesson #1 takeaway from our experience at Eccoes? The rewards of a Radical Decency business can only be achieved when the philosophy is fully, completely, and visibly embraced.

Lesson #2: Take your time, and exercise patience, as you build your staff and support team.

It's relatively easy to find people who know how to make money or, alternatively, people who put decency values first. But finding both together is much more difficult and, if either is missing, you will pay an unacceptable price.

For us at Eccoes, the most poignant example of a person stuck in indecent "business as usual" ways of operating was our first chiropractor, Brianna. Several months after we opened our doors, she started pushing for a larger share of the profits, arguing that our initial agreement didn't fairly reflect her economic contribution. Seeing merit in her position, we agreed to renegotiate. But Brianna was convinced we were trying to take advantage of her. So try as we might, we couldn't agree on a new deal.

Then, after weeks of stalled negotiations, something totally unexpected happened. Brianna learned that she had a progressive, debilitating disease that would, with time, make it impossible for her to continue her chiropractic work. At that point, we could have ended our relationship with her. But seeking to be true to our principles, we put together a new agreement that gave her the right: (1) To re tool in a less physically demanding healing modality – when that time inevitably arrived; and (2) to receive an ongoing percentage of the profits earned from the chiropractic practice she'd built to that point in time.

Needless to say, we thought this new agreement was a model of Radical Decency. But Brianna, stuck in her business-as-usual adversarial mindset, was never able to shake the belief that, even with this agreement, we were somehow taking advantage of her. Within months of signing the new agreement, she left the organization.

This was a difficult time for all of us at Eccoes. But we also learned a valuable lesson. Most everyone carries baggage from years operating in adversarial, "us vs. them" business environments. And for some, like Brianna, a shift to a different way of operating is impossible. In these situations, it's important to face up to that reality and move on.

At the opposite end of the spectrum from Brianna was one of our massage therapists, Mark. While he warmly embraced Radical Decency, he seemed to confuse these values with a lack of accountability, showing up late for meetings and, too often, cancelling sessions to tend to personal matters. Here, too, we placed too much faith in the power of our guiding principles, trusting that Mark, with gentle reminders, would come to understand that a disciplined approach to his work was integral to the philosophy. Unfortunately, that never happened and, eventually, we had to cut ties with him.

The key takeaway from these experiences: Pick your co-workers and collaborators with care. In the interviewing and evaluation process really try to get to know who they are, not just as workers but as people as well. And, if it is at all possible, test them out via a trial period before fully committing. Then carefully evaluate the evidence on both sides of the equation – values and productivity.

Lesson #3: Don't let fear of failure control you.

Suppose, after years of hard work, your radically decent business is doing well enough financially, but still remains a struggle. Haunted by all the things that could wrong, a gnawing fear of failure never quite leaves you.

Now a big contract or strategic alliance comes your way – one that could turbo charge your growth and profitability but will, inevitably, compromise your unique culture and ways of operating. At that moment, you need to remember why you began this journey in the first place: To create a workplace that makes better lives possible and meaningfully contributes to a better world. Operating just another business – no matter how profitable

– is a pale substitute for the payoffs a radically decent business offers. Don't settle for conventional success.

CHANGING BIG BUSINESS

As my experience with Eccoes Associates suggests, creating a radically decent business from scratch is a daunting task. But bringing Decency's 7 Values to established businesses – especially the corporate behemoths that exercise so much power in the world – is even more challenging. Their existing ways of operating are deeply entrenched and, financially at least, things look pretty darn good.

But most of the people who work there, even those at the top, are not leading nourishing and generative lives. In that regard, I always remember a social evening I spent with the long-time CFO of a large pharmaceutical company who, in her understated, matter-of-fact way, told me that, "at my level, every day is an unrelenting knife fight." With this reality in mind, the idea that lasting change can occur – even at these companies – is not as far-fetched as it might seem. After all, how many people, even highly paid executives, really want to spend the best days and years of their lives in the middle of a knife fight?

What follows is an analysis of Radical Decency's possibilities at larger, well-established businesses, using Big Law as an example. This sector has exploded in the last four decades, with the largest 100 firms grossing $96.6 billion in 2015 and the 10 largest earning more than $2 billion each. I'm choosing to use the legal profession as an example because of my intimate knowledge of that business, having spent 25 years at a series of big law firms, including 15 years as an equity partner or owner.

My friend, Carl, is a partner at such a firm. Several years ago, as he and his partners reviewed their budget for the upcoming fiscal year, the firm's managing partner revealed a proposed across-the-board cut to healthcare benefits. With an income in excess of $400,000 a year, these cuts were more than manageable for Carl. However, he was concerned about its effect on the support staff; people such as his secretary who made $50,000 a year.

The managing partner's response was a study in big business' masterful use of insincere expressions of empathy to mask its ruthless, bottom-line orientation, hiding it even – and especially – from itself:

> You make a great point, Carl, and, as you can imagine, we really struggled with this decision. But our continued growth depends on our ability to hire rainmaking attorneys, with big books of business. And we can only do that if we maintain our position as a top tier firm in terms of profitability. The unfortunate but inescapable reality is that, absent these cuts, our per-partner profit ranking will take an unacceptable hit, dropping from fifth to ninth in the region.

Rank-and-file partners like Carl, busy tending to their practices, typically defer to the firm's leadership when it comes to management issues. Thus, the managing partner went into this budget meeting with far more knowledge, a fully thought-out position and the support of key partners, carefully lined up in advance. He also benefitted mightily from a number of key unspoken, and unchallenged, assumptions: More profit for the partners is always better and the only way to remain competitive is to be highly profitable. In the end, the partners, Carl included, "reluctantly" agreed to make the cuts.

For me, this story chillingly illustrates how indecency works in a big business setting, and how deeply ingrained it is. It's not about people who openly and belligerently embrace a lying, manipulative, bad guy role. Instead, it thrives and extends its reach through innumerable meetings, quietly taking place in comfortable offices, where "reasonable" people delude themselves by "reluctantly" making "inevitable" choices because they "have to." Their unbridled greed and ambition – "we **always** need to make more money" – is almost never acknowledged. And the effect of their choices on the less privileged, even the secretaries sitting right outside their offices, is barely a blip on their radar screens.

Things CAN Be Different

The current reality notwithstanding, a radically decent approach to business is entirely possible, even in the highly competitive world of big law – and, by extension, at the largest of our corporate giants as well. But it can't be implemented on an ad hoc basis. If a big law firm's decency initiative is confined to an extra employee benefit here and a *pro bono* project there, its profit-first ways will remain intact and unchallenged. Then, when an inevitable down year hits, its experiment in being a little more decent will be quickly sacrificed to the god of six- and seven-figure partner incomes.

What we need instead is:

1. A systematic rethinking of every aspect of the firm's operations, including how power is distributed and exercised, what constitutes fair compensation, how performance is evaluated, how legal services are delivered and billed, how it contributes to the larger community; and

2. Concrete policies and procedures, clearly and forthrightly explained to all major stakeholders, that implement this radically decent approach.

Approaching the shift to decency in this way, our hypothetical law firm would be able to more effectively guard against the ever-present danger of sliding back into business-as-usual ways of operating. In addition, because mainstream businesses are so skilled at masking their avarice through high-sounding words, the visibility built into this approach would, hopefully, cement its reputation in the marketplace – and, thus, its competitive edge – as a firm that really does operate in ways that are different and better.

The change I have in mind would begin at the top. What I envision is a strong Managing Partner, with unquestioned leadership skills and a strong commitment to decency, using her power to initiate this change in direction and to steadily push for its implementation at every level.

And, ideally, she wouldn't be working in isolation. Understanding that the firm's new ways of operating work a lot better for them, the department chairs and the attorneys in charge of the various practice groups – the kinds of mid-level managers discussed earlier – would enthusiastically support her initiatives. And, so too, the associates and support staff who, delighted to be working at such a firm, would reinforce and deepen the firm's decency commitment through the kind of "bottom up" leadership discussed earlier.

At a policy level, the list of things that would need to change at our hypothetical law firm is a long one, affecting virtually every area of operations. But the good news is that, because many of these changes would do away with transparently exploitative and manipulative practices, they would have a powerful upside in the marketplace, reinforcing the positive message about what it's like to work with, and at, this firm.

Billing is a prime example. Big Law's current norm – cost plus hourly billing – is an open invitation to over-lawyering and padded time sheets; patently indecent practices that individual attorneys find almost irresistible since they so effectively drive up fees. If our firm dropped hourly billing entirely, it would send a powerful and unmistakable message to every potential client: At this firm, there is no need to worry about over-hyped conflicts and over-litigated cases, or bills that seem calculated to maximize rather than minimize expense.

Another good example of a place where fundamental change is needed is in how lawyer's account for their time. Most firms "officially" encourage community involvement but, at the same time, require attorneys to bill up to 2,100 hours per year to full-pay clients. A policy that gave full credit for time spent on *pro bono* projects – and at an ailing family member's bedside – would send a powerful, positive message to attorneys seeking a more humane, values-based place to work.

A final, truly transformative initiative would involve use of the extraordinary algorithmic tools that are discussed in Chapter 1 – not to exploit others but, instead, as mechanisms to track and expand Radical Decency's reach. Using data science's extraordinary ability to gather vast amounts of information, and to understand the correlations within it, a radically decent firm could, for example, simultaneously evaluate hours billed at three levels: (1) Revenue generated (the traditional approach); (2) success in achieving clients' stated goals; and (3) the project's contribution to the larger public good.

In this way, the firm would be able to provide far more cost-effective legal services to clients, thereby enhancing its competitive position. In addition, with its more civic-minded clients, it would be able to demonstrate, in a concrete and quantifiable way, the project's contribution to their public-spirited goals. Finally, taking its values-based approach to a new level, the firm could make knowing choices about which cases to take on, factoring in not just profitability but also the work's larger societal contributions. In this way, it would be able to create a client base that is increasingly congruent with its commitment to Radical Decency.

Initiatives such as these, effectively implemented and backed by high-quality legal work, would decisively refute the old small-bore, profit-obsessed concerns that dominated the thinking at Carl's firm. And extraordinary human beings would be drawn to such a firm; clients and attorneys alike. It would even attract that special breed of big rainmaker who, seeking a better life and not just more money, would look beyond the firm's per-partner profit numbers and enthusiastically come on board.

CHANGE BUSINESS, CHANGE THE WORLD

When it comes to Radical Decency in business, there are a number of key takeaways. First, we're are all in it together. It will require aware and courageous choices from everyone – from owners and CEOs to middle managers and workers.

The second takeaway involves the scope of the challenge. Business exercises unprecedented power in our lives and world – and is thoroughly dominated by the mainstream culture's compete-to-win values. Thus, getting from "here" to "there" is a daunting task. In his 2012 book, *The Signal and the Noise: Why So Many Predictions Fail – but Some Don't*, Nate Silver, the well-known statistician and writer, observes:

> New ideas are sometimes found in the most granular details of a problem where few others bother to look. And, sometimes, they are found when you are doing your most abstract and philosophical thinking. Rarely can they be found in the temperate latitudes between these two spaces, where we spend 99% of our lives.

When it comes to business, this dual perspective is essential. We need to immerse ourselves in business' most granular details, as illustrated by the billing and cost-accounting examples just discussed. However, we also need to think big, challenging our taken-for-granted ways in every area of our operations.

But while the challenge is great, so too are its rewards. With Radical Decency as business' new norm politicians, media outlets, nonprofit entities, and places of worship – all so heavily dependent on business' money – would be powerfully pushed in that direction as well.

Thus, as we do our decency work in this vital area of living, let us be sustained by this powerful reality: Change business and the world will change with it.

CHAPTER 10

Values Based Politics: Getting Beyond Us vs. Them

Needless to say, Radical Decency's across-the-board approach requires us to forthrightly deal with politics and public policy. Failing to do so, the problematic values that are so dominant in that realm will, inevitably, invade the small islands of decency we seek to create with family, friends and neighbors, or at our (fortuitously) family friendly workplace.

At the same time, however, the risk for many is in the opposite direction. Sucked in by the loud and very visible drama that is our politics, they:

- Become nonstop consumers of political news, compulsively following every twist and turn in the latest scandal, policy fight, or upcoming election; and,

- Continually rehearse in conversation, and in their agitated brains as well, their grievances and strategies for defeating the "bad guys."

This passionate hyper-focus on politics is worrisome for two reasons. First, many people believe that the fight to create a more decent world really is all about politics and nothing else. If we can just elect better leaders, they tell themselves, or persuade the people in office to make better choices, our problems will be solved. But this hoped-for outcome is a mirage. How can we expect elected officials – in power because they play the compete-to-win game really well – to pass laws that seriously undermine the very system that brought them to power?

My second concern is that even people who understand that getting from "here" to "there" involves more than politics can be sucked in by the (largely false) sense of urgency that is the hallmark of our politics. They, too, can often wind up pouring far too much attention and energy into the partisan political arena.

And here, I speak from experience.

For years, during Presidential elections, I was consumed by a desperate need to elect "my person" and to defeat that dangerously flawed candidate on the other side. And this obsession would persist for months on end even though my more thoughtful brain knew that my nonstop ruminations would have no perceptible impact on the election's outcome. More worrisome, however, is the fact that my endless rants about the "other" guy's immorality and stupidity diverted me from values to which I aspire – respect, understanding, empathy, and so on – effectively short-circuiting the kinds of initiatives, discussed later in this Chapter, that might more effectively model them in the political realm.

When it comes to politics, then, we can't afford to go to either extreme. We can neither ignore the partisan political realm nor delude ourselves into thinking that, standing alone, it's the path to our salvation.

•••••

With this important caveat in mind, how can our political initiatives become a more effective front in this larger fight to create a more decent world? I begin with a key insight offered by Robert Reich, the well-known economics professor and former Secretary of Labor. In his 2015 book, *Saving Capitalism: For the Many, Not the Few*, Reich urges a shift in the taken-for-granted framework in which our current political discussion operates; a shift that would allow for a far more constructive response to the rampant indecencies that riddle that world.

CALLING BS ON OUR POLITICAL SHELL GAME

The starting place for Reich's analysis is his frustration with the question that so often comes up at the many political events he attends: Do you favor the free market or greater governmental regulation?

Since this question has long framed our conservative/liberal political debate, you may be surprised, as I initially was, by his frustration. But, as he points out, this question is a devastatingly effective distraction from a more pertinent political conversation that needs to take place.

Transfixed by this issue, people on the right passionately argue that the free market's competitive efficiencies will allow everyone the opportunity to prosper and that most governmental intervention inhibits this process. Meanwhile those on the left argue with equal fervor that, while the free market is our economic cornerstone, its excesses result in unacceptable levels of suffering that urgently need to be corrected through governmental action.

Reich stands apart from this standard liberal/conservative debate. He argues instead that the shared assumption of a "free market," is a deeply misleading. To the contrary, all that exists is an intricate, ever-evolving web of rules created, enforced, and modified by our legislative and administrative bodies that, for better or worse, guide and govern our behaviors. What he's referring to are the many rules that, for example, allow you to own your house, require a license if you want to be a pharmacist, or reduce the annual tax bill for owners of NASCAR racetracks and private jets (by $40 and $400 million respectively).

When we pull away from the noisy, ever-present debate about how the "free" market should operate and focus on these rules, the dominant political story of the last 40 years is all about a series of under-the-radar rule changes – implemented with support or tacit complicity from both Democrats and Republicans – that have greatly increased the ability of the wealthiest 10% and, especially, the top 1%, to retain and augment their riches.

A number of important examples were described in the last Chapter: Changes to the antitrust, bankruptcy, usury, and banking laws; the expansion of patent and copyright protections; and the steady reduction in business, capital gains, and estate taxes.

And this list only begins to scratch the surface.

Consider, as well, the series of bipartisan rule changes made back in the Reagan and Clinton years that now allow senior executives at our largest corporations to take large chunks of their income as stock options. With these shifts in place, executives can now line their own pockets by engineering massive buybacks of their companies' stock; a maneuver that predictably drives up the price of the large pile of stock they now own.

In the years since these rule changes, stock buybacks have exploded. In 2013 our largest corporations spent $500 billion on stock buybacks, and by 2018 they'd reached $910 billion, almost doubling the already massive amount of buybacks made just five years earlier.

And make no mistake about it – these events have had massive social consequences. According to Reich, the 2013 buybacks diverted *a third of our largest companies' available cash flow into private hands*. Do you have any doubt that the *trillions* of dollars pulled out of corporate coffers by these buybacks, in the last 20 years, would have done a lot more good if they had been invested in product development, price reductions, new jobs, or additional pay for workers?

Another example, also drawn from Reich's book, illustrates how deeply this massive tilt toward the rich has been embedded in the country's operating rules. Did you know that while the average governmental subsidy for public university students is $6,000, the subsidy received by students at Princeton (with a median family income of $186,000) is nine times greater, standing at $54,000?

I suspect your initial reaction, like mine, is one of shocked disbelief. But it's true, made possible by policy choices buried deep in the tax code, that allow by way of example:

An income tax deduction for people who donate to our (ironically named) nonprofit universities, such as Princeton, which effectively means that a third of these gifts actually come from the government; and

A tax exemption for almost all of the massive amounts of money that Princeton earns on its $23 billion endowment.

•••••

The marketplace vs. pro-government mindset that dominates our partisan political debate deeply obscures this story. Wedded to their side of this ideological divide, Republican policies rely on outcomes produced by an unfettered free market, augmented by private choices. Meanwhile, Democrat offer programmatic solutions that reflect their "regulate the free market" mindset: Re-training programs for displaced workers, rules limiting the most visibly destructive choices that private financial institutions and health insurers would otherwise make, affirmative action programs designed to level the playing field for minorities, and so on.

It's important to note that each of these approaches has merit.

- Republicans by emphasizing: (1) The good outcomes that can result from a competitive economic system; and (2) the risks involved in an over-reliance on state interventions.

- Democrats by: (1) Promoting programs that seek to deal directly with the many indecencies that currently litter our society; and (2) pushing back on the belief that we can rely solely on market forces to right these wrongs.

But here's the problem. In our current setup, each side, overly enamored with its partisan position, overlooks their sides' flaws and pitfalls. Thus, many conservatives are committed Christians, sincerely guided by teachings of Jesus including this from Luke 14:12-14:

> When you give a lunch or a dinner, do not invite your
> friends or your brothers or your relations or rich neighbors .
> . . . No; when you have a party, invite the poor, the crippled,
> the lame, the blind; then you will be blessed, for they have no
> means to repay you and so you will be repaid when the upright
> rise again.

And these words, directed to the rich man from Mark, 10:21-22:

> Go, sell everything you have and give to the poor, and
> you will have treasure in heaven. Then come, follow me.

Living by Jesus' loving set of values requires a fearless, ongoing reckoning with our strong tendency to slide back to the culture's self-absorbed, me-first norms. But when you look at what mainstream Republican politicians are actually saying, here's what you'll find: Nearly all of them steadily promote the Party's pro-market perspective. However, you'll be hard pressed to find any who meaningfully discuss the complementary, private choices they should also be making as committed Christians.

And make no mistake about it, an analogous partisan myopia is at work on the Democratic side. In this case, it grows out of their refusal to move beyond the myth of the "free" market that Reich so effectively unmasks. Taking the market's centrality – and, with that, its unrestrained greed – as a given, Democratic policy initiatives are mostly tepid, after-the-fact patch-up jobs that seek to correct the market's "unfortunate but inevitable" side effects.

But these efforts will never come close to undoing the damage being done by the steady drumbeat of under-the-radar rule changes that are forever benefitting the rich. Thus, for example, despite decades of trying,

Democratic programs have failed to increase the availability of low-income housing. Nor have they meaningfully affected the gutting of the economies in Appalachia and our urban ghettos.

Nevertheless, the Democrats, like their Republican counterparts, claim the moral high ground – based on these tepid, inadequate programs – even as their more consequential policy choices unerringly align them with the economic self-interest of their wealthiest supporters, a reality exemplified by:

- President Clinton's welfare "reform" initiative and complicity with the rule changes, described above, that allow executive compensation via stock options;

- Obama's refusal to take on the big banks after the economic meltdown of 2008; and more recently,

- Democratic opposition, in the 2017 tax bill: (1) To any limitation on the property tax deduction available to people owning higher-end properties because its greatest impact is on people in liberal-leaning Northeastern states; or (2) to a modest 1.4% excise tax on multi-billion college endowments because it disproportionately affects liberal-leaning universities, such as Harvard and Princeton.

●●●●●

This shared partisan myopia is not some unhappy accident. To the contrary, when it to comes our mainstream politicians, it works quite well, allowing them:

- To attract the votes they need by convincing their supporters that they're dedicated to making things better; and, at the same time,

- To get the money needed to finance their campaigns through quiet complicity with the rigged rule changes that so richly reward their wealthy backers.

RADICAL DECENCY

Locking this cynical shell game in place, both parties then ignore the obvious shortcomings of their own policies and instead virulently blame the other side.

- "If only those venal and corrupt Republicans would stop obstructing our efforts, we'd pass more and bigger 'patch-things-up' programs. Then everything would be fine."

- "The only thing that stands in the way of continued growth and prosperity are the deeply misguided entitlement programs those arrogant and elitist Democrats insist on keeping on the books."

Understanding this, here is the reality we need to confront: If we continue to look to our mainstream politicians for guidance – and parrot their policy prescriptions – we'll never be able to move our politics in a more decent direction. What is needed, instead, is a fundamental shift in perspective at a grassroots level. Both progressives and conservatives need to wean themselves from their partisan mindsets, replacing them with a more constructive political conversation and, with it, more humane public policies.

WALKING THE WALK: TOWARD A MORE DECENT POLITICAL CONVERSATION

You might recall my earlier description of how Sunny Shulkin, the couples therapist my wife and I saw in the mid-1990s, described a typical couple's fight. The woman speaks and the man listens – but in a special way – carefully sifting through her words for ammunition so that when her mouth finally stops moving he can fire back. Then as he counter-attacks, she is busy collecting her own ammunition so she can return the fire as soon as he stops talking. And around and around they go.

Sunny was, of course, describing the behavior of our fight-or-flight brain in the context of a couple's fight. But when I think about our current political dialogue, I find it hard to improve upon Sunny's description. Seeking a fundamental shift in our politics, this is where our work needs to begin.

Even in a marriage where both people are earnestly trying to do better, it's difficult to overcome our fight-or-flight habits. But in politics the challenge is even greater. This is after all an area, like business, in which the culture's compete-to-win ways – wrapped in "this is what we need to do to win" rationalizations – are too easily condoned and, in many places, actually celebrated as good, smart politics.

But there are ways of dealing with it, even in the infertile soil that is our politics. In the discussion that follows, I offer five guidelines that, as I see it, are key to accomplishing this goal. Given where things now stand, the kind of changes I describe below might seem quixotic. But the past 40 years demonstrate that doubling down on our current "discredit the bad guys" approach will never work. So who knows? Because our politics are so deeply flawed, and because the strategies I describe below make so much good sense, they might actually catch on. Indeed, they might even infect our mainstream politicians who – understanding we expect better – might feel compelled to change as well.

1. The art of not getting sucked in

Our adversarial fight-or-flight political dialogue is, of course, deeply rooted in our over-identification with our partisan tribes. Going into a typical political discussion, nearly everyone has already chosen sides and communicates it either explicitly or through well-understood social cues. Moreover, if you try to avoid labeling yourself, others will do it for you.

Take me for example. Even if you've forgotten that I "outed" myself as a Hillary voter back in Chapter 3, I suspect you've long since pegged me as a member of the progressive tribe. Why? It likely has something to do with what you know about me. I'm a Philadelphia-based psychotherapist who attended a series of elite Northeastern universities. But beyond that, I suspect you just feel it in your bones.

If you do, you're on target. Progressivism is my home tribe, dating back to 6-year-old Jeff watching Adlai Stevenson accept the Democratic Presidential nomination, on our new Sylvania halo glow television, as my parents sang his praises.

The problem with partisan labeling is that it's a slippery slope that shrinks our ability to absorb subtleties and to explore new possibilities. So, for example, when I share with others the ideas in this Chapter, I'm often greeted with the following sorts of reactions, either explicitly or through an unmistakable shift in tone and affect:

- (From someone on the right) "You pretend to be something else, but I see through your carefully crafted 'nice' words about decency. You're really dishing out the same old arrogant, 'I know what's best for you' liberal bullshit;" or,

- (From someone on the left) "What's wrong with you? Why are you so critical of us and so eager to paint Republicans in a benign light? You totally miss the point. The real problem is those cynical, venal, grasping Republicans."

Our first challenge, therefore, in seeking to craft a less adversarial conversation is to avoid getting sucked into these stereotyping mindsets. With many of our conversational partners stubbornly sticking to their familiar partisan scripts, our strong temptation is to respond in kind. The better reaction? Politely but firmly refuse to engage in this way. Doing so, you'll avoid these tit-for-tat exchanges that almost always leave us frustrated and rarely change anyone's opinion anyway!

Avoiding this partisan trap is, however, just the first step. As developmental and comparative psychologist Michael Tommasello – author of *Why We Cooperate* (2009) –reminds us, we have been wired by nature to be empathic, understanding and cooperative:

In most primate groups, competition is the norm, with cooperation mostly among kin. But we humans truly sacrifice for one another on a very large scale and not just with kin. We donate blood for unknown others, risk our lives in war for our countrymen, and make sure the less fortunate have enough food and medicine. We also obey all kinds of pro-social norms when we really don't have to – from helping older people with their luggage to allowing others into line in traffic. And when we don't, we feel guilty or ashamed, a sure sign that Mother Nature has crafted us to be cooperative.

Building in this hopeful reality, we need to develop strategies that allow these better instincts to emerge. Here's an example of what I have in mind.

Suppose I'm in a conversation with an entrenched conservative who says: "How do you feel about abortion? Are you pro-choice or pro-life?" My initial instinct, reflecting my progressive tribal roots, might be to simply say, "pro-choice." And this would be an honest answer, if our only choice is to either allow abortion or to ban it. But refusing the partisan bait, I might offer the following response:

> I really feel discouraged when the conversation is reduced to this either/or choice. A great majority of women who face this decision really want to do the right thing. They care about their own future, of course. But they are also deeply connected to the beginning of life so powerfully growing inside them. What we need are policies that attend to the needs of these good people, while also addressing the really complicated questions that inevitably come up: When does life begin? What does it mean to be compassionate to the born and unborn? When it comes to abortion, I think we can do a whole lot better than a simple yes or no.

Given where we are today, talking about politics in this less adversarial way is a big challenge, to say the least. This pretty little speech of mine might well be derailed mid-sentence by a partisan zinger. Moreover, even if I'm able to finish the thought, it will regularly be greeted with skepticism that, if not said out loud, will be palpable in my conversational partner's tone: "Okay, I get it. You're trying hard to sound different. But I'm not fooled. You're just another arrogant, self-righteous, card-carrying liberal trying to manipulate me."

So that's the bad news. Doing this work we'll often feel frustrated and have no apparent impact. But on the more hopeful side, there will be other conversations that go differently and better. Thus, we need to tolerate our uncertain progress and persist, trusting that the possibilities inherent in this approach are well worth the effort.

●●●●●

I end this section with this heartfelt message to my fellow progressives: We, like them, are highly partisan and have a lot to learn about being better listeners. Thus, we need to respond thoughtfully when these initiatives come from conservatives – and persist even when they use language we find offensive. Our passionate desire to root out every manifestation of sexism or racism is understandable. But we can't allow our tendency to call others out on every perceived lapse to derail us from our larger purpose.

2. Focus on values

Most of us would agree that manipulation, insincerity, and ambition permeate our politics. But we also see it as mostly a problem on the other side. Thus, for example, when shown a series of video clips in which Obama and George W. Bush made almost identical warlike statements, the response of Trevor Noah of "The Daily Show," after a moment of stunned silence, was: "Well, they're completely different! Obama had to say those things! We all know he didn't mean it!"

The truth about our politics is that self-serving and duplicitous ways of behaving are endemic on both sides – but only when it comes to our professional politicians. The millions of ordinary people who vote, consume the news, and talk about politics aren't similarly motivated by greed and a lust for power. To the contrary, as noted earlier, it is in their very nature as humans to be decent and cooperative. But like "The Daily Show" host, they're too easily sucked in by the rhetoric of their partisan tribe, assuming the best about their "team" and the worst about the other side.

What we desperately need, then, is to bring our common purposes out of the shadows and into the forefront of the political conversation. And that is where values come in. Without regard to political orientation, there are a series of values that are shared by most ordinary voters. Moreover, while partisans might place greater emphasis on one set of values over others, the many well-intentioned people on all sides of the debate are likely to agree that all of them are worthy of consideration.

A number of thoughtful people, liberals and conservatives alike, have attempted to enumerate these values. For example:

- Marshall Rosenberg, a liberal, in *Nonviolent Communication: A Language of Life* (2003), describes eight Universal Human Needs: Autonomy, Connection, Integrity, Interdependence, Physical Well-Being, Play, Meaning, and Peace;

- William Bennett, a conservative, in *The Book of Virtues* (1993), lists six values essential to good character: Responsibility, Courage, Compassion, Honesty, Friendship, Persistence, and Faith;

- Jonathan Haidt, in *The Righteous Mind: Why Good People are Divided by Politics and Religion* (2012), offers a list of the values that operate across the political spectrum: Care, Fairness, Loyalty, Respect for Authority, Sanctity, and Liberty; and, of course,

- Radical Decency identifies seven fundamental values: Respect, Understanding, Empathy, Acceptance, Appreciation, Fairness and Justice.

While the words used in each of these lists vary, what is so encouraging are the lists' similarities. Each encompasses: (1) personal rectitude; (2) cooperation, respect, and concern for others; and (3) some form of greater meaning or spiritual grounding.

Focusing on these shared values can go a long way toward clearing our hardened political arteries. In this regard, Haidt's analysis is eye opening. In his book, he emphasizes our differences, proposing that liberals focus on Care and Fairness while conservatives incorporate, to a greater degree, Respect for Authority and Sanctity (by which he means reverence for communal rituals). For me, however, the more important point is this: If we take the time to consider all of these values, our respect for the perspective of others will grow. And, with that, our strident, party-line allegiance to our way of viewing things will, hopefully, decline as well.

That has certainly been the case for me.

Like many members of the progressive tribe, I'm not deeply religious. As a result, it's easy for me to demonize the Christian right by latching on to outlandishly debased public figures who loudly proclaim their Christianity: Pedophilic priests and their enabling bishops; or Pat Robertson who railed against Bill Clinton's oval office as a sexual playpen but, then, excused Trump's sexually predatory past as "just a guy acting macho." When I focus on Sanctity, however, I am reminded that there are millions of people including, of course, many conservatives who are deeply nourished by Christianity's teachings and sustained by its traditions and rituals.

In the past, my instinctive response to a conservative Christian's position on gay marriage was, like many liberals, dismissive: "There's no talking to this person. She's a brainwashed, unreasoning bigot." But supported by my values-based orientation and Haidt's insights, my outlook has shifted. I now understand that, on this particular issue, the importance of the Sanctity of traditional marriage – unimportant for me in this context – is very much in play for her. With that, my ability to constructively engage with her, on this topic, is greatly enhanced.

A similar paradigm shift is also possible for conservatives. While Haidt is probably right when he suggests that progressives place a greater emphasis on Caring and Fairness, most conservatives would agree that these are important values. It's just that when those particular values conflict with Sanctity or Respect for Authority, conservatives are likely to give these latter two principles a higher priority.

So, for example, while conservatives typically oppose racially based hiring quotas, most would likely agree that poor African Americans, living in economically devastated ghettos, aren't getting a fair shake and need a helping hand. By focusing on values instead of policy positions, these thoughtful conservatives can better appreciate their liberal counterparts' good intentions, while still opposing their ultimate policy solution.

Needless to say, this values-based approach is no magic cure. Locked into fight-or-flight mindsets, many people won't get it and others will continue to insist that their underlying values perspective is the only right way. In these cases, the wisdom-stretching element of Radical Decency really comes to the fore: Never stop looking for ways to redirect the conversation in a more values-based way, trusting that this approach can chip away at virulent partisanship even in the seemingly most unpromising of situations.

3. Get Personal

When we put our political hat on, it's so easy to forget that we're people first. And yet, that's how most of us live. Consider, for example, that cherished friend or relative who you see regularly but with whom you diligently avoid any talk of politics. Why do you continue to see this person? Because you recognize that, lurking below his strident political views, is a person you deeply care for and who cares for you as well.

It is this reality that leads to my third guideline: ***Get personal***. When it comes to politics, and especially the hot-button issues that divide us, find ways to be more open about the underlying emotions that so deeply affect the outlook of others – and our own as well.

Our current norm is to avoid these emotionally sticky discussions. So, when Uncle Joe shows up at the family picnic and launches into his intolerant rant about African Americans – or Hillary Clinton or Donald Trump – our strong instinct is to avoid this uncomfortable topic. Most of us remain silent or, at most, offer a few mumbled words of agreement or demurral.

But the Gestalt psychotherapist and social theorist Philip Lichtenberg, in *Encountering Bigotry: Befriending Projecting People in Everyday Life* (1997), counsels us to go in the opposite direction. Instead of creating distance, get interested. Listen to Uncle Joe's racist rant, not with embarrassment and impatience, but with real curiosity. Then, as the situation allows, invite him to explore the deeper emotions that lie beneath the surface with questions such as:

- A whole lot of your energy is focused on Black people. What's that all about?

- Have you always felt this way? Where do these feelings come from? Are there things you've experienced in life that make them especially strong?

- I am with you in respecting self-reliant people and your annoyance with people who game the system. What's your take on the Black people like Michael Jordan and Colin Powell who seem to model self-reliance?

- Do you ever have moments when you see Black people in a different light?

Needless to say, Uncle Joe has been regularly confronted and dismissed by people "like you." So, when you start asking these sorts of questions, he's likely to be suspicious of your motives and attuned to any hint of insincerity. With this in mind, let him dictate the tone and pace of the conversation.

In that regard, a good rule of thumb is to talk less and listen more. Faced with a torrent of provocative words, you'll be tempted to include a little speech before your next question: "Since we all know that many urban schools are woefully underfunded, I was wondering if..." If you give into this temptation, however, Uncle Joe will immediately pick up on your shift from true curiosity to crypto-advocacy. So keep your questions short and manage the reactivity you're bound to feel when he responds in his uniquely Uncle Joe way.

Note, importantly, that Lichtenberg's vision for the conversation doesn't end here. His larger goal is a relationship that, based on mutual trust, can lead to a far more constructive conversation, even on a highly sensitive topic such as this one. Thus, after Uncle Joe (hopefully) begins to sense your sincere interest in him as a person, the next step is to add your deeper feelings and perspectives to the conversation. In my case, it might look something like this:

- My background is very different. At age 13, my parents took me to a civil rights rally at Jackie Robinson's house and, at 16, to the March on Washington where Martin Luther King delivered his "I Have a Dream" speech;

- My favorite camp counselor, Bob "Botticelli" West, was a totally cool and endearing African American who had a way of making me – a troubled and combative pre-adolescent – feel safe, cared for, and appreciated;

- When you think about Blacks you tend to see scam artists and dangerous people. When I really think about it, I can see that, given my history, I tend toward the opposite extreme, assuming that they're all good people who are being treated badly.

When we take the time to share our deeper feelings, we facilitate a natural coming together, even when we're talking with people whose perspectives are very different than ours. After all, we all share the full range of human emotions and have a deep reservoir of shared values. So instead of jumping into a partisan-tinged discussion, ask your conversational partner why he got interested in politics or what he hopes to accomplish. In a surprising number of cases, you'll find that you have a lot in common.

That approach was taken by a friend of mine; a longtime advocate for the rights of special-needs children. Recently, she chaired a meeting in Philadelphia of people representing groups with a major interest in that issue, including the teachers' union, parents' groups, school administrators, and state regulators. Typically, these meetings are very contentious. But on this occasion, she took a very different tack. Instead of moving directly into the agenda, she began the meeting with the following:

> We sometimes forget how much we all care about these kids. Before we start, I'd like to go around the room and have each of you tell us, briefly, why you got into this work and what you hope to accomplish.

This approach was not a magic pill. Strong differences remained. But she told me later that there was a distinct shift in tone that led to a far more productive meeting.

4. Focus on what you can do right, not on what they're doing wrong

Having worked as a marriage counselor for many years I'm very aware of how many couples are caught up in the culture's "I'm right, you're wrong" mindset. She talks endlessly about his inattentiveness: His long hours at work, failure to show up for the kids' school events; and curt one-word responses as they converse on the way to our counseling session. He, in turn, goes on and on about her bitchy behaviors.

These issues are, of course, important and need to be addressed. But so long as the couple is rooted in a constant replay of past breakdowns their potential is sadly limited. To really grow and heal they need to shift their focus from what went wrong in the past to how they can make things better in the future.

When they do, a heartening byproduct is that each partner gets increasingly interested in what they can do differently and better. The reason? Because they realize that a continued focus on what their partner is doing wrong and how he or she can change too easily triggers their partner's defensiveness and, thus, a reversion back to the old tit-for-tat exchange. On the other hand, focused on more loving choices that can be made today and tomorrow, they're far more likely to evoke similar loving choices in response; setting up a virtuous, reinforcing upward cycle.

Our current political conversations, like those of my stuck couples, are almost always about how wrong the other side is. Thus, when the talk turns to politics with my fellow progressives, the topic is almost always Trump's latest outrage. By contrast, there is far less discussion about how the policies our guys are promoting can be improved. Even more striking, in its absence, is any discussion about how we can improve our ability to talk with those on the other side through strategies such as those I describe in the first 3 guidelines.

A shift from what the other does wrong to what I can do right is hard even for couples who are highly motivated to make this shift. Needless to say, it's much harder in the political sphere where so many people have no interest whatsoever in pursuing this goal. But this reality simply underscores the importance of the work. There's no excuse for not trying.

5. Never leave "kindergarten"

Since the problems we currently face are incredibly important, we need to participate in our current partisan fray, working for those flawed candidates and public policies that we believe are our best current options. Doing so, conservatives will continue to push mostly for Republican candidates and progressives for the Democrats; though, hopefully, with growing discernment that allows them to embrace the truly values-based politicians within their partisan tribe.

But here's the thing. We also need to focus a lot more time and attention on the "kindergarten" work described above; that is, the basics of how we interact with and treat one another. Doing so is wisdom stretching, often unacknowledged, and regularly disappointing in its immediate effect. But the hard truth is this: If we put these basics aside, any chance we have of creating a more decent politics will be dismally small.

VALUES-BASED POLITICS: TWO HOPEFUL STORIES

If you see the world of politics and public policy through our current partisan prism, you'll immediately think that Judy and Rollin have nothing in common. Judy Garson, my sister, is a stereotypical liberal. Now in her early 80s, I recently asked her if she'd ever voted for a Republican. Her response: "I think I did once, back in the 1960s. She was a mayoral candidate in New Jersey where I was living at the time. And, remarkably, my fingers didn't melt when I pulled the lever!" On the other hand, my dear friend Rollin Van Broekhoven voted for Reagan, Dole, and both Bushes. He is pro-life and, as a legal scholar and retired judge, describes himself as "a legal theorist in the tradition of Antonin Scalia."

But their stories reveal a shared approach in the public/political sphere that is far more significant than their partisan differences. Judy and Rollin have never met. But if they did, I'm sure they'd deeply admire the choices the other has made as an actor in the public sphere. Why? Because each of their stories exemplifies the values-based, relationship-focused approach I describe above.

Judy, a nun, and Rollin, a "missionary kid" raised in Guatemala, share a religiously based outlook on life. This is, I think, no accident. While our major religious traditions don't have a corner on the values market – and too often lead us astray – they can also offer a powerful source of sustaining inspiration.

Trained as a teacher, Judy was asked in the mid-1970s to serve as member of the Central Team, a group of four nuns that ran her Order, the Society of the Sacred Heart. During her six years in Rome, Judy visited the Order's convents around the world. Doing so, she learned firsthand about the state of our world as she traveled from poverty-stricken villages in the desert of northern Chile to the desperately poor slums of Entebbe, Uganda.

Returning to New York when her Central Team term ended, Judy reinvented herself professionally. Having seen so much suffering in her travels, she sought a position where she could support the neediest among us to move, in her words, "from poverty to self-sufficiency." For the next 25 years, she worked as the Executive Director of a social service agency run by the Little Sisters of the Assumption, in East Harlem; a religious order whose motto is "the power of growth is in relationship."

And that is how Judy approached her new job. A fledgling agency when she took over, it began to grow and flourish as she cultivated strong cooperative relationships in the community. She collaborated with the city government, local hospitals, and a half dozen Catholic religious orders with special skills supportive of the agency's work including, for example, nursing and respite care. And crucially, she cultivated a thoroughly collaborative relationship with the people she served.

Many of the agency's clients, working mothers and recent immigrants from Mexico, were separated from their extended families and in desperate need of affordable childcare. As a result, one of her early initiatives was a volunteer grandmother program. These volunteers quickly earned the trust of the agency's clients, giving it invaluable insight into its clients' needs. And, to their great credit, Judy and her coworkers never stopped listening and learning.

As Judy explains it, "everything grew organically from there." These ongoing home-based relationships soon uncovered, for example, serious asbestos problems and roach infestations, leading to advocacy work with local landlords and the City's licensing and inspections department. In addition, Judy's agency was among the first to identify a mysterious and devastating "flu" – later identified as AIDS – when it started appearing in East Harlem in the early 1980s. Finally, with financially strapped local schools struggling to support to their Spanish-speaking students, the agency began offering English language tutorials for parents so they could more effectively help their kids with their homework.

When it comes to politics, what is my takeaway from my sister's life's work? Sure, Judy's a liberal. But when you look at how she actually involved herself in her community, the partisan categories that so preoccupy our attention melt away. Judy's life is rooted in values most all of us share: Personal rectitude; respect, cooperation, and concern for others; and spirituality. It's hard to imagine a thoughtful conservative who wouldn't support and celebrate her work.

And, flipping the equation, the same can be said about liberals regarding Rollin.

Circumstance, not ambition, brought Rollin into a leadership role in the public sphere. In the late 1980s and early 1990s, the Center for New Era Philanthropy became a power in the nonprofit world. Posing as the middleman for a group of anonymous donors, New Era invited charities to provide it with a sum of money to be used to cover its operational expenses. The money was then returned to the charity six months later, along with an equal amount supposedly provided by one of its anonymous donors.

If this "double your money" scheme sounds too good to be true, it was. New Era was a classic Ponzi scheme that ensnared thousands of victims, including a Who's Who of the country's best-known charities: The Red Cross, the United Way, the Boy Scouts, the Rockefeller Foundation, the Salvation Army, the New York Public Library, Harvard, Yale, Princeton, and Duke. At the time of its sudden bankruptcy filing, in May 1995, New Era had just $80 million in assets available to repay $551 million in debt.

New Era's entrée into the charitable world grew out of its founder's evangelical roots. As a result, its bankruptcy hit that world with special force, with about 3,000 out of the 5,000 affected nonprofits being evangelical. For this reason, the crisis landed squarely on the shoulders of Rollin who, at the time, was the Chair of the Evangelical Council for Financial Accountability, the community's accrediting body.

The rules that govern Chapter 7 bankruptcies are a poster child for our culture's compete-to-win values. If you're a "winner" in a Ponzi scheme – that is, if you've received more money that you put in – you'll probably be sued. If, on the other hand, you're a "loser," your job is to elbow your way to the front of line to get back as much money as possible. In other words, a Chapter 7 bankruptcy is an every man for himself free-for-all.

But Rollin was determined to do something very different. From the outset, his goal was to create an outcome that was fair and just for all. And under his leadership, that's exactly what happened.

The bankruptcy was filed on a Monday, and by Thursday Rollin had convened a meeting in Atlanta, attended by about 40 key evangelical leaders including both New Era winners and losers. Also at the meeting were a handful of bankruptcy lawyers, including me.

I'll never forget that meeting. Going in, I assumed we lawyers would take charge, patiently explaining to everyone else the new realities that would now govern their lives. But Rollin moved us in a very different direction, proposing instead an approach based on a series of Bible-based values: Unity (Psalms 133:1); Love (John 13:34); Comfort (II Corinthians 1:3-7); Witness (John 17:21); Stewardship (Ephesians 5:15-16); Wisdom (Proverbs 15:22); and Impact (Leviticus 26:8).

What happened over the next three years was a tribute to the power of a values-based approach to public policy. Understanding the vital importance of relationship building, Rollin created United Response to New Era, a coalition that came to include more than 2,000 of the victimized evangelical organizations. Cultivating open and heartfelt conversations within his home community, Rollin created a deep reservoir of support for his approach. Within a few months, an "evangelical" proposal emerged that ultimately became the blueprint for New Era's reorganization.

At the same time, Rollin was careful to build bridges to the "secular" nonprofits. He supported the early organization of a Creditors Committee, cooperatively co-chaired by a "secular" attorney and me, as the evangelical's representative. He was also instrumental in the appointment of a consensus trustee who enjoyed strong support from both sides of the evangelical/secular divide. As a result, when our evangelical plan was unveiled, it had already been agreed to by many of the key secular nonprofits.

The plan itself was simple – but unprecedented in a Chapter 7 bankruptcy. The "winners" would give back enough money so that everyone, winners and losers alike, shared equally in the pain. In addition, following through on our informing Biblical values, any entity unduly burdened by the required payment could apply to the trustee for a "hardship" exception.

Looking at this proposal from the outside, it seems ludicrously naïve. How could we possibly expect thousands of entities to voluntarily give back millions of dollars, just because it was the right thing to do? But that's exactly what happened.

Why?

To begin with, our effort to be fair, just, and caring really did make a difference. It brought out people's best instincts in a surprising number of cases. But Rollin's tireless relationship-building efforts were our secret weapon. In literally thousands of meetings and phone calls, he listened and empathized as people described New Era's often-devastating effect on their organization's mission and fears for the future.

The bankruptcy's ultimate outcome was a tribute to the wisdom of Rollins' approach. With only two out of the 5,000 affected entities opposing it, our plan was easily ratified at the final court hearing. In the end, every victimized entity recovered (or retained) 91% of the money it had invested in New Era.

●●●●●

Bringing Radical Decency's values-based approach into our public/political engagements is a daunting task, to say the least. But I am deeply sustained in this work by the examples Judy and Rollin offer – and not just because it helps to know that good people like them exist. The deeper take-away from their stories is that they were extraordinarily effective actors in the public sphere *precisely because of their values and not in spite of them*.

The alternative story we can too easily tell ourselves is that when it comes to politics, we need to play the game, doing what we have to do to win. Then, and only then, can we get to the really good things we hope to accomplish.

But history teaches us that this approach seldom, if ever, works. If our goal is meaningful and lasting change, our political work needs to include an unwavering and determined focus on creating a political environment based on the values that Judy and Rollin's stories exemplify:

- A deep sense of service to others;

- An ability to listen with understanding and compassion; and

- An abiding belief in the best instincts of our fellow humans.

Just imagine the impact this would have on the quality of our political debate. Consider as well the far more creative, values-based public policies that would surely be its byproduct.

PART 4

THE WAY FORWARD

What we know is heavily influenced by where we've been in life. My own background, for example, has helped me identify how individuals can re-direct their lives in more productive ways. After all, I've spent the last 20 years working with individuals as a psychotherapist and the 25 years before that as an attorney, representing clients in lawsuits, bankruptcies, and business negotiations. So it's no accident that this book focuses on individual choice. That's what I know best.

But because we are creatures of habit, deeply influenced by our compete-to-win culture, the direction our individual lives take isn't enough. We also need to change: (1) The families, nationalities, ethnicities and religions into which we're born; (2) the schools that teach us so many of our life skills; (3) the places where we work; and (4) the many and varied communities and informal networks through which our interests and passions are expressed.

What unifies our work in these areas is its thoroughly systemic nature. What these institutions and communities are, and what they'll become, is determined by forces that go far beyond the accumulated choices of its individual members. Instead, as Daniel Kim, co-founder of the MIT Center for Organizational Learning pointed out in his 1999 book, *Introduction to Systems Thinking*, they consist of "interacting, interrelated, interdependent parts that form a complex and unified whole."

Recognizing this reality, the book's final two Chapters make the case for a systemically focused approach as the key to unlocking Radical Decency's potential as a force for change in the larger world: The way forward.

Chapter 11 discusses the importance of bringing our Radical Decency practice into the communities of which we're a part; infusing our churches, schools, businesses, professional organizations, and social networks with its 7 Values.

Chapter 12 describes how, when we pursue these values with focus, persistence, and guts, it impels us toward collaborative initiatives that are virtually endless in their possibilities and potential including, for example:

- Radically decent clergy, business people, and academics deeply immersing themselves in each other's different but mutually reinforcing perspectives and skills; and

- Enlightened political activists, psychotherapists, and artists actively engaging with each other's wisdom.

Given my background there is a lot I don't know about how to effectively pursue different outcomes in the systematic contexts to which I now turn. I trust, however, that I will be seen as a helpful collaborator, offering insights – based on my specific skills and life experiences – to those with more extensive expertise and wisdom in these areas.

● ● ● ● ●

For many, this systemic orientation will require a significant shift in perspective. The reason? Our individualistic culture actively promotes the belief you're doing your part if you're a good spouse, parent and friend;

recycle and shop at the local coop; and/or focus on being the best possible teacher (lawyer, lab tech, artist). But while these are all good things, this "do your own thing" approach to societal change is not enough. Some are fond of saying that, given the interrelatedness of the universe, the flutter of a butterfly's wings in Tokyo will inevitably impact events in New York – and that may be true. However, its effect is cosmically small. And so it is, as well, with our necessary and commendable but isolated acts of decency.

More consequentially, our comforting belief in the effectiveness of this individualistic approach to change – by discouraging collaboration, community building, and other organizing activities – is devastatingly effective in derailing larger reform efforts. If we hope to meaningfully change the environments in which we live, we need to move decisively away from this mindset, adopting instead more systemically oriented ways of operating.

How can we better engage in this process? Here are my thoughts.

CHAPTER 11

Making Our Communities a Force for Change

We humans are fiercely tribal. Think about all the people you know who are deeply wedded to their alma mater, favorite sports team, chosen religion, or political party or faction. Here in Philadelphia, the level of psychic pain I observe when the Eagles lose a football game is truly remarkable. And when was the last time you, as a Democrat or Republican, liberal or conservative, were able to convince someone on the other side that you were right – or vice versa?

In *Moral Tribes: Emotions, Reason, and the Gap Between Us and Them* (2013), Joshua Greene described a study that sought to understand how climate change deniers would be affected by increased scientific knowledge. The expectation: With more facts, they would moderate their views. The actual result, however, was very different. While there was no meaningful change in outlook, the arguments they brought to their side of the issue became far more sophisticated.

When we think in terms of our fierce tribalism, this outcome makes sense. Moderating their views on climate change would have risked alienating them from their political tribe; a major emotional loss. Thus, the more sensible move, in psychological terms, was to do exactly what they did.

A crucial takeaway from this study is that, in our efforts to become more effective change agents, we cannot ignore the compelling power of the tribes within which we exist. Instead, we need to become effective voices for decency within them.

RECLAIMING OUR COMMUNAL MOJO

In Chapter 5, we discussed the precipitous decline in our communal involvements since the middle of the last century. This trend, thoroughly documented in Robert Putnam's landmark book, *Bowling Alone*, was more recently highlighted in the 2017 "Social Capital Report" of the Senate's Joint Economic Committee. That report found "atrophied social capabilities" and a "diminished sense of belonging" that has left us "less equipped to solve problems together within our communities."

If we hope to become an effective force for change in our communities, the first step is, of course, to become active, contributing members. But because this decline in communal involvement has gone on for so long, even this seemingly simple step can be a big challenge. Many of us simply don't know what active communal involvement looks like – or how to do it.

That has certainly been the case with me. If you had asked me 30 years ago if I had a robust communal life, I would have said, "Of course." I was, after all, active on numerous nonprofit boards in Philadelphia's Jewish, legal, and civic worlds, and had lots of friends and acquaintances from these activities and through my legal practice.

But I would have been wrong.

My lesson in real community began in the mid 1990s when I participated in the Essential Experience Workshop; an intensive, four-day personal growth retreat that's been offered here in Philadelphia for the last 30 years. Readers may recall that my personal guide for living, discussed in Chapter 6, was developed in the context of the "EE" Workshop.

While the Workshop weekend inspired me to make significant changes in my life, the real eye-opener for me was the community I was invited to join afterward. Pre-EE, my "community" consisted of a series of one-to-one relationships. But the relationships that these people had with one another were haphazard and, often, nonexistent. It was up to me to maintain each relationship.

In EE, however, I became a part of something bigger than me; a community knitted together by an interconnected web of relationships. Even when I was preoccupied elsewhere, I knew the community was there; a home and refuge to which I could always return. And my sense of connection with others depended far less on the vagaries of my one-to-one individual relationships. Meeting an EE grad for the first time, I presumed a common outlook and shared respect, affection, and loyalty that were both general (to the community) and specific (to that member). And I reasonably expected these feelings to be reciprocated.

Key to my sense of belonging was EE's egalitarian structure and sensibility. As members, we were not slotted into an existing hierarchy. Instead, we were invited into a brotherhood/sisterhood of like-minded people, working together to create a shared environment of caring and support. Knowing that the community belonged to us – and depended on us for its continued vitality – we took great pride in what we'd created.

•••••

For me, EE was revelatory. But there was a time when this sort of community was a taken-for-granted reality. And, even today, there are places where it continues to thrive. This reality was highlighted for me, a few years ago, when I was doing service work in a small, rural Honduran village. Co-facilitating a discussion amongst the men in the community with Abraham, a younger man who was part of our group, one of the Hondurans asked about our relationship. I'll never forget their chuckles and looks of incredulity when we told them we'd met just six months earlier.

It turned out that the 20-some villagers in the room had known each other for their entire lives – and simply assumed the same was true for us.

Within our individualistic, first world culture, there are, needless to say, people who are communally gifted. Consider, for example, JoAnne Fischer, the woman who with her husband, Eric Hoffman, brought EE to Philadelphia.

JoAnne is our community's den mother – our "Saint with Earrings," the title playfully bestowed on her in a memorable "girl-talk" skit performed some years ago at an EE party. Through the years, JoAnne has nurtured and participated in the many dances, picnics, Happy Hours, service trips, and other gatherings that so vitally maintain and enhance our sense of community. We can always count on her to be present, warmly greeting both EE regulars and older graduates attending their first event in years. She is truly our communal glue.

But EE is only one example of her gift for community. Twenty-five years ago, she and a dozen friends (including my wife, Dale) started a women's group, known ever since as the "Wild Women." While they read and discuss books, the group is so much more. Every year they organize a weekend retreat in which a theme, drawn from a current book, is integrated not just into their conversation but also into the exotic foods served and outrageous costumes worn at their traditional Saturday night party. A rich mix of joyful camaraderie and thoughtful reflection, these retreats have powerfully cemented their sense of sisterhood.

The Wild Women also show up for each other beyond their organized gatherings. When an elderly member broke her arm and hand, they brought meals to her and stayed at her side throughout the crisis. Similarly, when Dale was organizing our daughter's wedding shower, a group of Wild Women transformed our living room and dinner table into a festive, Italian country vineyard while others helped to prepare the pasta, salads, cakes, and tiramisu (our daughter's favorite Italian dessert).

JoAnne's communal spirit is not the norm in today's *Bowling Alone* world. Far more common is the experience of many of my clients who have few meaningful friendships, an "in name only" relationship with a church or synagogue, and a Facebook account. If we hope to effectively translate our passion for decency into the larger world, we need to pay close attention to the many things that people like JoAnne do, large and small, to nurture a vibrant sense of community. Then, we need to apply those lessons in earnest to the communities in which we're involved.

LAYING BARE OUR INGRAINED "GO IT ALONE" INSTINCTS

As discussed in Chapter 4, almost every organization, institution and movement of any size and enduring presence – from our millennia-old religions to our established businesses and professional organizations – is deeply imbued with the compete-to-win values and individualistic mindset we're seeking to supplant. The result is a two-fold problem that deeply hampers a shift toward a more decent world:

1. It pushes these communal structures toward a status quo orientation fundamentally at odds with Decency's 7 Values; and

2. It fuels disengagement from them by the very people who are most needed, if we hope to move them in more decent directions.

Looking first at how mainstream values infect our communal organizations, here's how the process works. A group of well-intentioned people, fired by an inspiring vision of change, create a new organization to mentor start-up businesses in a City's poorest neighborhoods. In the beginning, the communal feeling, fueled by their mission, is palpable. But soon, real-world practicalities begin to impinge. With the organization's growing staff and expenses, how will it pay the bills and maintain its line of credit? How can it expand its network of supporters? How will it handle the seemingly endless onslaught of unexpected expenses, disgruntled employees, advice-giving funders, and byzantine legal and bureaucratic demands?

In these situations, there are a lot of mainstream-oriented experts, sincerely sympathetic with the organization's mission, ready to offer advice. And they're very good at what they do. The problem, however, is that, instead of working to maintain and enhance the entity's original mission, they offer the mainstream advice that has earned them their reputation as a capable accountant, attorney, financial adviser, or marketing expert.

So, for example, a mainstream fundraising person might offer the following bottom line, mission-diluting advice:

> Look, I appreciate your dedication to the poorest among us. But you won't be able to build your funding base unless you demonstrate measurable progress to your mainstream business supporters. So why don't you expand the project into more up and coming neighborhoods and include more established, more likely to succeed businesses. That way your "success" metrics will look better, and you'll have more of the feel-good stories that are so important to your fundraising success.

As the steward of the organization and its mission, it's awfully hard to ignore this sort of expert advice. This is, after all, a good person who is warmly supportive of your mission. And she is persuasively describing, from years of experience, the conventional costs incurred, and opportunities lost, if the organization doesn't operate in this status quo way.

With expert after expert offering this sort of advice, the organization's original, more visionary leadership slowly adapts to this more utilitarian approach – or is replaced by others more willing to do so. Sadly, the debris of this process is all around us. We are left, far too often, with:

- Mainstream religions that seem more interested in defending pedophilic priests than in Jesus' message of love and brotherhood, or in Israel's territorial ambitions than in "Tikkun Olam," Judaism's inspiring commitment to healing the world;

- Unions that, instead of fighting for expanded workers' rights, seek to maintain the modest economic gains already secured for their ever-diminishing membership; and

- Chambers of commerce that, instead of promoting enlightened business practices, work to extract every possible tax and regulatory break for its members.

●●●●●

This dismal trend, in turn, leads to a fundamental shift in the way in which we, as individuals, view these entities. Everywhere we look, we see organizations and movements that have become self-serving bureaucracies driven less by their original mission and far more by their narrow organizational and economic self-interest.

That, in turn, encourages a similar mindset on our part. Instead of seeing ourselves as committed members of the organization, we become consumers; showing up and contributing only when it's in our interest to do so; primed to leave as soon as it stops meeting our needs. The result – unfortunate and deeply consequential – is that the very people whose reform energy and creativity are most needed to maintain the organization's vitality are primed to abandon their involvement.

On its face, this seems like an irrational choice. Seeing the effects of this disturbing process, you'd think these reformed-minded people would redouble their effort to revitalize the organization. But, to an alarming degree, they don't. Instead, with the culture's individualistic, do-your-own-thing mindset informing their decision, they tell themselves that dropping out is a principled choice. "I'm dialing back on my involvement, not out of self-interest, but because I don't want to associate with the hypocrites and charlatans who run my church [or union]."

In this regard, my personal journey with organized religion is instructive. Coming of age as a Congregationalist, the religion of my mother, I was turned off by the tepid Christianity of our comfortable suburban church. But instead of raising my concerns within the church, I quit. And, tellingly, I did it with a distinct sense of pride in my "principled" rejection of its flawed values.

A few years later I converted to Judaism; a choice reinforced by my marriage to a woman whose deeply felt Jewishness reinforced my strong affinity for its outlook and traditions. Nevertheless, my wife and I have never found a synagogue or communal organization that lived up to our demanding standards. And living "righteously" apart from organized Jewry, we have largely forfeited our ability to influence its future.

LEANING INTO COMMUNAL POSSIBILITIES

Given our ingrained, individualistic habits of mind, a shift toward more communal ways of living is very challenging. We can't just say, "Okay, I get it. Deeper communal commitments are good. I'll do it." This approach is as likely to work as that New Year's resolution to lose 15 pounds or to get to the gym every week.

Instead of being one more item on our "to do" list, we need to make communal involvement an actively pursued aspirational priority. Embracing this approach, the measure of our success will be the regularity with which we make day-by-day choices that increase our communal involvements.

This is, you'll recall, a specific application of a mindset, central to Radical Decency's approach, which was first introduced in Chapter 2. In that discussion, I described committed Buddhists who focus on their breath every time they meditate, knowing full well that their focus will

inevitably falter, even after decades of practice. But their inability to eliminate distractions does not mean they've failed. To the contrary, persisting
in their practice over the years – trying and falling short, trying again and
"failing" again – fundamentally changes their outlook and way of being in
the world.

Pursuing our communal commitments and choices with this mindset, we can trust that our individualistic instincts will recede. With time,
we'll be far more active and empowered members of our chosen communities and, thus, more effective advocates for Radical Decency within them.

Here too, my experience is instructive. Like so many other people,
my ingrained instincts continue to be more go-it-alone than communal.
As a result, while people like JoAnne model steady, enduring communal
involvements, mine – even after my EE awakening – is still marked by periods of intense activity followed by extended periods of disengagement.

Nevertheless, I have found my way to a more community-based
way of living, centered on the EE community. It begins with my willing
involvement with the Community's core mission. I enthusiastically recruit
Workshop participants and, frequently, am part of the team that assists
in putting it on. And then, with this base of active involvement in place,
my communal work has grown to include initiatives that reflect my values-based passions.

For example, in the early years of my involvement, my wife and I
started a program that brought Community volunteers to Habitat for
Humanity on a monthly basis. I also co-led a men's support group, for 5
years, that offered a platform from which I could teach and model Radical
Decency's principles. My wife and I also organized a series of service trips
– to Haiti, Mexico, El Salvador, Honduras, and Guatemala – where we and
other EE'ers developed a far deeper understanding of the many ways in
which indecency impacts the world.

Another key element of my involvement in EE has been my willingness to take on not just leadership roles, but also the many mundane tasks

needed to maintain a community's vibrancy and growth. I run errands, make phone calls, and break down tables and wash dishes at the end of Community dinners. Working side by side with fellow Community members on all this "little stuff" enhances my sense of belonging. And, very importantly, it has cemented my position within the community, allowing me to have far more influence over its future direction.

WHERE DO I PLANT MY COMMUNAL FLAG?

If you agree that our decency goals require increased levels of communal involvement, the next obvious question is where? Which particular communities should I get involved in?

There is, of course, no right answer. The culture's network of communities is vast and varied. Communities exist in nearly every realm of life: Within our religious and spiritual traditions, our professions, our political parties and movements – and, even, with that group of neighbors who enthusiastically support the local high school's football team. Ideally, we would bring Radical Decency's outlook and operating principles to all of them.

So let's take a closer look at some of these possibilities.

In the realm of organized religion, many people, like me, have turned their backs on the religion of their forebears because of what we see as the current leadership's narrow-mindedness and hypocrisy. But here's the thing. For millions of people, these communities are at the very core of their identity. Thus, we greatly hamper our efforts to create a different and better world if we ignore them, leaving their direction to leaders who are far too comfortable with the status quo.

For people intent on working toward a more decent world, sinking their communal roots in their inherited religious tradition has an exciting upside. Most all of their histories include eloquent expressions of Decency's 7 Values, from the life and teachings of the Buddha and Christ to the more recent legacies of Gandhi and Golda Meir. What an inspiring platform from which to build your decency practice and to expand the influence of Decency's 7 Values.

If you are inclined in that direction, start going to services on a regular basis and work to become one of those dependable regulars that the community relies upon for its continued vibrancy. Then use the influence that flows from your more empowered position to advance the cause of decency within it.

Another option, rich in possibility, is to join a new organization or community. These entities are often the starting place for culture-altering movements, from the 19th century's abolitionist movement to Alcoholics Anonymous. EE is, of course, a good example of how fruitful this choice can be. Introduced in Philadelphia in 1989, it now – 30 years later – has more than 2000 Workshop graduates and hundreds of people who, like my wife and I, look to it for vital communal sustenance.

In seeking to increase our communal activity, let's also consider our places of business. Like it or not, work consumes the best hours of the great majority of our days and an enormous amount of our psychic energy. So while they're not commonly viewed this way, our workplaces are, in fact, communities to which we are powerfully bound – for better or worse.

Right now, business is a major roadblock in our efforts to create a more radically decent life and world. But it doesn't have to be that way. As discussed in Chapter 6, our workplace can become a vibrant, spirit-affirming community that nurtures Decency's 7 Values and expands its impact in the world.

A final point: Even though strategic considerations are important as we make our communal choices, we shouldn't ignore our innate passions and interests. Involvement in a particular community is very much an emotional choice – an affair of the heart. If it doesn't feel right to you, it will be hard to stay actively involved. So, as you choose, listen to your heart.

The bottom line: Understanding the vital importance of communal involvement, think about where and how you'd like to make a difference. Then, get involved – and stay involved!

WHY DO IT

When I reflect on community and its place in our lives, two key lessons stand out. First, if we're serious about creating a more decent world, we can't ignore the communal organizations that are so foundational to our way of living and that, cumulatively, so deeply affect how we live. We need, instead, to be actively involved so that, using our empowered position within them, we can deeply infuse our decency values into the ways in which they operate.

The second, very hopeful take-away is that a more communally oriented way of life has an enormous upside. At its best, it offers a safe home to which we can always return; a place that provides a sense of belonging that transcends, and is far more enduring, than the mundane strivings that otherwise dominate our lives. In this area of life, as in so many others, the choices that best serve our decency aspirations are, happily, also vital pathways to a more rewarding life.

CHAPTER 12

Collaboration: Expanding Our Vision

Everywhere we look, we witness indecency. We see it at work, in politics, in our day-by-day interactions with each other, and in the ways we push and judge ourselves. In addition, our ways of being indecent are endlessly complicated and ever evolving. It all feels like an endless game of whack-a-mole in which we make progress on one issue only to see new, even more disturbing manifestations of indecency pop up elsewhere.

Here, I'm going to state the obvious: When it comes to creating a more decent world, we can't do everything. Instead, we find a niche. Some of us focus on politics and public policy. Others focus on individual healing, becoming psychotherapists, nutritionists, acupuncturists, or other types of mind/body healers. Still others pursue a spiritual path, or become union activists, or values-based business owners. And, of course, a large number of folks express their more enlightened values in their own go-it- alone way – a sizable group, given our ingrained individualistic habits of living.

This multi-pronged approach is, of course, a good thing. In a compli-cated war, we need smart, dedicated soldiers on many fronts. But there's a troubling problem with this approach that lies not in what people are doing but what they *aren't* doing.

An obvious corollary to this single issue/expertise-focused approach to change is that, to maximize their impact, committed people from all walks of life should be in far more fruitful connection; learning from one another and supporting each other's work. Moreover, this deeper connection needs to happen not just between individuals but also, in line with the ideas expressed in the last Chapter, between the organizations and communities that are the context for so much of what we do. We need, in other words, to rethink what it means to be collaborative.

Most of us would, of course, agree in principle with this thought. But looming over it is a very practical question: Given our busy lives, and the immense challenge involved in promoting decency just in our limited area of activity, how can we find the time and energy to deeply engage with the reform efforts of others?

Weighed down by this reality, even the best of us – those who persist in the fight to create a better world – tend to walk down this well-worn path:

1. We focus on a particular issue we feel passionate about, usually reflecting our own life experience.

Then, further limiting the scope of our vision:

2. We become specialists – academics, political activists, reform-minded workers and business people, service workers, therapist/healers – telling ourselves that, in other areas, we need to defer to the experts.

Then, finally, cementing our isolation from one another:

3. Our interactions with people beyond our area of interest and expertise typically become intermittent, "when I have the time" explorations.

With each of these factors reinforcing one another, the possibility for meaningful, ongoing collaboration across areas of interest and expertise is pushed to the margins. Intent on doing our own entirely commendable thing, we see no compelling reason to seek out people whose focus is elsewhere. Instead, we assume that our unconnected, uncoordinated initiatives will, somehow, magically knit together into a coherent whole that, as it gathers momentum, will lead to a more decent world.

But this is exactly the mindset that Howard Lesnick dubbed "the avalanche theory of change." And the hard truth is this: If –comforted by this exercise in wishful thinking – we continue to subscribe to this go-it-alone approach to change, the likelihood of achieving a meaningful and lasting shift toward more decent lives and a more humane world will remain dismally small.

COMING TOGETHER THROUGH DECENCY'S 7 VALUES

Central to Radical Decency's approach is the belief that, with the culture's compete-to-win values driving so much of the indecency that litters our world, progress in one area of living will, almost inevitably, be short-circuited by the dominance of these values everywhere else. Thus, the philosophy's uncompromising message is that lasting change requires a commitment to decency in every area, from the most public and political to the most personal and private.

Informed by this perspective, Radical Decency is very supportive of the important, issues-specific work that so many are doing. But – and this is a vitally important addition – it seeks to expand its scope to include the crucial values-based work that promises to unify and, thus, to make these diverse initiatives far more effective.

And this is where collaboration comes in. If we hope to implement this vision of comprehensive values-based change, we will be impelled to reach out to people who have skills that extend far beyond those that we possess in our narrow areas of expertise. There is, quite simply, no viable alternative.

To illustrate this point, I begin by drawing on my long experience as a lawyer, offering two contrasting perspectives on what it means to be an ethical, values-based attorney: (1) The narrow and insular approach that is the profession's current norm; and (2) an approach grounded in Decency's 7 Values. Doing so, I highlight the dramatically different impact that this second approach will have on lawyers' collaborative initiatives.

LEGAL ETHICS: THE MAINSTREAM APPROACH

The American Bar Association's Model Code of Professional Responsibility provides the basis for the ethics courses most all lawyers take to maintain their licenses. And what do we do at these classes? We spend long hours learning how, based on the Code, to better locate the point at which our normal ways of doing business might cross an ethical line and, then, how to stay on the "right side" of that line.

For many years I, like most other lawyers, assumed that this was an entirely sensible way to approach our ethical responsibilities. But as my thinking about decency has deepened, so too has my exasperation with it.

Why? Because, when you think about it, it's no different than an attorney saying to his law firm's managing partner: "Look, I know our goal is to be profitable. So what's the minimum amount I need to do to stay on the right side of the profitability line?"

Needless to say, the managing partner's response would be less than positive. "Are you kidding?" he or she would likely say, "when it comes to profitability, you shouldn't be looking for the minimum acceptable bar! Your job, each and every day, is to find new and ever more creative ways to expand our profitability. Get the [insert preferred expletive] out of my office."

So why are profitability and ethics viewed so differently? Because profitability fully aligns with the culture's win-at-all-costs values, while a wholehearted embrace of ethics would inhibit them. As a result, the ethical explorations of mainstream lawyers are straitjacketed by this unstated assumption: Our headlong pursuit of more and more money, influence and prestige should be limited by ethics only when those restraints are unavoidable.

With this limitation in place, lawyers' ethics are highly constricted and self-serving. So, for example, Rule 1.7 of the Model Code begins with a prohibition on representing clients whose interests are adverse to one other. But then, with stunning cynicism, it goes on to tell us that these dual representations are just fine, so long as we "reasonably believe" we can competently represent each client and they give "informed consent." And with dismal predictability, our ethics courses – instead of focusing on client risks in these dual representation situations – offer detailed roadmaps for crafting airtight informed-consent letters.

Another egregious example is Rule 1.5 of the Model Code, which covers fees. While it purports to prohibit "unreasonable" fees, it is utterly silent when it comes to the profession's widespread practice of charging for every hour worked without regard to a case's outcome. Since most cases involve money and nothing else, the conflict of interest in this arrangement is glaring: Every dollar paid to a lawyer means one less dollar in her client's pocket. And yet, the Model Code makes no effort to regulate or, heaven forbid, to meaningfully restrict hourly billing.

Note, importantly, that this self-serving approach to ethics is not limited to lawyers. In my new profession as a clinical social worker, for example, a perennial hot topic is the danger in disclosing personal information; everything from the therapist's vacation destination to his struggle with depression – advising against the latter even when disclosure might offer much-needed support to a client struggling with the same issue. But with the consistent message being to avoid most any personal disclosure lest it unsettle a client and, as a result, expose the therapist to criticism or legal liability, one might fairly ask: "Who's being protected, the client or the therapist?"

Like lawyers, we social workers also rarely raise ethical issues that might interfere with our ability to make money. Thus, we ignore the ethical implications of ending therapy sessions at the end of an hour without regard to the client's emotional state. In addition, we are complicit with inpatient facilities that now terminate treatment, not when clients get better but, instead, as soon as their insurance coverage ends.

Standing alone, this debased version of ethics is a serious concern. But we also need to understand how it isolates and insulates us in our professional/vocational "tribes," deeply disconnecting us from one another.

Here's how that process works.

With career advancement and moneymaking as preoccupying concerns, each profession focuses on technical, profession-specific ethical issues, such as those just described. These issues are, needless to say, of little interest to people who aren't part of the profession in question. The result: Lawyers deal with their ethics; social workers with theirs; and academics, business people, journalists and so on, with theirs.

Since this arrangement allows them to pursue their self-interested goals without meaningful challenge from the outside, mainstream professionals are fully invested in it. So, for example, I have now attended annual ethics classes for an aggregate of 65 years (25 as a lawyer, and 20 more as both a lawyer and social worker) and not once have the organizers thought to include our clients! Equally absent, needless to say, are people who might bring different and broader perspectives to our ethical discussions: Historians, religious leaders, public-interest advocates, and humanistic academicians, among others. And the disquieting truth is that this way of operating is so thoroughly ingrained that it's hard for most of us to even imagine another way.

RADICALLY DECENT LAWYERS

Seeking to be decent to self, others and the world, at all times and in every context, radically decent lawyers would focus on a very different set of ethical issues, including the following;

1. Beyond the result in specific cases, do my services and products effectively advance my clients' broader economic and values-based goals?

2. Do the tactics I employ as an attorney align with my decency values?

3. Are my pricing and sales/marketing policies fair and transparent?

4. Does my law firm avoid overcompensating those at the top, unreasonably compromising the wages and benefits of lower level employees?

5. Is the firm accommodating the larger life goals of employees at every level?

6. Have we created, and are we maintaining, an institutional culture in which Decency's 7 values guide our choices, not just with co-workers and clients, but also with other law firms and their clients, vendors, and the public at large?

7. Given our financial capability and technical skills, are we responsibly contributing to the larger effort to create a more decent and humane world?

Dealing with these far more complicated, wisdom-stretching issues attorneys would be impelled toward collaboration with people who share their decency values but whose areas of experience and expertise reach far beyond the law.

Consider, for example, the challenge involved in making Decency's 7 Values the norm as we interact with co-workers, clients, and others. As lawyers, our special skill is to win arguments by jabbing holes in other people's arguments and constantly reiterating the rightness of ours. But this way of interacting exactly replicates the boundary-crossing, non-relational way of being – identified in Chapters 4 and 8 – that is the poster child for our compete-to-win ways.

Having now practiced and taught a different more relational way for many years now, as a therapist, I've dramatically tamped down my ingrained lawyerly instincts. But my journey is instructive. Detoxing from my lawyer's training has taken years, and even now my old habits will reassert themselves from time to time – as my wife would undoubtedly confirm.

In theory, radically decent lawyers can do this work on their own. But why would they? If they're willing to spend tens of thousands of dollars on marketing, accounting and computer experts in order to increase efficiency and profitability, it only makes good sense that they'd enlist outside help when it comes to this vitally important goal.

And this is just one of many examples. Seeking to make good on their commitment to across-the-board decency, they'd be motivated to reach out as well to:

- Business consultants who specialize in pricing and wage structuring issues as they work to implement fair pricing policies and an equitable pay scale;

- Philosophers; religious and spiritual leaders; and novelists and poets – who have so much wisdom to offer as they seek to accommodate their own and their employees' larger life goals; and

- Scientists who, using state of the art data harvesting and machine learning techniques, can measure and monitor the level of decency in every aspect of their operations; allowing them, in this way, to more fully make good on their decency aspirations (possibilities discussed in greater depth in Chapter 9).

One can only imagine the many ways in which lawyers would be challenged – and enriched – if, driven by their decency commitment, they were in deep collaborative relationship with these sorts of people. And needless to say, its impact on the profession and, thus, on the larger culture would be seismic as well.

•••••

Looking beyond this particular example, Radical Decency's varied and perplexing challenges will jumpstart collaboration between all kinds of people, with a wide variety of interests and specialized knowledge. In the next two sections, I describe two very important collaborative alliances that are likely to emerge: The convergence of the work of social activists and business people and a similar coming together between social activists and personal growth practitioners. Then, in the Chapter's final section, I provide additional examples to illustrate the far-ranging and truly exciting collaborative possibilities that might emerge if Radical Decency ever becomes the culture's new, taken-for-granted norm.

WHEN SOCIAL ACTIVISM MEETS BUSINESS

The relationship that currently exists between business people and social activists is, in the great majority of cases, an arms-length one. On their side, business people's interest in civic projects is typically motivated by a desire to advance their career-building ambitions by cultivating useful contacts, doing a favor for a client, or embellishing their resume. Lacking any real motivation to get involved in the nitty-gritty of social activists' work, most have little interest in creating a meaningful collaborative relationship.

And the standoffishness goes both ways. Fully aware of business people's modest and contingent interest, social activists typically view them as morally limited. Their default position is to not involve business people in the uncomfortable, status quo-challenging elements of their work. Instead, their interactions are measured, even manipulative. Seeking to preserve the flow of business' dollars to their projects, they mostly tell them what they want to hear.

One typical example involves the annual fundraising dinners that, in years past, I'd help to organize for groups such as Philadelphia's Public Interest Law Center and the American Jewish Committee. Invariably, we'd begin by finding a wealthy person who, in return for being our honoree, would write a large leadership check. Needless to say, these recruitment efforts were an exercise in ego-inflating flattery. Then, at the dinner itself, we'd lavishly praise the honoree as a model citizen, conveniently ignoring the typically problematic professional behavior that led to his wealth.

In a world in which social activists and business people are equally committed to Decency's 7 Values, their relationship would be very different. What would emerge, instead, would be a deep and abiding collaboration nurtured and sustained by their shared values.

Here's how that process would unfold.

On the activists' side, this shift would be facilitated by the fact its trust, and not on a lack of interest in what business has to offer, that keeps them at arms' length; the deeper truth being that, of course, business' core skills would be of enormous, potentially game-changing benefit to the organizations they run. With social activists and business people sharing a common decency-based approach, the activists' caution would dissipate. What would emerge, in its place, would be a close, collaborative relationship designed to take advantage of business' ever-growing arsenal of cutting-edge financial, organizational and operational techniques.

A similar impetus toward collaboration would emerge on the business side as well. Social activists are the people who, more than any others, devote their time and energy to grappling with society's big issues. As a result, their radically decent business counterparts would eagerly seek them out so they could best deploy their resources in ways that – moving beyond cosmetic, feel good initiatives – promote the deep structural changes required by their now whole-hearted commitment to decency.

WHEN PERSONAL GROWTH
MEETS SOCIAL ACTIVISM

Radical Decency will also foster a far closer relationship between these same social activists and people devoted to personal growth – therapists and life coaches, acupuncturists and other mind-body healers, mindfulness practitioners, and so on.

"But wait," you might say, "these are two sides of the same coin – one focusing on individual healing, the other on healing in the broader culture. Isn't close collaboration a given?" Unfortunately, in the great majority of cases, the answer is no.

Making this bold statement, I draw on extensive experience in both worlds. For most of my adult life, I've been deeply immersed in social justice causes, including Common Cause/Philadelphia, Philadelphia's Public Interest Law Center, the National Constitution Center, and Habitat for Humanity. Since the early 1990s, I've been equally involved in the personal growth world, including the Essential Experience Workshop Community, New Warriors men's training, and the Imago Couples and Gestalt therapy training communities.

In 2002 – just at the point when I shifted from the law to psychotherapy – a growing frustration came into focus for me. My years of experience made we realize how difficult it is to really change things in either world. On the personal growth side, brave words about living differently far too often dissipate when faced with the incessant demands of mortgage payments and work. Similarly, social activists work hard to elect a better leader, only to find her replaced, 4 years later, by someone even worse than the guy they ousted.

But despite these enormous challenges, the good people on each side of the personal growth/social divide seemed, mostly, to operate in separate worlds. And this, to me, seemed like an important lost opportunity. So, still naively hopeful, even in my 50s, I pulled together 20 friends and colleagues – 10 or so from each side – to bridge the gap.

It's a meeting I'll never forget; one I now describe as the worst I've ever facilitated in my life. It began well enough, with small talk over snacks on my porch, soaking in the bright sunlight and bracing breeze that make early Spring afternoons in Philadelphia so special. But when we began to discuss how to work together, things went downhill – and fast.

The personal growth people immediately started pushing for a relationship-building approach. "We need to bond as group, really get to know one another," said one psychologist. "Let's meet regularly and, perhaps, plan a retreat." The other personal growth types nodded.

As they continued to push this idea, I noticed growing frustration on the part of the social activists, culminating in this meeting-busting outburst from one of my particularly passionate friends. "This is ridiculous," he snapped. "Spending months navel-gazing and baring our souls is a complete waste of time. We already know how to get things done. Let's just pick an issue and start ringing doorbells."

What I didn't understand then was that their inability to work together was not some simple misunderstanding that could be easily fixed. To the contrary, each camp, deeply immersed in the culture's individualistic, do-your-own-thing mentality had little instinct to immerse itself in the outlook and approach of the other side.

As difficult as this meeting was, however, it did lead to a *Eureka!* moment. What I realized was that my friends were in fact united by a shared set of values. But because both groups were preoccupied with the immediacy of their special concerns, these common values remained below the surface, largely unseen and unarticulated.

This insight, in turn, led to an expanded, values-based vision of the work to be done on both sides; the approach to living I now call Radical Decency. And with that came the further realization that, when each side viewed the "other" in this new light – when they understood their deeply shared values-based goals – the close collaboration that seemed so elusive that day would become a cosmic no-brainer.

Pre-meeting, I assumed that social activism meant working to elect better leaders and to change existing laws. But this approach is too limited. To truly change the current system, we can't rely solely on the standard tools of a system which is rigged to reward the most powerful. We also need to directly challenge the system's underlying values, modeling and advocating Decency's 7 Values in every aspect of public life.

A similar narrowness of vision had also infected my outlook on personal growth. Before the meeting I assumed it was about "feeling better" or "feeling good." But we can't simply focus inward, on our feelings. If we do, the spirit-deadening, compete-to-win values in which we're so immersed will grind us down. Here, too, we need to systematically cultivate Decency's 7 Values in all aspects of life.

With this values-based approach in place on both sides, the gap between social activists and their personal growth counterparts no longer makes sense. Understanding that successful lobbying and electoral work depends on the relationship-building "kindergarten" work described in Chapter 10, social activists will become committed students of the best personal growth practitioners. And these healers, eager to understand how to deal with the indecencies of the organizations that dominate their clients' lives will seek out the special wisdom and experience of social activists – the very people who've devoted their lives to reforming these larger cultural institutions.

ENDLESS COLLABORATIVE POSSIBILITIES

Pulling the lens back from these particular examples, there is just so much wisdom and so many valuable skills to be assimilated into our toolkit as we challenge ourselves to be radically decent. Take the arts, for example.

Psychotherapists like me need to understand their clients' complex feelings and, to that end, exhaustively study: (1) Painful states of mind such as anxiety and depression, to which the current Diagnostic and Statistical Manual of Mental Disorders (DSM) devotes 42 categories and subcategories; and (2) aberrant behaviors and personality disorders, conditions that consume another 24 DSM categories.

But when it comes to a gut-level understanding of the searing pain of oppression, nothing in our training compares to the story of Sethe, an African American woman living in the South, in the 1860s, who Toni Morrison shared with us in her 1987 novel, *Beloved*. Nor is there anything to compare to the chilling insights into the mind of a pedophile that Vladimir Nabokov provides in *Lolita*. Seeking to truly understand what it feels like to be a person whose reality is very different from ours, the astonishing depths of understanding that artists like Morrison and Nabokov open up to us are, truly, an invaluable resource..

A second example involves the expanded vision that performance artists can offer to couples counselors like me. In a recent conversation with my daughter Julia, an experienced actor, she explained to me the art of improvisational performance:

> You always go with your partner's words and energy. He says, "Let's write a horror movie after the kids go to sleep." Instead of saying, "You're crazy," I might say, "That's great, I just bought new set of fountain pens and I'm dying to put some miles on them." Then, further building on my energy, he might say: "Yes, and maybe we'll put on the soundtrack to Nightmare on Elm Street to really get in the mood!"

As I listened to Julia, what hit me was that she and other improvisational actors, seeking to create the best possible performance, have developed an art form that has powerful lessons for relational experts like me. Because good communication is so predictably absent with the couples with whom we work, we therapists mostly teach unhappy couples how to listen with understanding and empathy and, then, to ask for what they want. But as important as these skills are, they aren't enough. What couples really long for are nourishing and joyful relationships.

That is just what improvisational actors are modeling. In their performance, Julia's partner asks for what he wants and she listens – for sure. But instead of focusing on an outcome, Julia's goal is to affirm and build on his energy.

Wow, what a powerful message. With Julia as my teacher, I'm now able to teach similar energy-building interactions to my clients. So the wife says, "Let's go to that Italian restaurant tonight." In the past, I might have coached the husband to say something like: "Sure, that's a good idea. But I'd prefer Chinese." However, since where they eat isn't all that important, he might opt instead for an energy-building response as they move into their hopefully delightful evening together: "Italian food sounds great. Let's do it. And then maybe we can seal the deal with fudge-drenched ice cream sundaes!"

●●●●●

Another less obvious area where collaborative possibilities exist is between the military and people like me. Needless to say, my customary ways of being and theirs are very different. Thus, the months I spent on active duty, as an Army reservist during the Vietnam War, were among the unhappiest of my life.

In basic training, my life was controlled by Drill Sergeant Mauney, a sadistic man who really seemed to relish our pain. After an exhausting double-time march to the rifle range under a blazing hot South Carolina sun, he would bark out "give me 10" – pushups, that is – and, then, "give me 10 more."

Needless to say, Sergeant Mauney had little use for a college kid from New York, like me. And I felt the same about him. Nevertheless, when we were on maneuvers, in simulated wartime conditions, his fierce loyalty and determination to keep his boys safe – me included – was like nothing I've ever experienced before or since. With blue tracer bullets whizzing over our heads, I'll never forget his firm, confident grip on my elbow as he steered me to the safety of a protective outcropping of rocks. This man, so different from me, had a lot to teach me about mission, service, and leadership.

●●●●●

Finally, consider insights that religion has to offer, even to secular people like me. Many years ago, when Dale and I were on a service trip to Haiti, we shared a guesthouse with the "two Marys" – spunky young nurses from St. Louis. Devout Catholics, they worked as unpaid volunteers for several months, each year, tending to the sick in one of Port-Au-Prince's poorest neighborhoods.

The Marys would begin each day at Mass and, one morning, Dale suggested that we join them. I had been to Catholic churches back home. But nothing from my U.S. experience – sitting through Masses in ornate sanctuaries with people who'd be spending the afternoon at their children's soccer games – prepared me for what unfolded that day.

This church was a cinder block room, punctuated with cutouts in the walls to let in Port-au-Prince's already hot, early morning breeze. The pews were straw mats thrown over a dirt floor. But in this unassuming environment, a lesson in the power of belief lodged in my heart.

Surrounded by a handful of Catholic lay workers and half a dozen Sisters of Charity, an unassuming Creole-speaking priest ran through the liturgy in a perfunctory way. But when my fellow congregants took communion – on their way to a day tending to some of the world's most desperately poor people – the power of Jesus' message hit me. These people really were taking in the blood and flesh of Christ and "embodying" Him in a powerful, indeed almost literal sense.

What I realized, in that moment, was that I was witnessing the breathtaking ability of communities of faith, at their best, to inspire and sustain the best within us. As I move through my days, seeking to do my part to create a more decent world, I can only hope that, true to their memory, I am carrying forward the lesson the two Marys brought into my life that day.

A JOURNEY OF DISCOVERY THAT NEVER ENDS

When I had the conversation about improv with my daughter, previously described, my immediate thought was, "Great idea, got it." But when I shared my first draft of this Chapter with her, I realized how wrong I was. Her art has endless subtleties built into it through long years of hard work. Thus, "getting it" was far more complicated than I'd originally thought. Hopefully, I've done a better job in the rewrite – and will continue to grow as I absorb what she has to teach me.

What this process brought home for me, with renewed and heightened awareness, is that to be truly collaborative, we need to listen with openness and a deep sense of not knowing. For many of us, me very much included, this is difficult work. We "know what we know" and have trouble opening space for other outlooks and sensibilities. But if we do, there is no end to collaboration's life – and world –changing possibilities.

FINAL THOUGHTS

From time to time, I'll tell a client: "What I'm telling you is something I've thought about a lot and, at least for now, it's my settled opinion. But that doesn't mean it's right."

Hopefully, you've found value in the ideas and strategies for living I've shared with you in this book. But and this is – I hope – an obvious point: Don't stop there. Seek out other teachers, as I continue to do, and pay close addition to the many people like Karen, Bob, Ann, Judy, Rollin, JoAnne and Julia who have so much to teach us. And never stop adding your own wisdom to the equation as well.

I often say – though I can't prove it – that no one is radically decent. The world is too complex, the challenges too great, and we humans too awash in conflicting needs and emotions. But remembering that the future is inherently uncertain, it's enough to pursue our decency goals with focus, persistence and guts, forgiving our lapses, forever renewing our commitment to that ideal, all the while knowing that in the end Radical Decency is its own reward.